FLAT BROKE IN THE FREE MARKET

FLAT BROKE IN THE FREE MARKET

How Globalization
Fleeced Working People

JON JETER

W. W. NORTON & COMPANY

New York   London

For information about permission to reproduce selections from this book,
write to Permissions, W. W. Norton & Company, Inc.,
500 Fifth Avenue, New York, NY 10110

For information about special discounts for bulk purchases, please contact
W. W. Norton Special Sales at specialsales@wwnorton.com or 800-233-4830

Manufacturing by Courier Westford
Book design by Chris Welch
Production manager: Julia Druskin

Library of Congress Cataloging-in-Publication Data

Jeter, Jon.
Flat broke in the free market : how globalization fleeced
working people / Jon Jeter.—1st ed.
p. cm.
Includes bibliographical references and index.
ISBN 978-0-393-06507-7 (hbk.)
1. Free trade—Social aspects. 2. International trade—Social aspects.
3. Economic development—Social aspects. 4. Economic policy—
Social aspects. 5. Working class—Social conditions.
6. Globalization—Economic aspects. I. Title.
HF1713.J48 2009
306.3—dc22

2009005045

W. W. Norton & Company, Inc.
500 Fifth Avenue, New York, N.Y. 10110
www.wwnorton.com

W. W. Norton & Company Ltd.
Castle House, 75/76 Wells Street, London W1T 3QT

1 2 3 4 5 6 7 8 9 0

To my parents, Joan and Cecil Jeter

There is something about poverty that smells like death. Dead dreams dropping off the heart like leaves in a dry season and rotting around the feet, impulses smothered too long in the fetid air of underground caves. The soul lives in a sickly air. People can be slave-ships in shoes.

—*Zora Neale Hurston*

CONTENTS

OVERVIEW   xi

Part One CANARIES IN THE MINE

1   **A NEW DAY** • Zambia and Free Trade   3

2   **THE NIGHT SHIFT** • Argentina and Monetary Policy   25

3   **LIFE AND DEBT** • Brazil and Interest Rates   52

4   **POWER AND LIGHT** • South Africa and Privatization   75

Part Two CHICKENS COMING HOME TO ROOST

5   **NEOLIBERAL NEGROES** • Chicago and Democracy   99

6   **DEALS WITH THE DEVIL AND OTHER REASONS TO RIOT** • Malawi, Mexico, and Food   124

7   **THE PLAN** • Washington, D.C., and Housing   140

8   **THINGS FALL APART** • Chicago and Family   161

9   **SÍ; CAGO; VOY** • Chile, Venezuela, and Hope for the Future   183

NOTES   205

INDEX   217

OVERVIEW

Not just plain terrible. This was fancy terrible; this
was terrible with raisins in it.

—*Dorothy Parker*

By virtually any measure, the last quarter century has
been an unqualified economic disaster for ordinary
people worldwide.

Unemployment across the globe has climbed to its highest
levels since the Great Depression. In rich nations and poor,
employees are working longer hours for less money while the
companies' CEOs are banking bigger and bigger paychecks.
Corporate profits account for a larger portion of world income
than at any time in the postwar period, while wages have
plummeted to their smallest share since the beginning of the
Great Depression.

As a percentage of their budgets, nations spend less on
public education than they did twenty-five years ago. Families
around the world save less than at any time in the past seventy
years and spend more than ever on housing, food, gasoline,
and medicine. Household debt is at an all-time high.

With more cash spanning the globe faster than ever, 1.3 billion people now live on the equivalent of less than $1 per day. Half the world's population—3 billion people—survive on only twice that, or about 25 cents less than each cow in the European Union receives per day in government subsidies.

Per capita income in Latin America increased by 82 percent between 1960 and 1980 and only 13 percent from 1990 to 2005. The world's income has increased by nearly US$1 trillion since 1990; sub-Saharan Africa's per capita income has fallen by 20 percent in that same time.

From Argentina to Zambia, from Chicago to Soweto and D.C. to Rio, the restructuring of the global economy has ripped a hole through the earth, city by city, block by block, house by house. Globalization has widened inequality, corrupted politicians, estranged neighbors from one another, unraveled families, rerouted rivers, emptied ports of ships, and flooded streets with protesters.

It has created poverty where it did not exist and deepened poverty for women, people of color, and indigenous people. It has swollen prison populations and increased the price we pay for a phone call, a glass of water, a kilowatt of electricity. Globalization has changed the nature of work, the music we listen to, the clothes we wear, the language we speak. It has made the word "public" a synonym for inferiority and added to our narratives savage ironies and limerick-like contradictions: there is more food than ever, and yet more people go hungry; American dentists have never been richer, but Americans' teeth have never been worse; Wall Street's money managers, not Jimmy Hoffa or the mob, gambled away the Teamsters' pension funds. Lawmakers can find $700 billion to bail out corrupt bankers but can't come up with $7 billion to treat poor, ailing children.

At the dawn of the twenty-first century, the United States is giving birth to the first generation of Americans whose life expectancy will be shorter, not longer, than their parents'. Our system of global finance has put us on the precipice, teetering on ruin. As of mid-2008, the United States has bequeathed to the world the biggest speculative bubble, the worst housing crisis, and the gravest economic meltdown in nearly eighty years, and the response from America's political class has been the largest single transfer of wealth from the poor to the rich in at least a century.

Worldwide, the ghetto is in its ascendancy.

How did we get here? Mostly, countries simply stopped making things and started buying them. Since 2000, the United States has lost 3 million manufacturing jobs; Brazil has lost 2 million since 1998, South Africa nearly 1 million.

Argentina used to assemble televisions; now it purchases most of them from abroad. Mozambique packaged its cashews fifteen years ago; today the country ships its raw nuts overseas for others to bottle and can. Zambians made their own clothes in the 1980s; now they sort through bundles of clothes shipped from the United States and Europe. The Hunters Point neighborhood in San Francisco used to manufacture the ships that delivered American-made goods to the world; now the ships docked in the Bay Area's ports are mostly from East Asia, unloading foreign-made products for American consumers.

Where there are factories, they have been made the vassals of retail kings like Wal-Mart, who can demand more and more work for less and less money. Gone are the days when a job at the factory provided a springboard to the middle class. The capital of the industrial world is no longer Detroit but

Shenzhen, in coastal south China, and the men who migrated to the Motor City half a century ago for union jobs at Ford, GM, and Chrysler have been replaced by women who roam the world to take jobs as maids, nannies, prostitutes, and seamstresses.

In roughly a generation, the economic fundamentalism articulated by the World Bank, International Monetary Fund, and U.S. Treasury has set the world on a path to deindustrialization that has created a transnational underclass. This book takes the measure of that biblical cataclysm.

How do you measure such a thing?

You measure it by broken dreams and despairing hearts and ambitions that never find traction. You measure it by the laid-off Argentine factory worker who, with his family in tow, every evening sifts through his neighbors' trash for recyclable materials they can sell for a few pennies per pound.

You mark a catastrophe's progression by a frightfully thin Zambian woman who struggles to earn 75 cents a day selling tomatoes at an outdoor market overflowing with thousands of cashiered textile workers, so she can feed her family a single meal of vegetables and porridge; or by the hardworking Brazilian taxi driver in a slum named Judgment who lives hand to mouth and worries constantly that his country's broken schools, joblessness, and exorbitant interest rates will bequeath to his children the same grinding poverty that he inherited from his father, and his father from his father.

You can gauge a catastrophe by the growing number of prostitutes who roam the streets of Buenos Aires, Oakland, Lusaka, and São Paulo, the escalating crime rates in Montevideo and Cape Town, and the falling marriage rates in Buenos Aires, in Johannesburg, and on Chicago's South Side, where a black woman fears that she will never marry because far too many men from her neighborhood are jobless, incarcerated, or dead.

You can use as a yardstick the anger and disillusionment of black South Africans who vanquished apartheid only to confront unemployment rates approaching 40 percent and whole city blocks plunged into darkness because no one can afford the rising costs of electricity charged by the newly privatized utility.

You can measure a crisis by the size of the United States' historic trade deficit, or the $62 billion in bonuses collected by Wall Street traders in 2007, or the nearly $2,300 that every man, woman, and child in America forked over to them the following year to reward their spectacular avarice and stupidity.

You can assess the damage by the growing numbers of people who are behind in the mortgage payments, or by a widening class war, or by the neighborhood activists who can't get their elected officials to help with the most basic tasks while multinational corporations demand the moon and the stars and often get them.

Globalization is an international shakedown, and its targets are ordinary people across the globe, men and women made sojourners in the country of their birth by global finance and its missionaries.

THE ESSENCE OF this book revealed itself to me over the course of thirty years in a series of epiphanies, the last of them in Milton Friedman's glorious apartment high in the sky, with San Francisco Bay and the Golden Gate Bridge shimmering in the distance like a fresco of sea and mountains and heroic steel beams.

xvi   OVERVIEW

It was an early autumn morning in 2006, and Friedman, the Nobel Prize–winning economist and ideological father of neoliberal economics, had granted me an interview at his home. Ten minutes into our conversation, he leaned back in his chair and offered this assessment: "These last twenty-five years have been wonderful, truly excellent in terms of the global economy," he said. "It's been a period in which you've had a significant reduction in interference in trade, and the low-inflationary environment has really created unprecedented opportunities for investment and innovation."

It was two months before Friedman's death, at the age of ninety-four, and as I sat and listened to him talk, I found myself contemplating this iconic figure before me. He was much more pleasant than I'd anticipated, engaging and mod-est, not insincere. That he was hard of hearing made him a somewhat sympathetic figure, and his blunt-spoken manner and principled libertarianism gave the impression of a man who struggled honestly with the gravest issues of his day and settled on what he sincerely believed was the best possible solution in an imperfect world.

I was struck by how nimble and energetic he was for his age, and how absolutely tiny he was, a sprite of a man, barely breaking five feet in height. I was pondering the contrast between his physical size and his towering presence in the world when a feeling of déjà vu washed over me.

Six years earlier, while reporting on the political unrest that had begun to surface in Zimbabwe, I had sat down for an interview with Ian Smith in the living room of his home in the capital city of Harare. He was eighty-one at the time, and I remembered thinking how small he was—not short like Friedman, but gaunt, his chest almost caved in. When

I was a teenager and read about Smith in the late 1970s, I imagined him a colossus, the defiant Bull Connor of Africa, the prime minister of a country that had seceded from the British Empire and was known then as Rhodesia.

As with Friedman, I had expected—wanted—to dislike him. But he was, in our meeting at least, a rather genteel man, white-haired and frail, a recent widower who seemed genuinely hungry for company and spirited conversation. He replenished my coffee cup whenever it was empty, and he invited me to stay and talk longer than the hour we had initially scheduled for our interview.

"This country has never seen such lawlessness and corruption," Smith said to me at the time. "Blacks come up to me all the time and say that they were better off when I was prime minister. We had a fine country then, a strong economy that was the jewel of Africa . . . Our blacks were the happiest in the world."

Much as Smith's view seemed an alternate reality to me, so did Friedman's analysis of the global economy. For Africans living in Rhodesia or for workers anywhere in the world, Smith's and Friedman's words would have been not just untrue, but untrue in the most absolute terms, or the complete *opposite* of the truth as they had experienced it.

In the brilliant light of Friedman's apartment, it dawned on me that Smith and Friedman were, in a political sense, one and the same: two leaders in the twentieth century's twin imperialist movements, colonialism and globalization, the goals of which were—are—one and the same: service to the empire and to their own social class. They spoke for their constituents and no one else. They saw no gray and did not want to. The world they built and lived in was wonderful, not in spite of what had befallen Africans or Chileans or U.S. workers but because of it.

On editorial pages, television news, and public television, pundits, bankers, politicians, and professors often describe globalization as a train—inevitable, demanding, churning violently, but ultimately necessary for civilization. But that all depends on your point of view. If you are lucky enough to have a seat on the train, then it seems all in all a rather good idea. But if you are on the tracks, with the train bearing down on you, then the locomotive, from where you stand, is not all it's cracked up to be. If you own stock in the publicly traded company, then you cheer the stock market like the home team. But if you work for the publicly-traded company and the stock price just jumped because you didn't get a raise, or a thousand of your coworkers just lost their jobs, or your retirement plan was eliminated, then your view of the world in that moment is much less sanguine than Wall Street's. If your home is in foreclosure because you can't afford the usurious interest on your mortgage, then you can think of better uses for $700 billion than bailing out a bunch of supposedly supersmart rich guys who conspired to swindle you and your neighbors out of your hard-earned cash in the first place.

From where Friedman and Smith sat on the train, Africa did fine under colonial rule and the revamped global economy yielded extraordinary successes. Neither man's equation factored in ordinary people.

Like colonialism, globalization is fundamentally extractive, a process of "accumulation by dispossession" as David Harvey, an economics professor at the City University of New York, describes it. The difference between the two is minuscule. The stewards of colonialism demagogically rallied their countrymen against the Communist menace. Globalization's architects found their own boogeyman—inflation—and used it to bludgeon the poor and the working class in the same manner. To the question of who gets ahead, the movements provide almost identical answers.

Rhodesia's European settlers got from Africans free land and cheap labor to amass their fortunes; their heirs, both biological and sociological, buy stocks in banks peddling subprime mortgages. It is the modern equivalent of the hut tax, the rich exploiting the poor for no reason other than to fatten their pockets.

Through deregulation, the United States and scores of other countries opened the door for corporations to span the globe, shopping for the lowest labor costs and more customers. Privatizing state-owned industries and utilities generated huge profits for investors but ate away at jobs and drove up the price of electricity and water.

To curb inflation, countries like Argentina, Brazil, and South Africa have strengthened the value of their currencies but in the process erased the price advantage their domestic manufacturers held over superior—and often subsidized—goods made in the United States and Western Europe. Foreign loans finance bridges, hydroelectric dams, and generators that largely benefit the country's elites but saddle taxpayers with crippling repayments. Rising interest rates lower inflation but make bank loans too expensive for working-class families who want to start a small business or send their children to college. Reductions in corporate taxes, soaring debt payments, and cutbacks in public spending wither credit unions, hospitals, schools, public transit systems, and land reform programs. Government transfers public property to private hands and private debt to public hands.

The poor are left with no way out. The ghetto metastasizes even while Wall Street rakes in record profits. Globalization has inverted the relationship between economic growth and the living standards of the poor, and today's investors have assumed the role of the landed gentry from the colonial era, cutting ordinary people out of the deal while they divvy up the booty among themselves.

CERTAINLY COUNTRIES THAT sell more of their goods abroad are better off than those that don't. But how do countries best position their economies to widen trade possibilities? Zambia, as one example, has since 1990 followed virtually to a T the ten-point plan, agreed upon by the World Bank, the IMF, and the U.S. Treasury (the Washington Consensus) for expanding the role of the market in the developing world, and sells half as much of its merchandise abroad as it did when it started.

The final chapter of this book is devoted to the growing efforts to reverse globalization's course. Led by a diverse coalition that includes rock stars, Bill Gates, South Africa's gay community, college kids in the United States, landless peasants in Brazil, and Venezuelan president Hugo Chávez, the movement that has emerged in the past decade is a high-tech version of the worldwide campaign to end slavery in the Belgian Congo nearly a century ago.

By providing a leg up to the poor both in his own country and abroad, Chávez has created the rarest of commodities: a government that responds to its citizenry more than to its corporate clientele. He is perhaps the most polarizing figure of the new colonial order.

The model for how best to manage globalization is Chile, which has had the fastest-growing economy in Latin America over the past twenty years. Contrary to conventional wisdom, it has accomplished this not by surrendering to the market but rather by tightening regulations on business and increasing taxes, the minimum wage, and public spending on education, health, and infrastructure. What Chile demonstrates is the central fallacy of globalization. The government's fingerprints are all over the country's prolonged prosperity. The plain and simple truth is that investors from abroad will no more rescue a sovereign nation's economy than a woman will be made whole by the attention of a man. To compete in the global economy, a country must first invest in its own workforce and industries, before outsiders rush in to assume a complementary and supervised role in economic development. It is Keynesian economics and good old common sense.

Numbers provide the skeleton that gives shape to any critical assessment of globalization: gross domestic product, inflation and jobless rates, trade deficits and mathematical formulas that measure inequality among populations. At its core, however, this is a book about jobs, decent-paying jobs, and the lack thereof, so it necessarily focuses on women and the darker-skinned people of and from the global South. They are, after all, the world's workers. And because of the central role they play in the global economy, there is also something of the blues in the marrow of this account. Like the tango in Argentina, the blues was born in brothels to Africa's sons and daughters, who put their heartache to music, a guttural wail of loss and longing. The blues are also a subversion, an act of defiance, sabotaging one's fear by singing out loud. Slaves in the American Deep South were far less likely to commit suicide than the slave owners, and the great jazz historian Albert Murray has posited that it was the blues, in its embry-

onic West African form, that sustained the slaves. Speak the
Devil's name and he loses half his power over you.

In distant lands and foreign tongues, whenever ordinary
people took the time to tell me their story, to describe their
sorrow and their hope, I always heard the blues. *This* is
what globalization feels like, and it is that feeling which has
eclipsed Coca-Cola, Detroit's cars, and Hollywood's movies to
become America's chief export to the world.

THE STORIES TOLD in this book are based on interviews I
conducted between 2001 and 2008. The seed, however, was
planted in my freshman year in high school, in 1979, when
my Latin teacher provided the class with the origin of the
word "ghetto." It comes, she said, from the Italian word
"getto," which means foundry. This, as I recall, jolted me
from the half-catatonic trance that was my way of coping
with the tedium of high school.

It is part of the family lore that my father was unemployed
on the day that I was born in 1965, at the apogee of the civil
rights movement and America's manufacturing sector. Laid
off from his job at a Howard Johnson hotel, he found work
two months later at the Chrysler plant on the west side of
Indianapolis. It was a foundry that made engine blocks.

The foundry, I knew even then, was a dangerous, dirty
place. But along with the post office, the automobile factories
and parts manufacturers on the city's west side were as good
as it got for black men credentialed with only a high school
diploma and a strong back.

My generation was among the first to be bused to school,
and so I knew that we didn't have what most of my white
classmates had. Still, my mostly black neighborhood was dif-

ferent from the ghetto. In my neighborhood, every man went to work in the morning. We had decent clothes, food when we were hungry, and medicine when we were sick. The ghetto was a few blocks away. It was overrun with men who had nothing to do in the middle of the day. Its landscape was of forbidding high-rises and shotgun homes that needed paint. The ghetto was a place of cheap liquor, bad manners, and worse teeth. The foundry was its antidote.

I became conscious of this just as American manufacturing was beginning its decline. In the early 1990s, while I was working for a Detroit newspaper, I volunteered as a mentor for a fifteen-year-old boy who lived on the city's poor east side. During one conversation, he blurted out, "You know, you are the only man I know who works. I know women who work, but I don't know a man who goes to a job every day."

A few years later, while writing about social policy in Washington, D.C., and its suburbs, it struck me that the women I interviewed for my stories on welfare had one thing in common: all had babies from men very much like my father, demographically speaking. Only now the foundry wasn't hiring, if indeed it existed at all.

In 1996 I interviewed a woman at a shelter in southern Maryland. She was poor, jobless, the mother of an eight-year-old girl, and she was describing for me her very simple dreams for the future. She wanted an apartment, new sneakers for her daughter, and a car, because her daughter was tired of walking everywhere and it hurt her to see her daughter walk.

And there was something else, she said.

"I want to see the ocean," she said. "I've never seen the ocean."

From where we sat, the Atlantic Ocean was not ninety minutes away.

I cannot remember her name, but I've never forgotten her face or the longing in her voice. Not a month passes when it doesn't echo in my head.

The ghetto, more than anything, exists in isolation, a half-lit world where people are estranged from their homeland, citizens unable to participate fully in the life of their city.

In 2003 I was interviewing a Brazilian taxi driver who was celebrating his forty-sixth birthday. His life was one of poverty, as was his mother's before him. He worked hard and he worried constantly that his children would not escape the poverty that he had inherited. He wanted to do so much for them, and as he drove me and my interpreter to a taxi rank one evening, he rattled off the things he would do for his family if he just had a little money: a proper wedding for one daughter, college for the other, a roof for his unfinished house, a ring for his wife of twenty-six years.

He paused, and then: "I want to take my mother to see the ocean," he said. "My mother has never seen the ocean. I don't want my mother to die without seeing the ocean."

She was at the time fifty-nine and had lived in Rio de Janeiro her entire life. From her home, the ocean was a twenty-minute drive away, due south. But it might as well have been a thousand miles. The taxi driver usually worked seven days a week, and if he wasn't paid a fare, the gasoline used for even a relatively short trip could mean that his wife and children went hungry later in the month.

This book is for everyone who has never seen the sea. And for everyone who wishes it for them.

Part One

CANARIES
IN THE MINE

1

A New Day

Zambia and Free Trade

Under free trade the trader is the master and the producer the slave. Protection is but the law of nature, the law of self-preservation, of self-development, of securing the highest and best destiny of the race of man.

—*William McKinley, 1892*

The old is dying and the new cannot be born; in this interregnum there arises a great diversity of morbid symptoms.

—*Antonio Gramsci*

Just a few miles north of Victoria Falls on Zambia's eastern border with Zimbabwe, there is a sprawling open-air market in a town named Maramba. It is on the edge of a two-lane highway that snakes through the city of Livingtone, past the two new luxury hotels and at least half a dozen shuttered factories, which rise like mirages in the shimmering summer air.

Long, uneven rows of vendors stretch far and wide, so if you walk from one end of the market to the other, you pass through a section of brilliant light, then shadows, then back into the light again. Near the front of the Maramba market, under the leafless baobab tree, where a shallow rut in the dirt forms a footpath, Rose Shanzi sits on a warped stool on a

February morning in 2002, with an angry tropical sun bearing down on her. She folds her arms across her waist as if she's been straitjacketed and rocks gently back and forth, her right foot tapping nervously in the dirt.

"Okay," she mumbles to no one in particular. "I am open for business now."

This is how the day begins for Rose, a sinewy woman with deep-set eyes and sharp features that jut like a sphinx's from under her black headscarf. She awoke with a start this morning, and the primordial question that was her first waking thought is stalking her again: will she and her children eat today?

It is always a compound question. She has five children to feed, and often there is not enough food to go around; sometimes tough choices have to be made.

Still, all the answers Rose is searching for today lie in the neat rows of tomatoes arranged by size, ripeness, and price on the wooden table standing at eye level before her. To buy enough food to get her family through another day, Rose will need to earn roughly 75 cents.

"If I sell my tomatoes, we will eat today," she says to me, matter-of-factly. "If I don't, we don't eat."

This is no easy feat. The 75 cents that Rose needs to make ends meet is about 50 percent more than she ordinarily earns from her vegetable stand in a twelve-hour day. Moreover, the competition at the Maramba market is stiff. After it opened in 1952, the number of vendors here remained constant for nearly forty years. Then, as unemployment swelled, it expanded to five times its original size within a decade. Rose is one of no fewer than four thousand vendors peddling everything from double-A batteries to zebra-skin loveseats to secondhand clothes. At least a few dozen women sell tomatoes just as red and ripe as Rose's.

And although the tomatoes cost just a few pennies per handful, customers are hard to come by. Jobs have evaporated, particularly since duty-free shipments of foreign-made clothes began pouring into Zambia in the early 1990s, shutting down all four of the textile factories in Livingstone and its environs.

"No one has money anymore," Rose is saying as she sizes up a woman who handled her vegetables but left without buying anything. "The town has no buying power. Selling anything is like squeezing blood from a stone."

The struggle of one woman in a remote African border town to earn what much of the world considers loose change reflects globalization's original sin: the doctrinaire opening of industrial markets to all comers has laid waste to local economies. Since Adam Smith published *An Inquiry into the Nature and Causes of the Wealth of Nations* in 1776, classical liberal macroeconomic faith has posited that favoritism saps vigor from the marketplace. When Smith's ideological heirs at the World Bank and the International Monetary Fund (IMF) sat down with foreign finance ministers to hammer out trade deals and loan conditions, beginning in the 1970s, the first order of business was inevitably the willy-nilly disassembly of tariffs that protect domestic industries from competitive pressures.

No country was a more enthusiastic convert than Zambia, a landlocked, butterfly-shaped nation of 12 million people with a landmass the size of Texas. Within eighteen months following the 1991 presidential election of Frederick Chiluba, a former trade union leader, the country dramatically reduced or repealed altogether its levies on more than 180 industrial products. Virtually nothing manufactured, bottled, or stitched together by Zambians was left untouched in the overhaul.

Had things gone according to the neoliberal blueprint, here is what should have happened next: Stiffer competition from abroad would have shut down some inefficient industries in Zambia, but many more would have thrived as manufacturers capitalized on its "comparative advantages"—say, topography or particular talents in the local workforce—to sell more merchandise to buyers in suddenly accessible overseas markets. Over time, liberalized markets would have reduced the ranks of Zambia's poor, first by expanding the number of workers participating in a modern economy, and second by driving down consumer prices, so that even when workers did not realize pay increases, they effectively earned more money by paying lower prices for the kids' breakfast cereal, shoes, and bicycles.

Here is how it actually went down: Zambia was overrun with foreign-made products and lost 800,000 jobs over the next decade. Too fragile to withstand competition for its own turf, too embryonic to produce much of anything the rest of the world wants beyond raw materials, the country's manufacturing sector was cut in half. Zambians today sell fewer products to global consumers than they did half a century ago, when the country was a British colony. Eight of ten Zambians today survive on less than $1 a day. In 1991 the ratio was four in ten.

Perhaps the most remarkable example of Zambia's deindustrialization is its textiles sector. Used clothing began to arrive here almost immediately after the government repealed import taxes in 1992. Since no duties are charged for used clothes—customs officials listed their value at zero—wholesalers realized they could create a new market by buying surplus clothing donated to charities like the Salvation Army for only pennies per pound, then shipping them by the bale to sub-Saharan Africa, where they are sold at markups of as much as 400 percent. Not especially efficient, Zambia's textile factories were overmatched by wholesalers delivering affordable, passable clothing, often made with subsidized materials in rich nations, without paying production costs, tariffs, or customs. The 140 textile manufacturing plants that Chiluba inherited in 1991 had been whittled to 8 when he left office in January 2002.

About 30,000 of the industry's 34,000 jobs disappeared, according to the Zambia Association of Manufacturers, and were replaced by a loose but crowded network of roadside and flea-market vendors beckoning shoppers to "rummage through the pile," or *salaula*, in the language of Zambia's majority Bemba tribe. The bales of old clothing shipped to sub-Saharan Africa by the United States alone account for nearly $60 million in sales annually and are by now so familiar that entirely new idioms have emerged. Partly in derision and partly because many Africans once assumed that the clothing belonged to the recently deceased, Ghanaians refer to the imports as "dead white man's clothing." Tanzanians dubbed the garments "dyed in America," and in Zambia the used-clothing stands are called "bend-down boutiques."

In the two generations since Africans began to free their countries from colonial misrule, nearly forty countries on the continent have liberalized their markets as part of the "structural adjustment programs" peddled by Western donors such as the World Bank and the IMF. In doing so, the continent has abandoned the industrial strategies designed to strengthen the puny manufacturing sectors left behind by European settlers, transforming Africa into a dumping ground for what the industrialized world no longer needs or wants, a deluge of secondhand clothes, used cars, old furniture, tools, and weapons.

The continent's transformation into a giant flea market is the trailer for a very bad movie. From the African savanna to the Andean Mountains to the American Midwest, global capital has taken a wrecking ball to the Rust Belt, its smokestacks, payrolls, and labor unions. The old economy favored production; the new economy favors retail, speculation, deal-making. Just as Chiluba bridged the gap between the two macroeconomic models in a single election cycle, America's political leadership traveled roughly the same political distance in little more than a generation, bracketed by the inauguration of two young, charismatic, skirt-chasing presidents, both Democrats. When John F. Kennedy took office in 1961, one of his top priorities was prodding Congress to create more factory jobs by rewarding corporate investment in plant improvements and new equipment with greater tax benefits. Thirty-two years later, Bill Clinton walked into the White House practically inviting factory owners to set up shop elsewhere by pressuring Capitol Hill lawmakers to pass the North American Free Trade Agreement, which demolished the tariffs for products manufactured on the other side of America's borders.

The shift is a critical detour from the path to prosperity, particularly for maturing economies. As the Norwegian economist Erik Reinert points out, "No nation has ever taken the step from being poor to being wealthy by exporting raw materials in the absence of a domestic manufacturing sector." Yet globalization's indiscriminate opening of markets has robbed undeveloped countries of what they most need for economic growth—an industrial strategy—and kicked the ladder out from under the world's poorest people just as they are beginning their ascent.

Sub-Saharan Africa's 800 million people represent more than 10 percent of the world's population but account for only 2 percent of global trade, a share that is smaller than it was even fifty years ago. Since 1990, manufacturing activity has declined by a third, per capita income by a quarter. During that same period, the growth of global trade has added nearly $1 trillion to global income.

Shortly after I first arrived in Africa in 1999 as a foreign correspondent, I began exploring a simple line of inquiry with academics, diplomats, and people in think tanks in Washington, D.C., and New York. Why is poverty so inert, so resolute on this continent? Why do Africans remain so stubbornly poor, their economies more primitive now than those of their parents?

The answers most often proffered to me pointed to Africans' corruption, a cultural ethos that does not encourage hard work or education like the West's, and the continent's abiding failure to prostrate itself at the altar of globalization. But the facts I saw on the ground bore witness to an altogether different failure. This border town on the banks of the Zambezi River demonstrates how globalization got it all wrong right from the start. Trade expansion does not trigger development, but rather widening trade *follows* domestic investment in infrastructure and industry. Africa in the twenty-first century remains in this sort of interregnum, surfacing from colonialism's indifference only to find its growth stunted again by another imperialist movement.

"We've made the mistake of confusing the free market with development," said Fred M'membe, executive editor of the *Post*, Zambia's only independent daily newspaper. "I'm not saying we should isolate ourselves from the world the way we once did, but we are not looking at how to develop our country. We are looking at how we can market our country to outsiders so they can come develop it for us. We are getting back to the same colonial equation where, in the land of our birth, Africans own nothing, control nothing, run nothing. We are soon to be aliens in our own country."

"IT SEEMS I just woke up one morning and everything was gone."

Rose is explaining how she got into the business of selling tomatoes. That was four years ago, after her husband lost his job as a firefighter when the government began restructuring the workforce. She had been one of the first batch of workers to lose her job when the textile factories began shutting down in 1992, and since then all forty had closed or so drastically cut back their operations that they employed only a handful of workers.

What was she to do? She was a forty-year-old woman with a high school diploma, with four children and another on the way. There was no work to be had, so she did not look. There was no dole, so she could not wait. There was no charity, so she could not beg.

"If I cry or go to my neighbors, what good would that do?" Rose is saying. "They have nothing either. They are suffering just as much."

Friends of hers who had also lost their jobs at the local textile factories had begun selling vegetables and charcoal that they purchased from wholesalers. Since her husband was too ill to work, Rose decided to join them.

"My husband was dying along with the town," Rose explains about her husband's slow disintegration from kidney failure. He died in 2001, a broken man in a broken town. "I think not being able to support his family is what really killed him. He was a proud man. He hated not being the breadwinner. But it was the only way we could make it. All of my neighbors work here at the market. For most of us, it is the only way to survive."

The littlest of Rose's children, three-year-old Betty, finished off the family's last dollop of porridge this morning. No one else in the household has eaten in nearly a day, leaving Rose unsure whether the knot in her stomach is hunger or anxiety, or both.

By noon she has not made so much as a cent, and she's been sitting here for more than two hours now. She passes some of the time gossiping with her friend, Judith Namakube, a vendor at the Maramba market who sells oranges and other fruits from a stand next to Rose's.

They both notice a young woman who seems to be flirting with a young man selling bottled juice, candy, and snacks at a stand maybe 25 yards from where they are stationed.

"This is the second time today she's visited him," Rose remarks.

"I don't think she is having much luck with him," Judith says.

"I don't think he wants what she is selling," Rose replies, an impish smile breaking across her face.

"This is a hard place for *anyone* to close the deal," Judith says. The two women chuckle.

There have been luckless days when Rose has gone home with nothing, and it is that possibility that begins to preoccupy her moments later. Eyes shut, hands clenched tightly together in her lap, she bows her head in prayer, silently mouthing the words.

Resurfacing, she smiles wanly, rejuvenated momentarily by faith, inspired by fear.

"If you are a mother," she says, her gaze fixed on the middle distance, "you don't know what suffering is until you have watched your babies go hungry. I have suffered many times."

Ask just about anyone in southern Africa what it means to go hungry, or what constitutes a food shortage, and they will say they are without "maize meal" or "mealie meal," depending on the country. Made from corn, it is all the same thing: the region's all-purpose, carb-heavy staple, used to make porridge for breakfast and *nshima* for lunch and dinner and any meal in between.

Nshima, called *sadza* in Zimbabwe, *pap* in South Africa, is the color of grits, the consistency of polenta. Zambians eat it with just about everything. Sprinkled with groundnuts, chopped okra, or maybe just some sugar, it is a meal in itself when little else is available, oftentimes the only thing standing between Africans and starvation.

"If you don't like *nshima*," said Judith, "you aren't Zambian."

Nshima is on the menu of the two gaudy South African—owned hotels that opened on the misty up-splash of Victoria Falls in 2001. The Zambezi Sun is a three-star property, the

Royal Livingstone a four-star luxury hotel where you can spend as much as $600 a night for a room in season.

With 173 rooms, marbled floors, and broad verandas, the Royal Livingstone especially tries to recreate the colonial experience for its visitors, mostly whites from Europe, the United States, and South Africa, who sip champagne and margaritas while watching the blood-red sunset from a beautiful cherrywood deck. The hotel assigns each guest his or her own butler, and white-coated Zambian staff members smile so intensely when turning down your bed or cleaning your room that it makes *your* jaw hurt.

In addition to *nshima*, the restaurant's offerings include a pork terrine with figs, pumpkin soup, pasta with pesto sauce and langoustines, and a nightly buffet; for high tea, finger sandwiches and mousse; and top-shelf single malt scotch and at least one brand of cognac that will set you back $1,000 for a bottle.

Out of sight of their bosses, the hotel's workers will often plead with you for a tip to feed their children. A waiter I once met at an after-hours drinking hole for Zambian locals told me that he and others were trying to unionize the hotel's workforce, but management had threatened to fire anyone who even broached the subject of unionizing on the hotel premises.

Of the roughly one thousand hotel employees, 40 percent are part-time. The average take-home pay is less than $100 a month. Executives at Sun International in South Africa say that their wages comply with Zambia's labor laws, which were watered down in the 1990s to allow for longer probation periods, fewer benefits, and longer workdays.

Globalization's supporters often contend that poor countries in the global South can rely on a growing tourism industry to bolster their economy in the absence of industry. But as the new and resplendent hotels here illustrate, tourism is no substitute for making things.

"The workers at the hotel work harder than anyone and they are treated horribly," Rose whispers to me as a friend who works as a maid on the property ambles out of earshot, shopping on her day off. "The hotel is for the whites. They come from South Africa, Zimbabwe, America, and Europe and they are treated like kings for a few days. And we Africans wait on them hand and foot because we are too hungry for just the small crumbs they throw us. It is really not very different from when the British first came here a hundred years ago."

Europeans dubbed Africa "the dark continent" because it was a vast and unknowable land, mysterious as the moon. Livingstone is named for the Scottish missionary and explorer David Livingstone, who in 1855 became the first European to conquer the dense jungle and lethal malaria to lay eyes on the towering waterfalls, the rainbow-colored mist, and the hypnotic gorge that make Niagara Falls seem like a wading pool.

Zambians call the falls the "smoke that thunders," or *mosi-oa-tunya*, in the Sotho dialect spoken here. Livingstone named the falls after Queen Victoria. Thirty-three years later, the British industrialist Cecil Rhodes negotiated mineral concession rights with unsuspecting tribal chiefs, and for the next thirty-six years Zambians were ruled not by the Commonwealth but by a single mining concern, the British South Africa Company. In all matters of the state, Rhodes and his lieutenants were the unelected and unquestioned rulers.

"No one knows better than Zambians about global capital," said M'membe, the newspaper editor. "Zambians were capital and the entire country was the property of a global corporation."

Rhodes relinquished control of Zambia in 1924 and Britain added the country and its mineral wealth to the empire's books. What made Zambia appealing was the copper, cobalt, and zinc buried beneath its soil, which by independence accounted for more than a third of the country's gross domestic product and 80 percent of its export earnings. The mines employed, in one capacity or another, almost half the workforce. Africans' curse has always been the abundantly rich earth beneath their feet. Whether gold, rubber, diamonds, oil, or coffee, all that colonial conquerors needed to turn a profit was cheap labor, a hole in the ground, and a railway to the sea. When they began leaving in the 1950s, colonial rulers left behind little of lasting value.

Copper, for instance, is one of the more versatile metals of the industrial world, a good conductor of heat and electricity, used in the manufacture of flatware, plumbing fittings, doorknobs, frying pans, ships, and batteries. The British, however, made none of these products in Zambia, preferring instead to ship the raw product overseas, where it would be processed and assembled into finished goods, earning higher wages for their better-trained workers and fatter profits for their factory owners.

This largely explains why development in Africa lags greatly behind that in other colonized lands in the Southern Hemisphere. The continent as a whole lacks the kinds of "value-added" industries that characterize prosperous economies. For example, Africans grow about one tenth of all coffee sold on the world market, selling the unprocessed beans for less than 25 cents per pound to roasters in London, Chicago, and Berlin. Starbucks sells the finished product to consumers in the United States and Europe for fifteen times that amount. There are no industrial roasters anywhere on the African continent.

Without firing a shot, Zambians won their independence in 1964, but Kenneth Kaunda, the country's liberation hero and first democratically elected president, inherited a country with no colleges or universities and fewer than a dozen college graduates. (Similarly, when neighboring Congo won its independence from Belgium three years earlier, there were no blacks there with college degrees.) For the twenty-seven years that followed, Kaunda pursued economic policies that joined government and the economy at the hip, jump-starting industrial development with a policy known in economic circles as import substitution, in which a country begins to manufacture for domestic consumption products it would otherwise buy from abroad. Kaunda nationalized the mines, expanded the manufacturing and agricultural sectors through state spending, and walled them off from foreign competition with daunting trade barriers, massive state subsidies, and onerous business regulations.

To improve the productivity and skill level of its workforce, the government provided free health care and primary education. Literacy levels rose. The economy grew. Because the settler regime had merely purchased whatever it needed from abroad, there were no large-scale textile producers in the country in 1964. Within six years of Zambia's independence, nearly 85 textile manufacturers employed more than 10,000 workers.

Then the bottom fell out. Copper prices plummeted just

as world oil prices climbed, and Kaunda turned to the donor community in 1973. "We had refused to borrow, but now we had no choice," Kaunda said in an interview. "I approached both the IMF and the World Bank and said, Look, we are in this precarious situation. Can we borrow? Their reply was, Well, we think that copper prices will soon rise again, so please feel free to borrow."

He did, but copper prices continued to plunge. Inefficient and unproductive, propped up by foreign loans and dragged down by plunging commodity prices, Kaunda's socialist system slid inexorably into collapse. Fed up with constant shortages of food and fuel and with Kaunda's authoritarian leadership, Zambians forced their stubborn patriarchal independence hero to allow elections, then voted him out in 1991 in favor of a trade union leader promising reform, Frederick Chiluba.

Officials with the World Bank and IMF joined British and American development officials to promise Zambia billions in loans if Chiluba would only eliminate tariffs on foreign goods, wean farmers off practically all government subsidies and supports, and sell more than three hundred state-owned enterprises, including the country's copper mines. Virtually overnight Chiluba replaced a centralized economy with undiluted capitalism.

The payoff so far is an economy fueled by little more than grit and guile, practically devoid of valuable commodities. By 2001 Zambia's debt had reached $6.6 billion, and its annual payments were three times what the government spent each year on primary education. Unable to pay the new fees charged by local schools, many parents simply stopped sending their kids. Dropout and illiteracy rates increased sharply.

The unemployment rate climbed to more than 40 percent, and many Zambians resorted to selling whatever they could get their hands on at markets like the one in Maramba—or on the streets after dark. Police say crime and prostitution have skyrocketed, especially in urban hubs such as Lusaka, Livingstone, and Kitwe.

The work in the textile factories was hard and the paychecks were small, Rose says. "But it was nothing like this. You worked eight hours and you went home. It was enough to put food in our children's bellies every day. The factories had reading classes to teach illiterate women how to read. People felt like we were progressing, maybe just an inch or two each day, but still, we were moving forward. Now we just pray that God will get us through this day."

Working with a Canadian cousin, Jim Ebrahim, the managing director of Central African Traders Ltd., ships a truckload of secondhand apparel into Zambia, Congo, and Tanzania at least once a week. "We pay $35,000 for each container," he said. "When we first started six years ago, we would clear about $6,000 profit for each shipment. But now there is so much competition that we only clear about $2,000 profit on each container."

Zambia's textile producers simply could not compete with the influx of Western clothes. Even used, most of the clothes were made with superior machinery and cheap cotton subsidized by Western governments or in East Asian sweatshops. "It was stylish. It was cheap. It was better made," said Mark O'Donnel, chairman of the Zambia Association of Manufacturers. "Our industry didn't have a chance. We would have preferred for the changes to be phased in to allow our textile industry a chance to catch up to the rest of the world and really compete."

"It's not just clothing," said Ramesh Patel, director of SWAPP Ltd. Clothing in Ndola, the heart of Zambia's struggling copper-belt region. "We used to have factories everywhere, but Ndola is a ghost town now. We are one of the lucky ones who have managed to survive, but there's no comparison. We used to supply retailers with 3.5 thousand tons of clothing annually; we're down to less than 500 tons now. We had 250 employees eight years ago; we're down to 25 now."

"You can walk for miles at a time here and not see anyone wearing anything remotely resembling African clothing," said Howard Gatchell, chairman of the Chamber of Commerce in Zambia's second city, Ndola.

Other countries in the region can sympathize with Zambia. When the World Bank prodded Mozambique in 1996 to repeal taxes that discouraged growers from selling their cashews on the world market, ten of the country's fifteen cashew processing plants shut down, leaving 7,500 of the industry's 12,000 workers unemployed. World Bank officials argued that abolishing the import tax would lower the price of processed nuts while increasing the price that peasant farmers could demand for their unprocessed cashews in a more competitive market. They were half right. Without protectionist measures, foreign processors were able to outbid Mozambican factories for locally grown cashews.

But Mozambique's isolated peasant farmers, accustomed to selling their nuts at a set price to government agents, had no idea how to negotiate with buyers, no clue about how to get their products to market without government assistance, and no hint, really, of who, what, or where this free market was. By 2001 Mozambican growers were getting less for their nuts than they were before the government lifted its export tax.

Savvy foreign traders—mostly Indian—were reaping the benefits of the higher cashew prices, buying the nuts from peasant farmers and then selling them abroad.

Mozambicans old enough to remember the country's post-independence socialist economy often repeat a refrain that I heard again and again from Zambians, Malawians, Brazilians, Argentines, and people in most any country that had witnessed the shift in industrial strategy. "Before, there was nothing on the shelves but everyone had some money in their pockets. Now the shelves are full but no one has any money to buy."

"You won't find many Zambians old enough to remember it who would want to return to the Kaunda era," said M'membe. "But you won't find anyone who will say that we're better off now than we were twenty years ago. No one alive today has ever seen such poverty. How do you run a modern economy when the vast majority of your earners are taking home pennies a day?"

IT IS SHORTLY after noon and Rose is turned toward me when she is ambushed from her blind side by a lithe figure with braided hair and a featureless, torn sundress, who appears as if dropped from the sky, hurtling into Rose's lap with playful fury.

"Mama, I am hungry," ten-year-old Ennelis says as Rose gathers the girl up in her arms. It is the girl's summer vacation, and she awoke to a house with no food.

"Then help me work," Rose says to her.

The girl is like a talisman today. Within thirty minutes of her arrival, three customers appear at the tomato stand, forking out about 8 cents apiece for a handful of the medium-sized tomatoes. Ennelis, who worked the vegetable stand

alone for three weeks last year when her mother was bedrid-
den with malaria, rips scraps of paper from one of Zambia's
independent newspapers, the *Monitor*. An editorial laments
the failure of Chiluba's economic policies. Ennelis wraps the
tomatoes inside.

Rose hates to count money during the day. She is afraid that
there are too many idle young men around, waiting to snatch
a day's revenue from some unsuspecting woman's hand. So
she usually hides the crumpled, faded bills underneath the
plain white doily on her table. The newspaper provides Rose
with both something to do in between customers and an idea
of how business is going that day.

"If you are just reading bits and pieces of a story at the end
of the day, you have made good money," Rose is saying. "If you
have a lot to read at the end of the day, then you have not made
very much money. If I have used up most of my newspaper
today, I will be able to buy maybe two small bags of maize
meal, and that is all I need to make me happy today."

Relatively speaking, Rose does better than many other
Zambians. Her husband left her with a two-bedroom home.
She has no electricity and relies on kerosene lamps and
candles for light, charcoal for heat and fire. But with a tap
in her back yard, she does have access to clean water, which
saves the time it would take to fetch water from faraway
wells or risk waterborne illnesses such as cholera.

And Rose has been able to make the most of her meager
earnings by joining a relief agency project that provides small
loans to poor entrepreneurs. The money is not much, maybe
$20 every six months. But it tides Rose over in particularly
rough times, ensuring that she has a steady supply of tomatoes
to sell.

"It is not a lot of money," said Joshua Tom, a project coordinator for CARE, the U.S.-based relief agency that runs the micro-lending fund. "But it can mean the difference between life and starvation for a lot of people here."

Living on $1 a day makes budgeting difficult but also reduces it to a few simple priorities. Of Rose's profits from the stand—roughly $12 to $18 per month—half goes for food. About $2 goes for the fees charged by Ennelis's public school. Rose pays $2 a month for water, another $1.50 in property taxes, and 50 cents for the government's health insurance plan. Whatever is left goes to pay off her loan from CARE.

Health insurance for the whole family would cost double what Rose pays for herself, so whenever other family members get sick and need to go to the clinic, they simply pretend to be Rose. That works fine for Rose and her four daughters, but when her twenty-year-old son came down with malaria last year, employees at the local clinic wanted to know how he came to have a woman's name.

"He told them that his parents really, really wanted a girl," Rose explains, dabbing her eyes while laughing at a rare triumph.

Water, education, and health care were free during most of Kaunda's rule, and it rankles her that she now has to pay for basic services. "That's money I could spend on meat," she says testily. The family eats meat only once a year, usually at Christmas, when Rose splurges. "It's rubbing salt in our wounds to take jobs away from the people and then make them pay for things they cannot afford because they're not working."

Another customer wanders by, followed by another maybe an hour later. By 3 p.m., Rose has earned a little more than half of what she needs to buy two three-pound bags of maize meal, meaning that the market's end-of-the-day rush will make or break her.

The few people in town with jobs usually stop at the market on their way home, but it's anyone's guess whether they will need any tomatoes or whether they will choose Rose's over those of the other vendors who sell them.

Still, Rose is feeling confident. Perhaps more important, she wants Ennelis to feel confident, safe, to believe that she will have food today. "Children should not live with such grown-up worries," she will say later. So she gives the girl the equivalent of about 12 cents and sends her off to buy vegetables for this evening's *nshima*—an act of faith.

"Pick out what you want to eat with the *nshima* and take them home for you and your sister to chop," she is saying to Ennelis, whose right hand is outstretched in anticipation. She skips off happily.

By 4 p.m. the market is a hive, snatches of color and sound and chaos that flit across the landscape: young men pushing wheelbarrows; an old toothless man holding a squawking chicken in a plastic bag; barefoot children weaving through the vendors' stands, chasing one another; women squinting in the sun from their misshapen stools. Rose is beckoning to a boy to fetch her a cup of tea for a nickel. It has been nearly twenty-four hours since she last ate anything.

"This is what I usually have for lunch," she says. "It settles an empty stomach."

Then, a flurry of customers. Rose springs from her stool. A woman buys one of Rose's biggest tomatoes for about 12 cents. A young man in a tie buys another. A woman who attends the same church as Rose palms three of the small ones and hands Rose about 8 cents.

"Rose, I am skinny, but you are really getting skinny," she remarks as Rose wraps her tomatoes in newspaper. "You are going to look as old as me if you don't eat."

"This life we live makes us old before we are ready," Rose replies as she hands the package across the table.

The sun is setting when Rose returns to her stool and retrieves the scraps of newspaper from underneath her table. She sizes up her surroundings and, seeing no signs of danger, pulls the wrinkled bills from underneath her doily. She melts into her seat while she counts: 3,900 Zambian kwacha. About 97 cents. Rose is smiling as she rises from her stool to go buy the maize meal that she promised her daughter, then start her thirty-minute walk home.

"Ah," she says as she stretches her arms toward the sky, "today we are rich."

2

THE NIGHT SHIFT

Argentina and Monetary Policy

> Got a stone but didn't get a nut to crack, got a nut but
> didn't get a stone to crack it with.
> —*Ghanaian proverb*

The dying light of an autumn day pierces Sylvia Ozuna's one-bedroom apartment like shards of glass, and the darkening sky above Buenos Aires jars her as if from sleep.

She is late.

Hurriedly, she dabs on a final coat of lipstick, barks instructions to the babysitter, plucks an open pack of Marlboros from the kitchen table, and bounds down four flights of stairs in what seems like a single fluid motion. Her heels click purposefully on the sidewalk's broken red brick as she strides past hulking walkups with laundry drying on the window ledges, dusty thrift stores, and hotels that charge by the hour and blink VACANCY in neon lights. In her head she does a quick accounting: the breeze is warm, the sky clear, and it is the first Friday of the month—payday for many of her customers. "Should be a good night," she says as she ducks into Charly's, an all-night greasy spoon that the girls use as a break room.

The fry cook with snow-white stubble and slits for eyes glances at her from behind the counter as she walks in. "Hello, honey," he says with a wide grin.

"Hello, Bruno," Sylvia answers as she opens the door of a closet-sized restroom with the letter "M," for *mujeres*, hanging crookedly from a plastic hook on the door. She tears off her khakis and emerges two minutes later wearing a pair of hip-hugging, sheer white leggings. She hands her folded khakis to Bruno to put behind the counter for safekeeping.

"Good luck tonight, honey," Bruno says. Sylvia waves without turning back.

Just blocks away, Miguel Machado is arriving for work at almost precisely the same moment. The ghost train pitches forward and then back before trembling to a halt in the city's Belgrano neighborhood. Hauling rucksacks, pushing grocery carts and makeshift dollies, *los cartoneros* tumble to the platform in clots, then scatter through the twilit neighborhood of leviathan high-rises and condominiums to sift through the evening's garbage for soda bottles, cardboard, newspapers— whatever the recyclers will take off their hands.

Miguel is among the first to exit. He is forty-six, square-jawed, Rock Hudson handsome, and in a hurry. Since he lost his job at the flour mill, picking through other people's trash for recyclables has been the family business, and the Machados are shorthanded tonight. His wife is home with the babies, both of them sick, leaving Miguel alone to supervise the couple's five oldest children. Since recycling fetches only pennies per pound, every hand counts.

"Mario, come on," he says to his lanky sixteen-year-old

son, who is pulling the hood of his gray sweatshirt over his head and pushing one of the family's two dollies. Miguel has the other one. He quickens his step, lowers his head, leans into it. "It's time to go to work."

This is the night shift in Buenos Aires, Argentina's teeming capital city, where workers in the most viable industries are the roaming bands of *los cartoneros*—literally, "box men" in Spanish—and *los gatos*, the swarm of prostitutes who occupy neighborhoods like Constitution in cheap leather, loud lipstick, and fuchsia.

Twenty years ago, Argentina's was the most prosperous and industrialized economy in Latin America and virtually everyone who wanted a job could find one. Then in 1991, with the blessing of the world's two most powerful financial institutions, the IMF and the World Bank, Argentina's investor-friendly government decided to root out inflation by fixing the exchange rate of the local currency: one peso for one U.S. dollar.

Within two years, the move had sharply curbed inflation, from a rate of 84 percent annually to one of 7.4 percent. But it also effectively raised prices on locally-produced goods, making Argentina's products too expensive to sell abroad and products shipped into the country artificially cheap. Much like the disillusioned, bankrupt protagonist of Ernest Hemingway's *The Sun Also Rises*, Argentina went broke, "gradually at first, and then suddenly."

Confronted with a deluge of foreign products and unable to sell their merchandise abroad, Argentina's manufacturers scaled back or went under. The very nature of work changed. By 2003 the country's auto industry was producing fewer cars than at any time since 1965. The nation's unemployment rate quintupled. Since 1997, three of every four jobs created here have been in the informal sector, meaning that they are off the books, on the margins, and often in the shadows.

Across the city, that means a nightly scramble for johns and scrap metal. On any given night, government officials estimate, as many as 40,000 *cartoneros* are working in Buenos Aires. That number has increased more than tenfold since 1993. So many *cartoneros* converge on the city from its rust-belt perimeter that in 2003 provincial transportation officials removed the seats from a fleet of trains solely to accommodate the workers and their equipment. No one knows who coined the term, but before long the trains were dubbed collectively *el tren phantasma*, the ghost train, because it's as if, Miguel says, the *cartoneros* "don't exist in this world."

The tragic truth is that there is not enough trash to go around. Miguel likes to arrive early and stake out his turf. "People will fight you over the garbage," he says as he stands under a streetlight with his children, poised and waiting for the night's rubbish to be hauled out. "We are living like animals now. This is not the life I wanted."

His goals are simple: to buy a house, take his children to see the ocean, buy them decent clothes. "This is the best I can do for now," he says.

On the corner of Pavon and Santiago del Estero, in the neighborhood known as Constitution, the white women from small towns in Argentina, Paraguay, and Peru stake out their territory. A block away the black women from the Dominican Republic, Cuba, and Haiti saunter. More seem to arrive each day—so many that Sylvia grudgingly had to lower her prices a few months back just to stay competitive.

"How much?" a merchant marine with hands the size

of hams and the rumpled face of a shar-pei dog asks Sylvia as she stands beneath a streetlamp, twirling strands of her waist-long honey-blond hair between her fingers. This is what she does when she's nervous.

"Thirty pesos" she says—roughly $10. "Plus another ten for the hotel."

A nod and they're off for fifteen minutes of sex on a lopsided queen-sized bed in a dark flophouse, after Sylvia demands that the manager at least change the sheets before she forks over the cash.

The merchant marine is her first customer this evening. Before the night is done, she will have sex with eight strangers —a good haul, considering that hardly anyone in Constitution has any real money to spare and there are seven other women working at this intersection alone.

"He smelled like bad meat," Sylvia says, grimacing, as she sits on a plastic chair at a wobbly table in Charly's sipping coffee and taking a puff from her sixth Marlboro of the night. It is 8:44 p.m. and she is complaining to her friend, Cecelia Cordon, who usually works the same corner as Sylvia.

Cecelia smiles, first at her friend, then at me and my interpreter. "The Paraguayan," she says playfully of Sylvia. This is the nickname affectionately given to her by the other streetwalkers. Sylvia moved here six years ago from Missiones, a cow town in neighboring Paraguay, contemplating medical school and marriage to a man she met shortly after she arrived in the city. She worked nights cleaning offices and attended premed classes during the day at the University of Buenos Aires. Tuition was still free; she only had to pay for books. But the maid service gradually cut back her hours. When the peso was devalued, Sylvia was earning $1 an hour for twenty hours of work each week. She quit school. She had a baby with her boyfriend, but their relationship flickered until he vanished from her life so abruptly and completely that she sometimes wonders, even now, if he weren't a hallucination.

She and a coworker were mopping an office floor together one evening when Sylvia shared her concerns about money. Her coworker told her that she earned extra money by working as a prostitute at a bar. "They're always looking for new faces," the coworker said.

Sylvia turned her first trick a year ago. She is twenty-seven, a single mother with a junebug-sized mole on her right cheek and carved features that are more handsome than pretty. She can be dour, almost joyless at times, and this is precisely why Cecelia and the others dubbed her *la paraguaya*, to needle her about her somewhat imperious bearing, her aloofness. It is their way of telling her to relax, to get over herself.

"I know they say I am very serious," Sylvia says. "I try to keep a low profile. I don't drink. I don't do drugs. I save. This is my job. That's how I have to look at it. I know some girls come here with the intention of being prostitutes. I didn't. But this is the only way I can feed my daughter, send money home to my father."

"None of us want to be out here, Sylvia," Cecelia chimes in. She is forty-seven and has worked as a prostitute on Constitution's streets off and on for more than a decade now. "We're all out here because of the crisis. We're all here because we have children to raise alone, without husbands. We're all here because there is no other work for us in Argentina. There are a lot more women on the streets now than there were ten years ago.

"And to do this you don't even need a uniform," she says, smiling broadly to defuse a slightly tense moment with her friend. "All you need is a short skirt."

Sylvia exhales a cloud of cigarette smoke, dashes the butt in an ashtray, and leans forward. "But Cecelia, I don't want this to be my life. I don't want to be too comfortable here. I would quit doing this tomorrow if I could find a real job somewhere that would pay me what I can make out here. I would—"

"We all would," Cecelia says.

"But I—" Sylvia begins to answer, but Cecelia cuts her off.

"Let's go," she says, rising suddenly from her chair. "Let's go back to work."

NOTHING HERE IS as it should be. The dry calculus of globalization's monetary policy is the author of countless operatic tragedies. Beginning in 1973, following the military coup that brought the conservative Chilean dictator Augusto Pinochet to power, the United States and its corporate envoys have dangled loans and trade pacts as bait to persuade scores of countries to stabilize prices by increasing the value of their local currencies. Like many developing countries, Argentina had experienced bouts of hyperinflation in the postwar period, and above all things, the global investor hates to have inflation eat into his purchasing power, the resale value of his building or fleet, or the returns on his stock and bond portfolios. But a "strong" currency policy is overkill, like using an elephant gun on a mouse. The number of casualties outweigh the benefits.

In Argentina's case, the country's fixed exchange rate, like

the gold standard, guaranteed that for every peso in circula-
tion, the treasury held US$1 in reserve, causing the money
supply to contract sharply. The central bank could no longer
pay debts simply by printing more notes, because each peso
had to be backed by US$1 in its vault.

The shift in 1991 meant that Argentines were suddenly
playing with the house money. The pesos in their pockets
and bank accounts were effectively transformed into U.S.
dollars. The added buying power meant that American
goods and products were suddenly accessible to the Argentine
middle class. Travel agents here were inundated with calls
from Argentines wanting to take the family on their first
trip to Disneyland. But this windfall was short-lived. Just as
Disneyland was suddenly affordable, so too were American-
made televisions, cars, clothes, shoes, and other merchandise
shipped into Argentina. Brands from the United States flew
off the showroom floors and store shelves. Conversely, the price
of Argentine-made goods tripled. Sales both here and abroad
dried up as consumers gobbled up foreign products which
were suddenly cheaper than their Argentine competitors.

INFLATION, TO BE sure, is no good for anyone. Poor people
hate to see higher prices for a loaf of bread or a bag of rice
as much as the rich hate to see a smaller dividend check. But
studies have consistently demonstrated that economies can
withstand moderate levels of inflation, even as high as 30
percent annually, with no adverse impact on growth or jobs.
To a worker, lowering inflation is a Pyrrhic victory if it costs
you and your neighbors your paychecks.

Preoccupied with inflation but unconcerned about the jobs
climate, Milton Friedman and his coterie of advisers from

the University of Chicago coaxed Pinochet in 1974 to fix the exchange rate of the Chilean currency at about 1.4 pesos to the U.S. dollar. Within two years the country's jobless rate had climbed to 33 percent. Pinochet dismantled the fixed exchange rate, known as a peg, and Chile switched to an exchange rate that allowed the central bank to adjust the currency's value frequently. Maintaining a healthy equilibrium between inflation and unemployment with a slightly undervalued currency has helped Chile's economy grow faster than any other in Latin America since 1990 and China's grow faster than any in the history of the world over that same span. China's central bank adjusts the value of its currency, the yuan, daily to keep inflation at moderate levels while making Chinese products a good bargain on the world market.

With a mounting trade deficit, and borrowing heavily from foreign donors to buy the dollars needed to prop up the peso, government officials in Argentina decided in 2001 that the country could no longer sustain its one-to-one peg and devalued the peso as Chile had done more than twenty years previously. The difference was that the United States and international lenders helped bail Chile out of its immediate jam but offered no such assistance to Argentina. Argentines saw two thirds of their savings disappear overnight and, afraid they would lose it all, tried to withdraw all of their funds at once, triggering a run on the banks like the one that followed the 1929 stock market crash and led to the Great Depression. When her Bueno Aires bank would not allow her to withdraw even a portion of her life savings, one woman set herself afire in its lobby.

"Getting the money wrong," as the Argentine economist Alan Cibils says, is globalization's most lethal poison, the surest way to stop any economy, rich or poor, in its tracks. Argentina's inflexible, nineteenth-century approach to combating inflation underscores how laissez-faire capitalism is anything but, and proponents of such strategies often misrepresent critics of globalization as "protectionist." With few exceptions, globalization's critics do not question *whether* countries should engage in international trade, only *how*.

"Inflation is immaterial if you don't have any money to spend," said Mark Weisbrot, an economist with the Center for Economic Policy, a Washington, D.C.–based think tank. "But you can see how the average bondholder might not be as invested in how high unemployment rates climb. If they were honest, they'd tell you that they just don't want unemployment to go so high that there is civil unrest, because that can jeopardize their investment even more than inflation. Globalization choked off economic growth to get inflation under control. We've allowed the financial sector to unilaterally determine economic policy for the rest of us."

Followed to its logical conclusion, this policy of appeasing speculators has culminated in an all but unregulated banking industry in the United States and the housing crisis that almost crushed the global financial markets under a mountain of bad mortgage debt in 2008. Nixon abandoned the gold standard in 1971, which, like Argentina's monetary policy, caused money supply to contract, but which used gold rather than the U.S. dollar as the peg. A decade later Ronald Reagan entered the White House intent on restoring the value of the dollar through market interventions such as aggressively buying back treasury notes. Clinton's first treasury secretary, the investment banker Robert Rubin, continued to boost the dollar, driving up its price by nearly 30 percent against the value of the United States' trading partners. That worked, effectively, as a 30 percent tax on exports and a 30 percent subsidy for imports, punishing domestic manufacturers.

But Clinton went even further in servicing Wall Street's whims, in 1999 demolishing the New Deal–era legislation that was a firewall separating investment banks and depositors' cash in commercial banks. Suddenly commercial banks were free to make loans to practically anyone with a pulse, because investment banks were climbing over one another to take the debt—bundled into complex securities—off their hands. It was 1928 again—until it wasn't. When Wall Street's accumulation of trillions of dollars in bad debt deterred banks from extending credit in the summer of 2008, Treasury Secretary Henry Paulson, a Goldman, Sachs man, and Congress stepped in to use taxpayer money to buy the bad loans at market price. Unlike the New Deal's response to the financial crisis of the day, neither Paulson nor Congress offered refinancing or relief to homeowners who could not afford to pay the fraudulent loans with exorbitant interest rates, nor did they offer to recapitalize banks by purchasing on behalf of taxpayers preferred shares in the troubled Wall Street firms that could pay dividends down the road.

In the game of global finance, ordinary working people are the suckers more than ever. And for them, the financiers and their bagmen in Washington have nothing but contempt.

This constant reworking of the rules to favor capital has changed Argentina's essential character, demolishing what was once the continent's safest and most prosperous country just as deftly as a team of bulldozers.

For most of the twentieth century, Argentina was both ridiculed and envied by its Latin American neighbors. With its august theaters and bookish cafés, Buenos Aires was regarded by many of its continental neighbors as a smug European outpost, the Paris of the global South. On a continent where the chasm between rich and poor is wider than anywhere else in the world, eight of every ten Argentines were middle-class as recently as 1990. For the forty years that immediately followed the end of World War II, workers and their bosses split the nation's income exactly in half: wages accounted for 50 percent of the gross domestic product, profits the other half.

When voters went to the polls in 1946 and elected their former labor minister, General Juan Perón, as president, they ushered in an era of prosperity that was both unprecedented and unrivaled in the Southern Hemisphere. Perón may have borne an eerie resemblance to Boris Karloff, and he had an unnerving fetish for fascists, but he created the modern industrial state in Argentina, nationalizing key industries, spending heavily on health care and education, subsidizing agriculture and public works. Between 1946 and 1990, the number of Argentines living in poverty did not eclipse 5 percent. The national unemployment rate never climbed higher than 6 percent. Three of every four workers belonged to a labor union. Whatever Argentines wanted or needed—cars, televisions, candy, shoes—Argentine factories and employees assembled it, bottled it, shipped it, repaired it.

With the cold war winding down and Argentina emerging from *la guerra sucia*, or dirty war, between the country's conservative military junta and leftist dissidents, voters went to the polls in 1989 and elected a flamboyant, Ferrari-driving attorney who was the darling of Wall Street and Capitol Hill. Before the second of his two five-year terms ended, Carlos Menem's administration had given birth to a new nation. By the time he left office in 1999, this virtually all-white country bore a stark resemblance to some doppelgänger American slum.

As of this writing, Argentina is five years into a robust recovery, marked by a return to many of the trade policies introduced by Perón. Yet a third of the country's 40 million people remain poor, or unable to afford a weekly basket of staple foods and household products, as the government defines poverty. At the height of Argentina's financial meltdown in 2003, 56 percent of the population was impoverished. The unemployment rate leapt as high as 24 percent; it remained at about 10 percent in early 2008, according to official government statistics, though economists say that both figures are artificially low because they do not include more than a million households that have shuttled on and off the dole since the federal government first extended cash subsidies to indigent single mothers in 2001.The gap in income between the wealthiest Argentines and the poorest has widened by a factor of 400 since 1989, and the coupling of inequality and poverty has peeled from the country's once solid midsection a desperate underclass.

In less than a decade, the nation's crime rate soared by more than 300 percent. At the height of the crisis, thieves in Buenos Aires and its suburbs stole 275 cars a day in a province of 13 million people, and police investigated, on average, four "express kidnappings" per week, in which rogue taxi drivers or roaming bands opportunistically abducted victims at gunpoint and then forced them to withdraw cash from an ATM. The nation's crime rate has subsided some since 2004, but Argentines have turned fearful of one another. The number of gated communities doubled in the 1990s. It is not difficult to find an Argentine who acknowledges that he regularly danced the night away or rarely locked his doors at home in the years before Menem was elected; now many say that they seldom leave home in the evenings. At the peak of the crime wave in 2004, Argentines from all walks of life staged ear-shattering protests against crime by beating their cookware with spoons or other utensils.

The country's skyrocketing crime rate is primarily attributable to juveniles and young adults. Prisons and juvenile detention centers here are increasingly overcrowded. High school dropout rates have increased, and the numbers of Argentines between the ages of fifteen and twenty-four who are neither enrolled in school nor working has doubled since 1990. With nowhere to go, youths have often turned to marijuana and beer, which are cheaper than Argentina's rich wines and promoted heavily by multinational breweries who capitalized on globalization's aperture to grab market share.

In the concrete shantytowns known as *villas miserias*, or misery villages, clots of young men in hooded sweatshirts and skullcaps gather on street corners, downing bottles of beer, passing spliffs, and complaining that police harass them and employers shun them. With so few opportunities, Argentine youths see in *fútbol* what African Americans see in basketball: their last chance.

"My favorite movie is *Boyz n the Hood*," a young man once told me as he tinkered on a friend's beater of a car in a Buenos Aires slum, referring to the 1991 cinematic classic on violence in south-central Los Angeles. "To me, that's how we're living."

The loss of decent work has thinned Argentina's marriage pool. The divorce rate in this overwhelmingly Catholic country has held steady since divorce was legalized in 1987, but the country's marriage rate has dropped by nearly a quarter since 1990. The number of households headed by an unmarried woman has almost doubled, from 14.6 percent to 27.1 percent. The number of babies born to teenage mothers has inched up from 14 to 20 percent of all live births.

The unraveling of families has poisoned the air. Women here often complain about how unreliable their children's fathers are, failing to provide material support or to visit. Men complain that women pressure them to deliver precisely what they cannot, or aren't sympathetic to their struggle. The rumblings from a rearranged Argentine society sound unmistakably like the Spanish-language equivalent of what has been popularized on bad sitcoms in the United States as "baby's daddy's drama" or "baby's mama's drama."

Sitting on a Buenos Aires park bench one Saturday morning in the early winter of 2003, Lorena Peralta and her ex-husband Herbert Robaldo spoke about their failed marriage.

"What's done is done," Lorena said as she breast-fed their eighteen-month-old son.

"No, really," Herbert asked, "why couldn't we stay together?"

He always does this to me, she told me and my interpreter—coyly slips the question into our conversation, as if he doesn't know the answer, as if he hasn't asked it a thousand times before and received the identical answer each and every time.

"You know why," she said to him, sounding at once exasperated and amused. "You drank too much."

"It's true," Herbert acknowledged to us. "But I drank because I could not find work and take care of my family. If I had a job, many things would have been different."

"I know," Lorena answered. "But what's done is done."

That their four-year marriage ended badly was no longer her most pressing concern. She had moved on. What preoccupied this girlish-looking twenty-year-old was how she would get through the days and years to come, raising two children on a maid's salary, alone.

"All Herbert ever wants to talk about is when we were married," she told us as Herbert rambled off to chase their other son, four, through the park's tall grass. "My problem now is that I am a single mother with babies to feed. So many families are breaking up now. It is horrible. This crisis has made us all crazy."

She sighed and turned her gaze to the street, where young men stood outside a convenience store in a haze of smoke, talking loudly as music blared from a radio.

"It is a bad time to be in love in Argentina," she muttered, almost to herself.

The parallels with the American ghetto are ironic, because Argentina has far fewer people of color than most of its Latin American neighbors. Fifty-three percent of all Argentines claim Italian ancestry; 97 percent identify themselves as white, which for anyone who has spent so much as a day in the country seems far too low.

The country's plantations never relied on African slaves as much as say, Brazil's, Cuba's, Colombia's, or Venezuela's did. Since the country needed workers for its growing industries, Argentina's immigration policy for most of the twentieth century heavily favored newcomers from Europe. When the country went to war against Paraguay in the late 1800s, it manned its frontlines largely with soldiers of African descent, but few returned. (Those who survived or stayed behind had a lasting cultural impact: they began a new dance called the tango in the brothels of Buenos Aires.) So rare are blacks here today that when a black woman tried to board an international flight at Buenos Aires' main airport in 2002, immigration officials detained her, solely because she had an Argentine passport. Newspaper accounts reported that a black woman holding an Argentine passport aroused suspicion.

The paradox of Argentina is that this homogenous population and its unraveling provide a profound lesson on race relations in the United States. Conservatives and elitist African Americans like the Harvard sociology professor Orlando Patterson, the journalist Juan Williams, and the comedian Bill Cosby contend that the woeful state of black Americans results primarily from a subculture that does not value hard work, education, or responsibility. But what then should we make of Buenos Aires, a city that not twenty years ago was poised to become another Vancouver or Vienna but today shares more in common with Baltimore and Oakland? Either Argentines share cultural traits with African Americans or the traumatizing loss of manufacturing jobs in both south-central Los Angeles and South America is the common denominator.

At a barbecue I attended in Villa 31, one of Buenos Aires' most feared and fastest-growing slums, several women voiced their grievances to me and my interpreter, an American journalist whose Spanish was much better than mine, while we sipped *mate* and sat on the dirt floor of a scrap-metal shanty with bootleg cable television and a sloping tin roof. It was hard for them to find work, they said, because employers can discern from the address on their application if they live in a Buenos Aires slum. "If they see that you live in a *villa miseria*, they will not hire you, because they believe you will make trouble for them or steal from them," said one of the women.

Still, they said, that is no excuse to stop looking for work altogether, as some men do. "We call them couch pussies," a woman said, with nods of agreement from the others. And some of the women are no better, they said, bearing babies out of wedlock as a ruse to collect government welfare checks.

"We have really lost our way in Argentina," said one of the women, Fatima Prieto, the live-in girlfriend of Oscar "Paulito" Domingo, a grocery store clerk. The couple has two children.

Argentine women are actually having fewer children now, said Orlando D'Adamo, a pollster and sociology professor at the University of Belgrano in Buenos Aires. But the growing friction is typical of Argentina's dysfunction. "We've been introduced to the culture of not working," he said. "There are a lot of people who are no longer connected to society in the way that Argentines typically have been. The damage is happening house to house, neighborhood by neighborhood. The quality of our relationships has declined along with our quality of our life."

Said Artemio Lopez, a polling director for Equis, a research firm here, "When you talk about the failures of this new global trading system to benefit countries like Argentina, you cannot just measure it in terms of gross domestic product. You have to talk about what a destabilizing agent it has been for families."

"WILL YOU TAKE a check?" a bearded man in a sleeveless black T-shirt asks Sylvia as she twirls her hair between her fingers while standing underneath the streetlamp. It is shortly after 1 a.m.

"Pardon me?" Sylvia says and leans toward the man.

"Do you take checks?" the man asks again.

Sylvia smiles broadly. "No, I don't take checks."

The man smiles and continues on his way.

"I get all kinds," she says: the downtown lawyers who've wriggled momentarily free from their wives; the widowers who don't know what to do with their solitude; the damaged, vulnerable men who only want to be held like babies in her arms. One regular customer is a heroin addict who pays her to spend the entire night with him while he shoots up, nods off, and shoots up again. "He just wants someone he recognizes to be there when he wakes up. Otherwise he freaks out," she explains. "He gets paranoid, afraid really, like a lost little boy."

Sylvia certainly understands fear. It is with her constantly. She once got in the car with a john who pulled a knife on her. At a stoplight she jumped out and ran for her life, and to this day if she gets into a car with a man, she keeps one hand on the door handle at all times.

"I ask myself all the time how I got here," she says.

Her father was a veterinarian in Paraguay, but when he retired he couldn't stretch his pension far enough to take care of Sylvia, a brother, and four sisters who remained at home. He looked for another job but found none.

Sylvia decided she would have to get a job, but she had no more luck than her father. Her two older sisters had left for neighboring Argentina a year earlier, and because their paychecks were effectively in dollars, they were able to send some of their earnings home. Sylvia got on a bus and headed south.

Similarly pushed by falling wages in their home countries and seduced by Argentina's strong peso, Sylvia was joined by 844,797 other women from Latin America and the Caribbean who moved to Argentina in the 1990s, according to government statistics. Slightly more than 770,000 men migrated here over that period.

A great migration is under way, not unlike the waves of Europeans and blacks from the American South who moved to the American North to work in stockyards, factories, and mills beginning in the late nineteenth century. But the new world economy does not need men's strong backs so much as the comfort provided by women like Sylvia. Globalization has feminized immigration with a growing service economy fueled by nannies, maids, and prostitutes. Offering or soliciting sex for money is a crime in Buenos Aires, but police seldom enforce the law. When they do, according to relief workers, it is selective, usually targeting migrant sex workers.

The Constitution neighborhood is as synonymous with prostitution as it is with the train depot that was built more than one hundred years ago to deliver Argentina's wealthy rural landowners and workers to the city. A highway dissected the neighborhood in the 1970s, demolishing its commercial heart. Stores and warehouses closed. The neighborhood lost a third of its population. Housing prices plummeted, and immigrants who began to pour into the city in the 1990s found rents affordable.

"The neighborhood has been mutilated," said Emilion Vareso, forty-four, an architect and president of the neighborhood association. "There have always been prostitutes here. When I was a kid growing up, I might see ten prostitutes in a day. Now I can see that on one corner."

With foreign cash pouring into the country to buy bonds and state-owned utilities in Menem's first term in office, Argentina's economy grew by nearly 51 percentage points, but all of it was at the expense of the manufacturing sector. The number of people living in poverty jumped by 51 percent as well. Three years into Menem's second term, the economy had slid into a full-blown recession, just as Sylvia arrived in Buenos Aires.

MIGUEL ONCE WORKED the sugarcane fields up north but fifteen years ago moved to the city, where he got a job at a flour mill and made some good money. His take-home pay was $600 per month. "I've never been afraid of work," he says. "Whatever you got, I'll do it. Just give me a chance."

The mill shut down two years ago, when grocery stores began stocking baked goods shipped from overseas. Miguel started picking through garbage. On a good night, the family can salvage $10, maybe $12 worth of recyclable goods. Four hundred pounds' worth. Better than nothing, but barely.

The doormen at the high-rise apartments in Belgrano have their favorites and will often separate the good stuff and set it aside for families like the Machados, good people who don't just rifle through the trash bags and leave a big mess for the doormen to clean up. But you have to be quick, or they'll leave it for someone else.

"The doorman has something for you," Miguel says to his son Lucas, nine, round-faced, chatty, and in the middle of putting his brother Jonathan, eleven, in a headlock. Miguel points to a figure standing in the shadows 30 yards away. "Go get it. Run. I think he has newspapers."

"Jose!" Lucas greets the doorman, Jose Ojeda, who has just

handed him a garbage bag. Lucas is staring intently at the bag as if it's a meteor that fell to earth. "Is there glass in here?"

"No, I don't think so," Jose answers, standing in the dim foyer light with his hands stuffed in the pockets of his jean jacket.

Lucas taps the bag with his foot. He does it again and again until he is no longer inspecting for glass but dancing a sort of triumphant samba with a trash bag.

The first thing you learn as a *cartonero* is that there is sometimes broken glass in garbage bags. The second thing you learn is that you don't want anything to do with the broken glass that is sometimes inside garbage bags. The third thing you learn is the sound of broken glass when you pat, shake, or kick the garbage bag before opening it.

"I've cut my hand twice," Lucas says. He is a fireplug of a kid, with long black hair that constantly gets in his eyes and shoes with holes so big you can see his toes. He knows all the doormen by name and argues with them about soccer. He doesn't really mind the work, he says. He likes being outside, likes being with his brothers and his father, likes the banter with the doormen. Sometimes the waiters at nearby restaurants hand him a plate of pasta or bread while he works.

Since his father lost his job, things have changed for Lucas. He used to eat yogurt and cereal for breakfast every morning. Now, if he's lucky, he might have cereal, and often dry at that. No milk. For dinner, when things are really tight, his parents have only *mate*, the traditional Argentine herb tea, which they sip slowly while the children finish what's left of the food.

His parents argue more now, Lucas says.

The Machados work six nights a week, five hours each

night, rain or shine. They divide twenty buildings among them. Miguel takes eight, the biggest and most affluent ones, which produce the most volume. Nothing stirs so much joy in him as when he stumbles on a stack of newspapers, which sell for the equivalent of nearly 8 cents per pound, or maybe an old lamp that he can sell to a secondhand dealer for 75 cents. "Their garbage," he says. "Our blessing."

The children—Lucas, Jonathan, Mario, Romina, and Maria—split the other twelve buildings. "The kids," says Miguel, bending over a bag filled with nothing more than grimy Styrofoam, "they want to play. I know this is not a good time to be a child. But they don't always understand that this is my job. This is our job. If we do it, we eat. Nothing more, but we eat. They don't always understand that."

Except Romina. She is fifteen, lithe as a ballerina but strong as a bull and bossy when need be. "She's like our mother," says Jonathan.

"I put a lot of trust in her," Miguel says. "She's more responsible than the others."

"They are lazy," Romina says of her brothers and her sister, who is twelve, as she uses all her weight to push the nose of the dolly down so it is resting solely on its wheels. She says she can handle a dolly with as much as 400 pounds by herself. The trick, she says, is balance and alignment. Always keep the wheels straight in front of you; otherwise, she says, "it will attack you."

When she first started working on the streets, she woke up sore for a week. "But the body gets used to it," she says. Once a passing car nicked the dolly as she was pushing it. Just about broke her arm in two, she says: "You have to really watch the cars."

She has a boyfriend she met a few months ago at her fifteenth birthday party. He is seventeen and a *cartonero* as well, working with his father in a neighborhood not far from here. She wishes they had more time together.

She talks as she works, sifting through garbage bags, loading the dolly.

She wants to be a doctor, but it's hard to find time to study. She hates to get her hair dirty. Still, things are not so bad, she says. Half the children in her class at school are *cartoneros*, she says, so she's not embarrassed by it. She meets people on the streets, and she does like the energy of the city streets at night. She finds herself easily bored when she's home.

She pauses a moment, and then the words spill from her mouth like rain.

"Let me tell you what's hard. What's hard is waking up in the morning, fixing my father's *mate* and doing all the stuff that needs to be done around the house, going to school, coming home to study, then coming out here to work, getting home at midnight, then waking up six hours later and doing the same thing over again." She inhales. "Sometimes I do miss my old life, where I could just stay home and study."

"Is this a job?" Miguel says as he ties Coke bottles together with string. "No, this is a necessity. This is survival. This is so I don't have to steal to feed my family. This is only one step from that. I hate this. Everyone who does this hates it."

It is 10 p.m., and the streets are cluttered with *cartoneros* pushing their loaded dollies, beginning to head for the train or the recycling plants to sell what they've collected. Miguel and Romina push their loads slowly, robotically, while the others prance off in the moonlit distance.

"We're done," Miguel says as he makes his way toward the

train station for the thirty-minute ride home with garbage piled nearly 6 feet high. "We'll be back tomorrow."

AT A QUARTER to midnight, there were ten women on the corner of Pavon and Santiago del Estero: two sitting on a dark apartment stoop a few feet from where Sylvia was leaning against a tree, one on the corner adjacent to Sylvia, two more across the street, and four in Charly's Bar.

"Bruno, what do you have to eat back there?" a woman asked as she bounded into the bar and kissed three women sitting at tables.

"All these women, they have a story," said Bruno, sixty, a wiry retired factory worker with thinning white hair, a stubbly beard, and eyes that seem never to open fully. He works five nights a week, serving up sausages, dry toast, and coffee so black and hot that Sylvia and the others joke it could raise the dead.

"They have children, or they have husbands who left them," he said. "They do the best they can with what they have. They just don't have much to work with. Ask any one of them if she'd rather have a real job that paid decent money and she would say yes."

Sylvia walked in. She just had a customer, a married man she usually sees once a week. Most customers are married, and it is a running joke among the women how it is a waste of time for wives even to try to keep tabs on their husbands. If they want to cheat, they will cheat. Exhibit A is one regular customer whose wife allows him to leave the house without her for only an hour each day, to walk the dog. When the women see him, leash in hand, they call for his favorite girl. They lock the dog in the bathroom at

Charly's for thirty minutes and the two are on their way to the flophouse.

"Fidelity is a dream," Sylvia said as she stared out the window to the street. A single streetlamp gave the darkness a yellowish glow. As she talked, a six-year-old girl walked into the bar, wearing flip-flops and sucking a popsicle. Without saying a word, she kissed Sylvia wetly on the cheek. Sylvia smiled, said hello, and reached into her bra for a few coins to hand the girl.

The girl is the daughter of a *cartonero* who works in Constitution. "She's in here every night," Sylvia said. "Another one of my regulars."

Sylvia said she feels a camaraderie with the *cartoneros*, poor people like her whose work is foisted upon them as much as it is found. In both their business and hers, there is little dignity. She tells almost no one what she does for a living, not even the nanny from Paraguay who watches her daughter while she works only two blocks away. "I am sure she suspects something, but she doesn't know for sure and she won't ask," Sylvia said.

She feels dirty. She won't so much as touch her daughter without first taking a shower. But showers don't wash everything away.

A Catholic, Sylvia won't take sacrament in Buenos Aires; she goes to communion only when she is visiting her family in Paraguay. During a visit to Missiones six months after she turned her first trick, her father asked how she managed to send home as much as $150 each month, three times what she usually sent home when she was working as a maid. "He knew," Sylvia said. "But I think he wanted to hear me tell him."

Sylvia says she started to leave the room but then steadied herself, breathed deeply, and blurted it out. "I sell my body," she told him.

Dead silence followed, for what seemed like forty days, she said, and to this day she is unsure whether the worst heartache she ever endured was telling her father that she was a prostitute or realizing that he accepted it because he knew it was the best she could do. "Please," she recalled him telling her, "promise me that you will quit the first chance you get."

As she tells this story, a man Sylvia recognizes taps on the windowpane, summoning her. She tends to him and then another and then another in rapid succession. When she returns to the corner, it is after 5 a.m. and daybreak approaches. She feels most ashamed in the first light of dawn, when she recounts in her head the night's business and her earnings.

"I hate this life," she says in a barely audible voice as she stands on the corner. "I hate it," she says and then rattles off the phrase again and again, her voice growing louder. "I hate it. *La odia. La odia. La odia. La odia.*

She cranes her neck and stares up at the sky for several seconds, as if wishing on the last star before it evaporates in the light. She sighs and looks down at her feet before saying once more, for good measure, "*La odia.*"

Two new women emerge from the shadows and take their places on the corner opposite Sylvia, who sizes them up and announces that it is time to pack it in for the night. She smiles and steps off the corner.

"Shift change," she says, and heads home.

3

LIFE AND DEBT

Brazil and Interest Rates

Ivan Ilych's life had been most simple and most
ordinary and therefore most terrible.

—*Leo Tolstoy, from* The Death of Ivan Ilych

In the final days of 2003, throngs of Brazilians advanced
on Rio de Janeiro's storied beaches for a solemn ritual by
the shore. Sculpting makeshift altars in the sand, they filled
the shallow warrens with votive candles, prayed for Iemanjá
to bless them in the new year, and cast out to sea toy sailboats
laden with trinkets, candy, and flowers.

With a population of 182 million people, Brazil has more
Catholics than any country in the world and more blacks
than any nation other than Nigeria, and it fuses the cultures
of both groups into a kind of hybrid catechism, deploying
West African deities as stand-ins for Christian idols.

Iemanjá is the African sea goddess who watches over her
worshippers, and like the Virgin Mary, she is the icon that
Brazilians most often turn to in their darkest moments, so
that the tougher the year, the more people who huddle at the
edge of the Atlantic Ocean, launching so many miniature

boats that they resemble a fleet from some Lilliputian navy
heading off to war.

Dressed all in white, Isabella Lopes da Silva stood in the
champagne-colored dusk of Barra da Tijuca Beach, head
bowed and eyes shut as she clutched the hand of her six-
year-old grandson. When she finished her prayer, she knelt
at the water's edge and nudged into the tide a single long-
stemmed gladiolus, then a tiny blue wooden sailboat onto
which she had loaded lipstick, a bracelet, and a hairbrush.
"Iemanjá is a quite vain goddess," she said, smiling as she
watched the boat drift slowly toward the horizon. "I hope
that my offering pleases her. This has been a very difficult
year, very difficult. I hope that she will bless Brazil in the
new year."

In 2003, Brazil's GDP contracted by .2 percent, its worst
year in more than a decade. Unemployment hovered around
13 percent, and every few months local television stations in
Rio and São Paulo broadcast scenes of thousands of Brazilians
waiting in lines that were two and three blocks long to apply
for a handful of available jobs at a warehouse or department
store.

"I lost my job in February," said da Silva, forty-nine, who
had been a secretary for six years. "My son-in-law lost his job
in March, and my daughter lost hers in May. It is all we can
do some days to come up with enough money just to put food
on the table."

Brazil's recession was triggered by its interest rates, the
highest in the world in 2003. Concerned that inflation was
lurking around the corner and would eat into the profits they
earn from the Brazilian bonds in their investment portfolios,
traders—through the IMF and World Bank—pressured

Brazil's central bank to raise the country's overnight lending rate higher and higher, peaking at 26 percent in 2003.

The rising interest rates subdued inflation but pummeled economic growth as well, by discouraging consumers from buying big-ticket items like cars and homes and drying up the credit that business owners rely on for start-ups and expansion. Moreover, because a country's lending rate determines the interest rates it pays on its bonds, the higher Brazil raised its lending rates, the more money investors put into Brazilian notes. By mid-year, Brazil's public debt had ballooned to 54 percent of GDP, meaning that for every dollar in income produced by the economy here, 54 cents went to service the national debt.

That left Brazil's newly elected president, Lula da Silva—a former lathe operator popularly referred to only as Lula by peasants and potentates alike—with little cash left over to pay for the social programs and public investments he had promised voters in his 2002 campaign. In his first year in office, his Workers' Party and its governing coalition slashed civil servants' pensions and transportation subsidies for students and dramatically scaled back plans to fund food vouchers, education, and land redistribution efforts. In a span of less than twelve months, the percentage of Brazilians who approved of Lula's job performance plummeted from 81 to 53 percent. It would have fallen far lower, pollsters and political scientists say, if not for Lula's charisma and "man of the people" bona fides.

It was a bad year all around, with two notable exceptions. As the underwriters for Brazil's bonds, the country's banking industry celebrated record profits, and the vendors who sell gifts and toy boats for the offering to Iemanjá said their

December sales were better than in any year they could remember.

"Look at this," said Paulo Roberto, a cabdriver parked by the side of the road in Barra da Tijuca, simultaneously reading a newspaper article on the banking sector's windfall and watching Iemanjá's worshippers trek to the beach while he waited patiently for a fare to return. "You see, this is the story of Brazil, year after year. The poor get poorer and the rich get richer and richer. It doesn't matter who is in charge of the country. It's all the same."

A pleasant man with a bantamweight's build and a broadcaster's smile, Paulo has a wife, four children, ulcers, and a lot on his mind as 2003 draws to a close. The son of a maid, he was born in a slum named Judgment, stumbled out of the gate, made up some ground through tenacity and hard work, but never managed to put any real distance between himself and poverty. His ambitions never found traction. And so on the eve of his forty-sixth birthday, he sizes up his life and this is what he sees: poverty behind him, poverty ahead, and no way out.

Worsening his anxiety is the announcement a few weeks ago by his supervisor that all the contract drivers for the four-star Marriott hotel on Copacabana Beach must upgrade their cars by the first of the year or they will be replaced. He figures he can fetch maybe $3,500 for the five-year-old Ford he purchased with the settlement he won when he was wrongly fired from his job as a bus driver. But a new car will cost him at least $9,000 more. With interest rates so high, there is no way Paulo can afford monthly payments on a bank loan. He is a poor man who knows only poor people. No friends or family can loan him the money. And finding another job in this economy is close to impossible.

He brings home about $400 a month from his job, just enough to feed his family and keep a roof over their heads. He wants one thing for his birthday: to lose no more ground.

"I'm just trying to hold on," he says.

Debt is the cornerstone of the new economy, and no matter how you look at it, debt is merely exploitation by another name, a way for party A to get over on party B, regardless of whether the parties doing the borrowing are sovereign nations or heads of households. Around the world, in their loan arrangements with countries like Brazil, the World Bank and the IMF persuade government officials to push interest rates up, sometimes to historic levels that no wealthy nation would ever tolerate. This accomplishes two very important goals of the neoliberal agenda. First, it strangles inflation by making credit unaffordable; fewer loans means business screeches to a halt and the money supply contracts. Second—and this in my mind exposes better than any other example just how the rules of international finance put in the fix—the higher the interest rate, the higher the returns on government bonds purchased by Wall Street speculators. Globalization's commissars use market liberalization and foreign exchange rates much as arsonists use power tools, quietly jimmying the works to provide financiers and bankers with a windfall. Jobs vanish in a plume of smoke; the forensic evidence is hazy. But interest rates are a much cruder instrument, like a tire iron wielded in a daylight smash-and-grab, enabling global investors to exploit poor countries like cheesy payday loan shops in America's ghettos peddling "Quik Cash" and "EZ Money" to down-on-their-luck blacks and Latinos.

It is usury, an uncomplicated swindle that threatens the futures of Paulo, his family, and millions like them just as menacingly as if they had gotten in over their heads with a neighborhood loan shark. In this way, Brazil's highly leveraged economy and resulting credit crunch was a precursor of the financial crisis that surfaced in the United States in 2008. When millons of American homeowners could no longer pay the high-interest loans on assets at artificially inflated prices, they defaulted, leaving the banks who purchased the bundled bad loans—and the insurers who guaranteed them—in the lurch. With so much toxic debt on their hands, banks become gun-shy about lending any more of their cash to businesses, state and municipal governments, and especially consumers who were already in over their heads. As in Brazil, the economy froze.

While Lula has pushed to give more and more of Brazil's money away to the country's creditors, public schools here remain dysfunctional, clinics scarce, hospitals threadbare. There is no savings-and-loan industry; there are no unemployment benefits, no GI bill, no Pell Grants or student loans, no effective effort to redistribute land from the affluent to the peasantry. Mass transit is an oxymoron, particularly if you live in the constellation of shantytowns, known here as *favelas*, that soar like hallucinations above Rio's bewitching coastline. In the cities, there are no jobs for the poor. In the countryside, there is no land for them to farm. Of all the public institutions that have historically helped poor people become middle-class, virtually none in this breathlessly beautiful country seem to work.

"This is why we turn to Iemanjá for help," Paulo says. "Because the state gives us nothing, not even some basic hope that if we play by the rules, maybe tomorrow can be better for us than today. I want for my children so much more than what I had. I tell them to study, to work hard, to obey the law. And I worry that it won't be enough."

THE BIRTHDAY PARTY is an unfussy, intimate affair—just Paulo, his wife, their two grown daughters, and his brother-in-law, squeezed in the kitchen of the family's split-level brick home here in this slum on the outskirts of Rio de Janeiro.

It is a comfortable house, easily the nicest on a bad block, but its dimensions are modest, the ceilings low and the roof half finished, leaving a four-foot aperture between its lip and a second-floor bedroom wall. The rain began to fall this morning, and its relentless patter on the corrugated tin and plastic tarpaulin sounds like an off-key call-and-response.

Shoeless and beaming, Paulo sits at the head of the kitchen table with his arms stretched wide in front of him, threatening to erupt in a fusillade of tears if anyone dares to sing another chorus of "Happy Birthday to You." This, everyone knows, is no bluff. He is a sentimental man with spartan appetites and downsized dreams, and the only joy he has ever really known is building this house brick by brick, putting food on the table, and knowing that his family is safe and warm and near.

"Okay," says Alaide, his wife of twenty-six years. "We better stop now or the floodgates will open. Let's eat."

"Yes," Paulo says, steadying himself, a sheepish grin on his face. "Let's eat."

He is taking the first blissful bites of his *feijoada*, a heavy pot-liquorish stew created by African slaves here, when Joequeline, his youngest daughter, mentions, almost in passing, that her fiancé quit his job.

Paulo freezes suddenly. He stops moving, stops smiling,

stops chewing, his spoon suspended in midair as if someone has cast a dark spell on him.

"What do you mean, he quit?" he asks, fixing his stare on Joequeline.

"He just couldn't do it anymore, Daddy," she says plainly, refusing to meet her father's eyes as she ladles *feijoada* onto her plate. "He's been doing it for four years, twelve hours a day, standing up the whole time in that factory. He is looking for another job."

"I didn't know he quit," Paulo says. His voice cracks, as if has been wounded. "It is hard for a young couple today. You have rent to pay."

"I know, Daddy," Joequeline says softly.

"It's more difficult now even than when I was starting out," he goes on, stiffly.

"Daddy, it will be all right," Joequeline reassures him. She reaches across the table to stroke her father's shoulder.

When Paulo was born, his mother was thirteen, unschooled and unmarried, working as a maid. So far as he knows, he has never laid eyes on his biological father. He was six when his mother married his stepfather.

He would have liked nothing more than for his mother to attend his small birthday party. Paulo paid a visit to her home this morning to plead with her to come. But while her husband snored in the bedroom, she held Paulo's hand and told him over coffee that his stepfather simply wouldn't stand for it. He kissed his mother goodbye and left, trying his best to hold back tears.

Paulo has a bitter relationship with his stepfather, who, when he was younger, parceled out beatings to Paulo, his mother, and his brothers as if they were interlopers in his home. The last beating was the worst, and Paulo swore he'd never let his stepfather lay hands on him ever again. He left home and lived on the streets and with friends.

He was fifteen.

In the nearly twenty years since he began building his three-bedroom brick house in this slum 14 miles northwest of Rio de Janeiro, his mother has visited just once, though their homes are less than 5 miles apart.

Alaide says that her husband's unhappy upbringing has made him fiercely protective of her and their children. Sometimes Joequeline will leave for work, and by the time she arrives forty-five minutes later, Paulo will have called the office where she works as a secretary as many as three times to see if she has arrived safely. When Alaide plans to go shopping or to visit a friend, he asks what time she thinks she will return. If she's fifteen minutes late, he is in the car looking for her.

When the drug dealers and their guns began terrorizing his old neighborhood, he moved the family into a shack on a patch of land here in São João de Meriti, another slum, albeit a noticeable upgrade. The shack was so small that he had to saw off the top of an armoire to open it. When it rained, everyone moved to one side of the shack to avoid the sheets of water pouring through the leaky roof on the other side.

Paulo razed the shack and began building the house the family lives in now, a modest two-level dwelling with blank gray concrete walls. It's a tight fit, but Paulo's three oldest children remember the shack and jokingly refer to their new home as "the castle."

When he left his mother's house this morning, Paulo stopped to visit his son at his $35-a-week security job. Jose was lucky enough to land a double shift today, but that means he won't be able to attend his father's birthday party in the afternoon. Jose has little time for anything. Two months ago he failed the police academy exam and he is studying to take the test again, and between work and poring over books, he has no time to date or go out. His father sometimes phones home from work to make sure he is studying, and Jose says he feels the pressure. "I don't want to let him down," says Jose. "He wants us to succeed more than I think any of us do."

Paulo knows as well as Jose does that what holds Jose back is his public school education. There were no computers at his schools, no nurse, no books for some classes, no teachers for others. With little money for construction, the government has built virtually no schools in the city in more than twenty-five years. It was not unusual for Jose to sit in a classroom with more than fifty students.

In high school, he once had a teacher who didn't teach: he would let the students talk quietly among themselves while he napped, sipped coffee, or read the paper. "His attitude was that we weren't going to amount to anything, so why waste his time," Jose said. "Our parents weren't doctors or lawyers and we weren't going to be doctors or lawyers. We could read, and that's pretty much all you need to be a maid or a chauffeur. He never saw us as being anything more than that."

Jose graduated from high school, but without taking any math beyond arithmetic and without ever working on a computer. "There is just a lot of stuff on the exam for the police academy that I had never seen before. I am trying to reeducate myself now."

As is true with Jose's test scores, the family's setbacks usually seem to come down to numbers that don't quite add up.

The $150-a-month tuition for Joequeline's nursing school is about $10 more than her monthly salary, and the provincial government and the federal government offer a combined $0 in college aid.

The twelve-hour days that the family's eldest daughter, Aline, twenty-eight, puts in on her job as a switchboard operator leave her without enough time to study, even if she manages to save the money she needs to go to business school. Brazil's unemployment rate has driven wages down by 10 percent in real terms over a six-year span, and where there are labor laws in place, the government has no money to enforce them. Aline does not dare to complain that she works at least two hours a day without pay.

"I have this theory," Paulo says as he sits at the kitchen table, "that the reason no one in my family ever gets sick is because poor people know they don't have health care or sick days. The mind conditions the body not to get sick. Brazil just doesn't present us with many options."

WHAT REDUCES POVERTY and gaps in income and enables ordinary Americans, Europeans, and Japanese to live better than their parents is economic growth. Between 1960 and 1980, Brazil's was among the world's fastest-growing economies, its per capita income increasing by 123 percent over that span when adjusted for inflation.

If the country had continued to grow at that pace, Brazil would now be one of the wealthiest countries in the world, with living standards comparable to Western Europe's. It didn't. Beginning with the military dictatorship and continuing with a generation of democratically elected governments, Brazil's political leaders started to turn off the industrial spigot in the 1980s, strengthening the country's currency, the real (pronounced ray-*al*), cutting tariffs, and borrowing heavily from abroad. Between 1980 and 2007, Brazil's per capita income increased 12 percent when adjusted for inflation, or less than one tenth the growth rate over the period between 1960 and 1980.

The slowdown in growth has exacerbated longstanding flaws in Latin America's most populous nation. Brazil's distribution of wealth has historically been among the most unequal in the world. Income for Brazil's wealthiest 10 percent is fifty-one times that of its poorest 10 percent, according to a 2007 United Nations report. (By comparison, the ratio in South Africa is 33 to 1; in Sweden it is 6 to 1; and in the United States, home to the most unequal distribution of wealth in the developed world, the ratio is 15 to 1.)

Compounding Brazil's stunning inequality is its lack of social mobility, which means that barring something terribly unlikely, Brazilians who are born poor will die poor, as will their children after them, on and on in what has essentially been one godawful national losing streak dating back more than five hundred years, to the day when the first Portuguese settlers came ashore.

Unlike Argentina's epic reversal of fortune, or the Zambian economy which has left virtually everyone impoverished, Brazil's economy is an elegy to stasis and immutable friction. The country's inheritance is the same hardscrabble life passed down from one generation to the next as surely as a weak chin, dimples, or a family heirloom. It is as if ordinary Brazilians are stock characters in a tragic version of the cult movie *Groundhog Day*, waking morning after morning to a feudal class system that has withstood colonialism, slavery, and a quarter century of neoliberal policies. "Brazil," goes the old national joke here, "is the country of the future. And it always will be."

The country's costly borrowing has only deepened the divisions that have defined Brazil since its birth. Blacks, women, and landless indigenous peasants have shouldered the brunt of the growing debt.

To work the cotton and coffee plantations, pan for gold, and cut sugar cane, Brazil imported six times more Africans than the United States did and double the number that went to either the Spanish colonies or the British West Indies. More abducted African slaves were delivered to Brazil than to any other country in the world, to work as porters, cooks, maids, nannies, and even soldiers. "The Brazilian dream was to have one or two slaves whose labor could be hired out for a price high enough to free the dreamer from ever having to work," wrote Pedro I, Brazil's first post-independence leader, in 1836. "Begging was preferable to work. Even beggars had slaves."

Brazil abolished slavery in 1888; it was the last nation in the Western Hemisphere to do so. Still, the country never legally sorted black from white in the fashion of Jim Crow laws in the United States or apartheid in South Africa. The census's crayon-coded racial categories include *preto* and *pardo*, the terms for black and mixed-race. Only 6 percent of the population chooses black on the census, but nearly half identify themselves as *pardo*. Lula's predecessor as president, Fernando Henrique Cardoso, an Ivy League—educated lawyer and by all appearances a white man, often described himself as "having one foot in the kitchen," a colloquialism for mixed ancestry and a Brazilian reference to the proliferation of black maids in white households. That kind of casualness about miscegenation contributes to a nationalist mythology in which Brazilians typically consider their country a "racial democracy" where skin color is largely irrelevant.

Yet race matters profoundly here. The unemployment rate for black Brazilians is twice that of whites. White Brazilians generally earn 57 percent more than black Brazilians working in the same field, and a white Brazilian without a high school diploma earns more, on average, than a black Brazilian with a college degree. Blacks in Brazil die younger, are more likely both to be arrested and to be convicted of crimes, and are half as likely as whites to have running water or a working toilet in their homes.

Law enforcement here is first and foremost a barrier separating the third-world *favelas* from the first-world cities that appear on postcards. Heavily armed, drug-dealing gangs shut down whole neighborhoods for days at time in shootouts with rivals or the police. Nearly two thousand civilians in Rio and São Paulo were gunned down in 2003 by law enforcement officers or the hundreds of vigilante death squads that are manned by off-duty and retired officers. Authorities describe the deaths as acts of resistance against dangerous thugs, but a 2002 study by Amnesty International found that 61 percent of all civilians slain by police were shot in the head at close range. Nearly all were black and poor.

In Morro do Borel, a *favela* that borders Paulo's, police in 2003 fatally shot four young black men in broad daylight on a crowded commercial strip in what witnesses describe as an ambush. None of the four men had criminal records; all were employed or in school. Witnesses described police as casually chatting to one another as one of the young men lay fatally wounded at their feet, pleading for help. "I am a worker," they described him as saying repeatedly. "I am a worker."

As in the United States, the disparate treatment of blacks by the criminal justice system is accompanied by deep fissures in Brazilians' education. Of the 1.4 million students admitted to universities here each year, only 3 percent identify themselves as black or mixed-race; only 18 percent come from the public schools, where most black Brazilians study.

"People here say that it's impossible to say who is white and who is black," said Jocelino Freitas, whom I interviewed in 2003, when he was twenty-five and a first-year law student at the State University of Rio. "Really? Ask the police. I bet they can tell you who is black. Ask any doorman who can go through the front door and who goes through the service entrance. I bet they can tell you who is black. What color is the maid? We may not spend a lot of time talking about who is black and who is white, but we live in color every day."

Freitas considers himself *pardo* and was admitted under a new government quota system to increase the numbers of university graduates who are black or mixed-race and poor. The government's lowering of admissions standards was a tacit admission that graduates of its public schools were unprepared to score as high as whites who attended private high schools.

Paulo has roughly the complexion of Halle Berry, and many Brazilians of his hue would identify their race as *pardo*. But when I ask him through my interpreter what race he considers himself to be, he answers without hesitation. "I am black," he says, smiling as he tugs on strands of his close-cropped Afro. "I must be, because my hair is nappy and I am poor."

Arguably, though, it is Brazil's women—and particularly those of color—who have borne the brunt of the country's indebtedness. They have given up their unborn children. In a generation, the family here has undergone a transformation of almost biblical proportions.

Thirty years ago, civil society joined with government officials in an orchestrated effort to raise families' incomes in the developing world by reducing the size of their families. Nowhere has the effort been more energized than here in Brazil, where doctors sterilize poor black women with neither their knowledge nor their consent in the hazy hours following childbirth. Employers routinely refuse to hire women who cannot prove that they are infertile, and politicians canvassing for votes during campaign seasons offer free sterilizations—surgical procedures known as tubal ligations—to women in exchange for their votes. In the *favelas* and on tribal reservations, vans bearing candidates' names and likenesses patrol like ice cream trucks in the weeks before a critical municipal or provincial election, a speaker promising via bullhorn to arrange the procedure for women of voting age if they will cast favorable votes on election day.

Government statistics indicate that nearly one of every two women of childbearing age has been sterilized, but many public health workers and women's groups say the ratio is likely closer to two thirds among poor women of color. In Brazil's northeast state of Bahia, where the population of blacks is densest, health workers say they have found entire city blocks without a single fertile adult woman. In a 1995 survey that has become infamous among women's organizations here, health workers found that all eighty-five women living on a small reservation of Guarani Indians in Bahia had been sterilized.

In 1980 a Brazilian woman of childbearing age had, on average, four children. By 2003 the number had dropped to half that, one of the steepest declines in history. The rub, of course, is that women lived up to their end of the bargain but got nothing in return from their leveraged economy. Women here are even poorer now than they were in 1980. Feminist groups and civil rights and health organizations complain that racism and not sound development policies propelled the country's sterilization efforts.

"I really see sterilization as an attempt to exterminate a problem, and that problem is poor people, and in Brazil that means black people," said Catia Helena Bispo, who is black, a teacher, and the former director of a community organization in Pernambues, outside the city of Salvador in northeast Brazil. "What's going to happen to black families if more and more women stop having babies? If you want to lift someone out of poverty, what is better, educating them or sterilizing them?"

Many women say that they later regret their contraceptive choice and that the surgery is costly to reverse. Women's groups and civil rights organizations have staged anti-sterilization protests over the past decade and in 1997 persuaded lawmakers to pass a law requiring that all women who undergo the procedure either be twenty-five years old or have at least two children.

In the country's northeast, the name and face most associated with free sterilizations is Mauricio Trinidade, a local councilman who campaigned successfully for a seat in the state legislature in 2004. A physician by training, the forty-three-year-old Trinidade estimated in a 2004 interview that he had arranged as many as 10,000 sterilizations over a political career that had at the time spanned more than a decade and four campaigns. Neither race nor racism plays any role in his efforts, added Trinidade, who is white. Quite the opposite, he said. "Poor women prefer this method. It's simple. It's effective. Wealthy women have always had access to family planning. It's poor people—black people—who don't."

He said that his approach has been instrumental to his political success, and that his efforts to decrease Brazil's birthrate preceded his first electoral bid. Few women regret their decision to be sterilized, he said, as he grew visibly irritated at the suggestion. "Oh, maybe sometimes some woman meets a man and he says he wants to have children and she gets a little upset that she can no longer conceive," Trinidade acknowledged. "But if you check back with her in two months, the guy has flown the coop, left her high and dry. She's not so sorry then.

"It is a priority because we live in a country where the birthrate is higher than the gross domestic product," he said. "In other words, what grew was the misery. In some areas of Brazil, you will find women with up to twenty children. It's simple math: a woman can provide more easily for one child than for two. Lowering the birthrate gives us an opportunity to increase per capita income."

Trinidade arranged a tubal ligation for Rosangela de Jesus Santos in 2001. When I met her three years later, she was thirty-three, a widow with a sixteen-year-old son, a fourth-grade education, and a live-in boyfriend. First she insisted that she had never regretted her decision to have the procedure.

"There is a problem with women having more children than they can take care of," she said. As she is unable to provide for her son, he lives with her parents, while she searches for work every day, without fail, she said.

She and her boyfriend had discussed marriage and having a child together. Her tone softened as she talked. "What I really need is a job," she said. "I go from one place to another all day long, but no one here is hiring. That's my number-one problem."

Of her sterilization, she modified her previous assertion. "I do regret it a little bit."

"You don't solve poverty by reducing family size," said Juanita Werneck, the executive director of Criolla, a woman's health organization. "You solve poverty by expanding the economy through greater educational opportunities, through land reform. You have to create opportunities for women, not restrict them. There are far too many black women who are told that the only effective method of contraception is sterilization. Some people are quite well-meaning, but there is a racist ideology behind it."

Bogged down by debt, Lula has left a string of broken promises to Brazil's poor. The poorest 40 percent own only 1 percent of the country's arable land, while a wealthy elite— roughly 20 percent of the population—owns 90 percent. This is a critical issue. Land reform is perhaps the crucial step in the industrialization process, from the U.S. Homestead Act of 1862 to China's Great Leap Forward in the 1950s.

During his 2002 campaign, Lula pledged to accelerate land reform efforts, but in his first year of office his government managed to resettle only one tenth of the 60,000 peasants he had planned to provide with 50-acre plots. In anticipation of the effort, 98,000 families moved into squatter camps in 2003, the greatest such migration in the twenty-five-year-old history of the Landless People's Movement, known by its Portuguese acronym, the MST.

Squeezed onto plots that are far too little to be viable smallholder plots, the 30,000 Kaiowá Indians who live on the Brazilian prairie in the state of Mato Grosso do Sul have experienced an epidemic of suicides among their young. Since 1995 nearly five hundred have taken their own lives, usually by hanging. The numbers would be far higher if guns and not garrotes were the preferred method. Unable to live off the soil, the traditionally agrarian Kaiowá work at the alcohol distilleries and sugarcane refineries that line the state's two-lane highways like grazing elephants. It is backbreaking work that pays little and requires workers—usually teenage boys and young men—to leave the reservation for months at a time, living in hostels far from home and from everything they know.

With the men gone for long stretches, women greatly outnumber men on the reservations for much of the year, which strains relationships, budgets, and families, which are historically close-knit. The unemployment rate on the reservation is more than 60 percent, and alcoholism, drugs, and malnutrition are rampant, a local police officer, Andrea Depieri, told me in 2004. Often left behind, adolescent girls and young women from the reservation increasingly turn to prostitution to support themselves or their families, she said.

The Kaiowá often attribute the suicides to a dark magic, a spell that finds its voice in a rustling wind that counts off the days you have to live. But the truth is far simpler, said

Luciano Arevalo, a tribal official whose fifteen-year-old niece hanged herself in 2004, followed within weeks by unsuccessful suicide attempts by her fourteen-year-old sister and sixteen-year-old boyfriend. "Our children look around them and look ahead and they see nothing worth living for. It is a curse to have to cut your children down from trees."

"HE HAS . . . THESE black moods. It's like he crawls into this dark cave inside his head and no one can reach inside and pull him out."

This is Alaide describing how her husband woke with a start the morning before his forty-sixth birthday. He mulled over his dilemma in the inky morning darkness, sitting on the edge of his bed, his head cupped in his hands.

Alaide tried to console him, rubbing his back softly. "You are a man of faith," she said. "Believe."

Paulo is a devoutly religious man, the result principally of a drunken barroom brawl sixteen years ago, when three men jumped him and beat him bloody. He went home to retrieve his gun. Alaide confronted him as he searched for his pistol, bruised and bloodied and high on cheap whiskey, and told him that if he wanted to get his fool self killed, then that was his prerogative. But vengeance wasn't going to feed their children, and whether he came home that night or not, she was going to church the next morning—and maybe he should too.

He did, and he hasn't missed a Sunday in years.

The plates have been cleared from the table and the family has moved on to the birthday cake, with vanilla frosting that is Paulo's favorite.

With their children grown now, Paulo and Alaide can foot

the $25-a-month tuition for a private Catholic elementary school for Marcos, Alaide's ten-year-old nephew, whom the couple is raising because Alaide's sister is disabled. Marcos usually does well in school, but he didn't on a recent test, and at Paulo's birthday gathering, Alaide recalled what the boy said when she pressed him for an explanation. "I prayed, Auntie Alaide," he said innocently, "but God didn't come through for me."

Paulo laughs until tears well up in his eyes. His mood has lightened considerably since the tense moment with Joequeline, now more than an hour ago, and he leans back in his chair, his legs crossed underneath the table, scraping icing from his paper plate.

The conversation careens from family to men to street crime to everyone's disappointment in Lula in his first year on the job. The expectation was that he would stand up to the World Bank and IMF, not fold like a house of cards.

"That is not Lula. I think the U.S. kidnapped him and they've found an impostor to take his place," Paulo says.

Talk of Lula leads to how few blacks are in top positions in his administration and then to the racism of daily life here. When Aline lost her job as an emergency operator nearly two years ago, it took her a year of poring over the classified ads every Sunday to find a job. Black Brazilians say that the term "good appearance required" is a subtle code that they need not apply, but Aline, desperate for work, answered several of the ads anyway, unsuccessfully. Once she showed up for an interview and was met with a line of more than two dozen women. After a while she had to use the bathroom, she said, and asked the only other black woman in line to hold her place. When she returned, the black woman was waiting alone. "They came out and took all the blondes," Aline recalled. "They told the rest of us to go home."

Later, when I ask him about it, Paulo tells me that it was at this point in the conversation that he decided what to do about finding financing for a new car. "I am going to pray this evening and first thing in the morning, and if it's not raining tomorrow when I leave work, I will go to ask Iemanjá to bless me and my family. I think Marcos had it right in asking God to come through for him. That's exactly what I am going to do. I have nowhere else to turn."

4

POWER AND LIGHT

South Africa and Privatization

The People Shall Share in the Country's Wealth
> —*Provision in the Freedom Charter,*
> *written by the African National*
> *Congress at its first people's convention*
> *in Soweto, 1955*

It is always the same. The darkness seems to surge over 65 Maseka Street, and in the first dizzying moments after she awakes, Agnes Mohapi panics, unsure for a moment or two of what to do. *Should I wake Flora? Or maybe I should wash first. No, maybe there's an outage in the neighborhood; I should go to the neighbors' to see if their lights are outa too.* Then it comes to her like a thunderclap, rattling her uncertainty into submission, a bracing clarity that steadies her hands and calms her mind. *Eskom has disconnected my electricity again. I will get dressed, walk to the pay phone, and call the people at the Soweto Electricity Crisis Committee to restore my power.*

There is a chill in the late-autumn breeze. It rustles the high veldt and stiffens Agnes's arthritic knee. She is fifty-eight, widowed, and lives with her twenty-four-year-old daughter here on this treeless, dusty corner where Maseka and Moema Streets intersect in Orlando East, one of the oldest districts in Soweto. She has no more furniture left to use as firewood, and even if she did, she says, she wouldn't.

"How do you say in America?" she asks rhetorically as she stands outside her hovel while two bootleg repairmen from the SECC hot-wire her electricity. "I am sick and tired of being sick and tired."

Here in this crowded all-black township southwest of Johannesburg, electricity bills have increased by as much as 400 percent since South Africans of all races went to the polls in the nation's first democratic election in 1994. Planning to auction off the public utility commission, known by the acronym Eskom, the government wants first to fatten the utility's bottom line to demonstrate to prospective buyers that they're getting a good deal.

Nervous of sparking the fire next time simmering in its townships during apartheid, the white-minority government charged a flat rate for electricity and rarely disconnected users for nonpayment. The African National Congress, South Africa's new, black-majority ruling party, has no such compunction. In Soweto alone, a community of roughly 1.5 million people, Eskom cuts off service to as many as 20,000 delinquent customers each month. On some days, residents say, entire city blocks here are dark.

Not 200 miles south of Johannesburg, in a village called Embabe in South Africa's KwaZulu-Natal province, Metolina Mthembu makes the shoeless trek to the river, walking past the tap that was installed just a few feet from her house two years ago. It is bone dry. What the peasants call "the river" is no more than a puddle, really, a shallow accumulation of muddy brown water at the bottom of a rocky knoll near the town of Empangeni. The river is maybe a quarter mile from Mthembu's mud hut, and to get there you walk through a breathlessly gorgeous expanse of green savanna, runaway hills, and sugarcane fields that tumble along the coast of the Indian Ocean.

With two jobless adult children to feed and only her pension of roughly $50 a month to support them, the seventy-year-old Mthembu can't always find the money to pay the equivalent of $7 a month for water. And so a well-rehearsed dance has evolved between the old woman and her local utility, a sequence that plays out every few months or so: she falls behind in her payments; the utility disconnects her tap; she turns to the river until she finds the money to pay her bill.

During what Mthembu calls "the old government," she had to walk half a mile to get clean water from a standpipe. She's glad the new government installed a tap outside her home, but now the water costs money, she notes, and people here are poor.

"There are no jobs. We must choose between food and water, so we buy food and pray that the water does not make us ill," she said on a late-autumn morning as a young girl in a formless yellow dress crouched in the river behind her, dipping her plastic bucket. "It is a bad gamble. I was a victim of cholera in February, and then my daughter and my neighbor became sick with cholera as well. Many, many of us have grown sick from the water."

The high price of water triggered the worst cholera epidemic in the country's history, which began days after the utility here began shutting off the taps in July 2000 for nonpayment. Villagers turned to the river and other sources of dirty water to bathe and drink, sparking the outbreak, which began here and fanned out to seven of South Africa's nine provinces, infecting some 145,000 people, most of them in the first two years.

In this nation of 46 million people, the effort to privatize the economy has constructed a sprawling Potemkin village often without water or light, the hollow façade of a country appearing to take a great modernizing leap forward when it is actually taking a step backward.

Since Nelson Mandela was sworn in as president, the ANC has built nearly 2 million new homes, expanded the electrical grid to include 4 million additional households, and reduced by nearly three fourths the number of South Africans without running water. But the government's surprising fealty to liberalizing markets, strengthening the national currency, and raising interest rates has pushed the country's unemployment rate to nearly 40 percent, pared the workforce of nearly a million jobs, and shaved per capita income by one fifth between 1994 and 2005. Adding insult to injury, bureaucrats at the World Bank prodded the ANC to pair its privatization efforts with a fiscal measure known as cost recovery, which requires public services such as water, electricity, housing, telecommunications, and schools to pay for themselves.

Tragically and paradoxically, life, materially, has only gotten worse since the end of apartheid, and the most visible change in daily life is that ordinary South Africans struggle more to pay their bills. A quarter of all South Africans live in households that have had their water cut off at least once since 1996. The number of evictions has doubled. Households earning less than $100 a month—roughly one in two nationwide—spend nearly a quarter of their income on utilities. In Soweto, 61 percent of all households with electricity have had their electricity shut off at least once within a twelve-month period. Ninety percent are behind in their payments.

South Africa's second intifada is against privatization. Grass-roots organizations in Durban have begun moving evicted families back into their homes, sometimes only minutes after authorities have piled their household goods in the street and bolted the doors. Unemployed plumbers in Cape Town reconnect their neighbors' water supply when it has been shut off because of nonpayment. Trade unions protest the government's plans to auction off the telephone and utility companies with placards that read: "We did not fight for liberation only to sell it to the highest bidder."

THE CLASSICALLY LIBERAL macroeconomic idea behind privatization is that the state lacks both the competitive drive and the profit motive that inspire innovation, lower prices, and improve service.

The reality has been far different. Across the globe, municipal and state governments play a smaller role in providing services, from electricity to road repair to prisons, than at any time in the past thirty years, yet the price of a local call, a kilowatt of electricity, or a liter of water is higher than ever, eats up more of consumers' paychecks, and draws more customer complaints.

Water privatization in England and Wales in 1989 produced rate increases of 46 percent when adjusted for inflation, and the number of shutoffs grew by 200 percent. In Pekin, a town in southern Illinois, the price of water has increased by 204 percent in the eighteen years since the water plant was sold to a subsidiary of American Water Works, Inc. Multinational firms have raised Nicaragua's water rates by 30 percent since

2000. Rates for water have increased by 200 percent in Saudi Arabia and by 87 percent in Brazil since 1997. Pressured by the World Bank, Bolivia sold its state water system to a consortium of British investors in 1999 for only $20,000. Within a year the buyers had tripled the price of water in Latin America's poorest country and, to ensure their monopoly, written a codicil into their contract with the state that legally prohibited Bolivians from collecting rainwater for personal use. Massive street protests in 2001 led the government to cancel the contract.

In 2004, Argentina's president, Nestór Kirchner, defied foreign donors by refusing to allow a 37 percent hike in electricity rates to the two Spanish-based conglomerates, Edesur and Edenor, that had purchased the rights to the utility in 1997. Kirchner argued that Argentine consumers could not afford the increase, and the utility, which had already increased rates by more than 25 percent in 1999, did not need one.

Brazil's privatization of its utility in the 1990s led to a 65 percent rate hike for consumers in that country and Peru's electric rates increased by a factor of 14 between 1992 and 2002. The cost of electricity in California has increased by 56 percent since the government deregulated the industry in 1998. In Baltimore, electricity rates have increased by 77 percent. The main utility company in Illinois, ComEd, pushed through a rate increase of 26 percent in January 2007 despite record profits the previous year. State officials in the United States said they were expecting record numbers of utility cutoffs in 2008, in many cases eclipsing the record set the previous year.

In South Africa, Eskom implemented cost-recovery measures in 1996 in which the price for each kilowatt of electricity is set according to how much the utility spends to provide it, said Jacob Maroga, the utility's executive director of distribution. He said that Soweto's electricity problems started when the boycotts of the 1980s bankrupted the apartheid-controlled municipal government, which purchased electricity and resold it to residents. When Eskom began handling the accounts directly, it spent about $75 million in capital improvements and wrote off nearly $37.5 million in household debts. "The idea is that we would do all the improvements and then the residents would start living up to their commitments. But we still recover only about fifty to fifty-five percent of the costs for the electricity we sell," Maroga said. "There are clearly customers who don't have the capacity to pay. But there is also this culture of nonpayment in Soweto where customers can afford to pay but they prioritize other consumptive spending. We need to deal with that."

Because Eskom sells electricity at discounted bulk rates, affluent municipalities in mostly white suburbs buy electricity and resell it to customers for roughly 30 percent less than what it costs Soweto's consumers. For the biggest users of electricity—industrial sites such as steel plants and coal mines—the rate for each kilowatt is roughly one tenth the rate for a household in Soweto.

Patrick Bond, professor of public management at the University of the Witwatersrand and codirector of the Municipal Services Project, acknowledges that it is expensive to provide electricity to the poor, who use little electricity and don't generate enough tax revenues to enable their municipal government to buy it in bulk, which results in duplicate costs for equipment, administration, and labor. But he said that Eskom could largely resolve the debt problem in Soweto by charging big industries a few cents more for each kilowatt of electricity, subsidizing a cheaper flat rate for poor customers. "Eskom has a rate structure that economically makes sense," Bond said. "But socially it makes no sense. Their structure is good for the northern suburbanites, but we'd like to see a structure that is good for everyone. That means smaller profit margins in the short term but a healthier society in the long term."

South African municipalities have auctioned off more than a dozen water plants, including that of Johannesburg, the nation's largest city, which has a utility district that includes Soweto and which entered into a partnership with the French transnational Suez and its subsidiaries in 2001. Suez's history of raising prices did not bode well for poor residents, especially since the new utility inherited an apartheid-era white elephant known as the Lesotho Highlands Water Project. This $8 billion scheme to build six new dams in the water-rich country of Lesotho, which is completely surrounded by South Africa, had already caused the cost of water in Johannesburg to nearly triple since the ANC came to power, and many residents in the township of Alexandra complained that they could no longer afford to pay their bills.

Conceived by the apartheid government, the project was supported by the World Bank and other international lenders, who sidestepped international sanctions to finance the deal in 1986. The ANC, then in exile, denounced the arrangement at the time, saying that it strengthened apartheid. But after the ANC took office in 1994, party leaders decided to plow ahead. The first of the six dams, the tallest on the continent, was completed in 1998. Developers expect to build the remaining five over the next eighteen years.

The project is partially financed by international loans

that will be repaid by passing the cost on to consumers. A disproportionate share will be paid for by residents of Alexandra. All-white suburbs, home to less than one tenth of South Africa's population, account for more than half the country's residential water use. But since these communities can take advantage of discounted bulk rates, a household in Johannesburg's white suburbs can fill its swimming pool and water its garden at less than half the cost per liter paid by a family in Alexandra. Unions, environmentalists, and community groups have appealed to the government to cancel the Lesotho dam project and repair the apartheid-era infrastructure instead. Blacks here are in effect paying for their oppression twice: first with blood, then with cash.

"We don't need the water from the dams," says Sam Moiloa, a conservation activist who lives in Alexandra with his wife and two children. "We lose half of our available water through leaks. We should just fix the leaks, and our government can use that money they're spending on dams for the rich to improve our standard of living."

So far, such protests have not swayed ANC officials, who say that making utilities profitable is critical to South Africa's competitiveness at a time when foreign investment is badly needed.

"There's a lot of polemics around this issue," said Mike Muller, the director general of South Africa's Department of Water and Forestry. "But the truth is that operating costs have to be recaptured, or there is no way to sustain basic services."

THE TOWN OF Empangeni derives its name from the Zulu word "phanga," which, roughly translated, means "to grab."

It is a reference to the uncommonly high number of crocodile attacks that once occurred on the Mhlathuze River. Home to South Africa's largest sugar mill as well as paper factories, aluminum smelters, mines, and upscale game farms, Empangeni is surrounded by Ngwelezana, an all-black township, and the villages of the Madlebe tribe, which during apartheid were autonomous black homelands, or bantustans, which provided white-owned business with cheap labor.

The Zulus, who make up South Africa's largest tribe, have historically had little use for dates. Instead, they mark time by great events, so if you ask a man what year he was born in, he may respond, "In the year of the great flood" or "In the time of the great famine." If you ask Josephine Mhiyne about her youngest grandchild, Nomsa, she will tell you that the toddler was born "in the time of the great cholera"—in 2000, the year the epidemic began.

"We all had it," she says, sitting on a rug in front of her mud hut while her granddaughter mauls a stalk of sugarcane. "We just thank God that no one died. I got it right after she was born. My stomach was running so bad. It was because we were drinking from the river. I live in fear of the river, but I still return to it for water every day. I have no other option."

Until the recent outbreak, the Empangeni region had not seen a major cholera epidemic since a bad drought in 1982, when some 12,000 cases—less than 10 percent of the number reported in the more recent epidemic—occurred. In response to that outbreak, town officials built nine communal taps providing clean water to nearby villages. It was not uncommon for residents to make several trips a day to fetch water, sometimes walking a mile each way.

In the months before the December 2000 nationwide

municipal elections, Mandela's successor, President Thabo Mbeki, and other ANC politicians took to the campaign trail and promised more water and electricity hookups for the poor. Within eight months of the vote, municipal workers in Empangeni completed the extension of the water pipes to about seven thousand homes in the outlying villages. There was just one catch: to use the newly installed taps, residents would have to insert a prepaid card into a meter. If someone fell behind in paying the water bill, municipal authorities would cancel the card, leaving the resident unable to access his or her tap.

Between August 2000 and December 2002, KwaZulu-Natal's public hospitals reported nearly 115,000 cases of cholera, more than five times as many as had been reported in the province over the previous twenty years combined. Nearly 260 South Africans died from the disease. Early on, cholera was so rampant that hospitals in and around Empangeni opened fourteen hydration centers, tents where medics worked in twenty-four-hour shifts to provide fluids to patients. When the city ran short of ambulances, the local government appealed to the South African defense forces for help, and for nearly six months soldiers shuttled patients to hospitals and makeshift clinics.

"We were simply running out of capacity and out of space," says Peter Haselau, the manager of the region's main public medical center. "We would get a handle on it in one place and it would break out somewhere else. We got to the point where we thought we might collapse if we got any more cases. The problem was that so many people didn't have money for water, so they were going to traditional sources of water. And that water's no good."

The government scored one major success in the epidemic: it kept cholera from killing most of its victims—a remarkable feat, especially given South Africa's high HIV infection rate. Only a quarter of 1 percent of those who contracted the cholera bacterium throughout the epidemic died, one of the lowest fatality rates on record in a major cholera epidemic, notes David Hemson, the research director for the government-funded Human Sciences Research Council (HSRC). But, he adds, "Even that came at great expense to the government, and it could have been offset with some adjustments in their policy of cost recovery. The cutoffs cost them more money in the end in dealing with the disease that resulted from it."

South Africa's cholera infection rate began to slow late in 2002—in part, experts say, because people became more cautious about the water they use. Still, Metolina Mthembu continues to make her daily trek to the river, navigating the hilly footpaths with an ease that seems impossible for a woman of her age and slight physique.

"Sometimes the river gets totally dry," she says, "and you have to walk for two or three kilometers to find water. Or you go without for days at a time."

Mthembu cannot imagine any hell worse than apartheid; she makes sure to preface any criticism of the government with that caveat. "But we still live with misery," she says as she climbs the hill separating her home from the copper-colored stream on which she once again depends. "If we could only get water, then we would be really free."

Said Hemson of the HSRC: "No one doubts our government's good intentions. But in the name of development, in the name of progress and modernization, we have exposed our most vulnerable populations to this very colonial disease, a disease that is by definition a byproduct of backwardness. What does that say about policies like cost recovery?"

ROYALS AND ROBBER barons financed the West's dissection of sub-Saharan Africa. But it was Europe's working classes that did the empire's heavy lifting. Laborers, castoffs, and soldiers returning from war came to Africa searching for a life better than what they were offered at home.

Today, the primary distinction between African nations is rooted in the difference in the European émigrés' state of mind when they stepped off the boat. In countries like Congo, Angola, Ghana, and Rwanda, colonialists arrived with no intent other than to plunder Africa's natural resources and exploit its labor before heading back home with their bounty. In countries like Zimbabwe, Kenya, and South Africa, the pattern was quite different. Whites in those countries were settlers who considered themselves Africans at least as much as Europeans. They came to stay, and on the backs of black labor built a country that their children and grandchildren could live in comfortably for generations to come.

The European settlers who most identified with Africa were the Afrikaners, the Dutch émigrés and French Huguenots who fled religious persecution in their own countries and headed south to the Cape of Good Hope beginning in 1652. Their strong ties to the land played an instrumental role in the development of the most industrialized country in sub-Saharan Africa, as central to the region as the United States is to the rest of the world.

Like the ethoses of the American West and the Australian outback, in which brave, resourceful pioneers struck out on their own and conquered hostile lands and savage people, the Afrikaners—Africa's Lost Tribe—constructed a similar nationalist identity. God and capitalism's consecration of the individual and his private property got the white man through.

Beginning in the 1830s, Afrikaners embarked on a series of mass migrations inland from South Africa's Western Cape region, by the Atlantic Ocean, in search of fertile farmland. The *Voortrekkers*—literally, those who move ahead to new lands to the north—encountered violent resistance from the Zulus, or "people of the sky," the indigenous warrior tribe that populates the mountainous coastal region of KwaZulu-Natal.

In 1837 Pieter Retief, a wealthy Afrikaner farmer, led his delegation of covered wagons over the Drakensberg mountains into KwaZulu-Natal, where he entered into negotiations with Dingane, a chief who became king of the Zulus after he murdered his brother Shaka Zulu in 1828. In the popular Afrikaans version of the meeting, the two men signed a deed (historians agree that it was written in English) bequeathing lands to the *Voortrekkers* if Retief recovered some cattle stolen by a rival tribe. Retief's repatriation of the cattle was feted with two days of feasting by Dingane and his chiefs, but the king turned on Retief and his party and killed them, and then sent his forces to massacre about five hundred Afrikaner men, women, and children camped nearby.

By and large, blacks tell a slightly different story. Dingane's was not an act of betrayal but one of self-defense when it became clear that there had been a misunderstanding between the two men. Dingane had intended for the *Voortrekkers* to farm the land but not to own it. An argument ensued. Retief threatened Dingane with a musket. The idea of property rights was foreign to Africans. No one owned the land, not even Dingane. The land belonged to everyone, and was to be parceled out—leased, if you will—as the king, its caretaker, saw fit. In a communal, agrarian culture that valued collaboration over competition, you could no more own the soil beneath your feet than you could own the sky or the sun or the water.

The confrontation between Retief and Dingane formed the template not just for apartheid but for the enduring relationship between tribes of the global North and South over private property and the public good.

Thousands of British prospectors and settlers streamed into South Africa following the 1885 discovery of gold in the Transvaal region, which now includes Johannesburg and which was colonized by the Afrikaners, perjoratively called Boers, or farmers, by the newcomers. The resulting dispute triggered two Boer wars, the last of which culminated in a decisive British victory in 1902. The British burned to the ground thousands of Afrikaner homesteads and jailed thousands of women and children, both black and white, whose husbands and fathers had taken up arms against the Queen. A postwar study concluded that more than 27,000 Afrikaners—mostly women and children under sixteen—and more than 14,000 blacks died from starvation, disease, and exposure in British internment centers (for which the term "concentration camp" was coined). In the wars' aftermath, Afrikaners were subject to British administrators and humiliated by their lowly status, forced to compete for sometimes menial jobs with blacks and even to work shoulder-to-shoulder with them.

When the Afrikaners' Nationalist Party reclaimed control

of the government in nationwide elections in 1948, the Afrikaners earned 60 cents for every dollar in British income; Africans earned only 30 cents. Within months of the 1948 election, the Nationalist Party had passed the laws that were the foundation for apartheid, and a decade later Afrikaners' income disparity with the British had been reversed. By 1956 the British in South Africa were earning 60 cents for every dollar in income pocketed by the Afrikaners, while incomes for blacks dropped to 20 cents on every dollar earned by the British.

There is, however, a very real irony in apartheid. The Afrikaners essentially created their segregationist state with a promissory note: to end poverty for their own. And they did it with the same ruthlessness that global financiers use to fatten their pockets in this global economy, but with strategies that are the exact opposite of those of the international trading regime.

Using a formula for white South Africans similar to Perón's strategy for all Argentines, the Nationalist Party poured money into whites-only schools, whites-only hospitals, and whites-only banking institutions. They nationalized key industries, subsidized strategic sectors of the economy, and deployed the civil service as a Keynesian buffer against unemployment. With the land they seized from Africans, they created one of the best classes of commercial farmers in the world, providing first-time farmers with seeds, equipment, training, and loans. When inexperienced white farmers couldn't turn a profit their first time out, the government often forgave their loan, gave them another, and told them to take another shot at it, on and on until they got it right.

When voters repealed apartheid, the percentage of whites

living in poverty in South Africa was exactly zero. By 2006, after a decade of policies designed to expand trade and create a more just economy, the figure had climbed to all of 1 percent. The face of South African poverty remains darker-skinned. Apartheid helped create two countries in a single border: one of 8 million whites living in a country that has living standards remarkably similar to Canada's, the other of 38 million blacks and Indians who are citizens of a country with a standard of living that is more comparable to Namibia's.

In its contract with international capital, South Africa's new black majority government has agreed to an economic program that does for the country's long-suffering black population precisely the opposite of what its white predecessors did for their own. This is fundamentally a nation in the midst of an identity crisis, torn between its communal African impulses and a Western value system that exalts the individual and his private gains.

For proof, look no further than the country's efforts to privatize its state-owned airline. Wanting to transform South Africa Airways into a moneymaker that could attract lucrative bids from investors, ANC officials were almost gleeful in 1998 when they hired an American turnaround specialist, T. Coleman Andrews III, to run the carrier. A Republican and a former candidate for governor of Virginia, Andrews was hired to nudge SAA into the global marketplace with some good old-fashioned American business know-how. He did just that, immediately sizing up the competition and setting his sights on Sun Air, a small but nimble regional airline. Slashing fares and flooding the skies with cheap flights, Andrews bludgeoned Sun Air into bankruptcy within a year of his arrival, leaving SAA to gobble up most of its passengers and expand its share of the regional market.

The ANC seethed. Sun Air was their baby, the government's first successful effort at brokering a deal to create a viable black-owned company after decades in which blacks were legally banned from owning property. Within three years Andrews had worn out his welcome. He left the country with a $24 million severance package—the largest in the country's history—and SAA with as much red ink as when he arrived. The $40 million profit that Andrews claimed on the carrier's 2001 balance sheet evaporated after auditors discovered an Enron-like accounting scheme that reported as profit the one-time revenues from the sales of planes and equipment. Those auditors said the airline actually lost about $73 million in 2001, roughly the same as in the year before Andrews arrived, when adjusted for currency devaluations.

"It was criminal," said Victor Nkosi, SAA's vice president for marketing. "The core business is not any more profitable than when he found it, once you account for the assets he stripped. We wanted an American to show us the ropes, and he took us for a good ride."

Similarly, South Africa's effort to redistribute land to the poor has lagged. With little money and a willing-buyer, willing-seller policy intended to mollify foreign investors concerned about property rights and public spending, the government has been unable to purchase at market prices much of the 87 percent of arable land owned by the country's white elite. At the current pace, experts say, it will take another 120 years to resettle blacks in proportion to their numbers.

Frustrated by the government's snail's pace, about 2,500

squatters in 2001 relocated to a patch of unused land owned by a farmer near Johannesburg. The ANC sent police in riot gear and armored cars to escort construction workers, who tore through the groves of tin shacks with crowbars, leaving one home after another in a heap of scrap metal and ripped tarpaulin. No one missed the scene's eerie similarity to those of the apartheid era, when the white-minority government bulldozed whole neighborhoods and throngs of foot-stomping blacks railed against it in the streets. Squatters shook their fists defiantly at the police, while women chanted antigovernment slogans and danced in protest, baring their breasts in a gesture of shame meant to taunt the demolition crews. "This," said Zakes Hlatshwayo, the chairman of an advocacy organization for the poor and landless, as he looked at the demolition from the roadside, "is just like the old days."

Land ownership plays a critical role in South Africa's HIV epidemic, which has infected an estimated 5 million South Africans, nearly a quarter of all adults. Without land, millions of South Africans have left the countryside for the city, settling in overcrowded slums like Soweto and sometimes working in the country's mines, which require young men to live in hostels for several months at a time. The combination of idleness and congestion caused by high urban unemployment and the promiscuity encouraged by the mining sector's housing policies fuel the spread of the disease through heterosexual sex, the primary mode of transmission here. Without health care, young men are unlikely to get medical attention for venereal diseases, which, if left untreated, increase the risk of HIV infection by a factor of nine.

President Mbeki and his advisers have been reluctant to offer anti-AIDS drugs to HIV-infected people, in part because he and others in the ANC's leadership—many of whom recall earlier sterilization efforts by missionaries and the apartheid government's secret chemical warfare program—are truly skeptical of the efficacy of Western medicine. But just as problematic is that top ANC officials have been slow to provide the cheaper generic versions of the medicine because they fear antagonizing foreign investors by either importing or manufacturing generic drugs that cut into the pharmaceutical companies' profits.

That fear is not irrational. Carrying water for the multinational drug companies, which are huge donors to the Democratic Party's coffers, then vice president Al Gore repeatedly threatened Mbeki with economic sanctions if the ANC were to bypass drug company patents. The World Trade Organization allows the manufacture or importation of generic drugs in the case of a public health crisis, but Gore's admonitions persuaded an already reluctant Mbeki, who shied away from getting on Wall Street's bad side.

In Johannesburg, a group of activists formed the Soweto Electricity Crisis Committee in 2001 to help poor households in the tin shanties and brick hovels that circle the bustling city built atop a mammoth gold reef like rows of rotting teeth. Asking nothing in return and relying heavily on laid-off Eskom repairmen who volunteer their time, SECC volunteers zip across the city five days a week, sunup to sundown, using a penknife, a snip here, and a splice there to reunite power and people. Since then, Operation Khanyisa, which means "to light" in the Zulu language, has unlawfully restored electricity to about 50,000 homes, though many are repeat customers.

"We shouldn't have to resort to this," Agnes Mohapi says

as she stands cross-armed and remorseless in the street, watching two repairmen work. Apartheid, she says, was a blasphemy. Nothing compares to it. But for all its wretchedness, apartheid never did this: it did not lay her off from her job, jack up her utility bill, then disconnect her service when she inevitably could not pay. "Privatization did that," she says, her cadence quickening in disgust. "And all of this globalization garbage our new black government has forced upon us has done nothing but make things worse. . . . But we will unite and we will fight this government with the same fury that we fought the whites in their day."

"We're getting about fifty calls each day from the community," Virginia Setshedi, an SECC spokeswoman, told me in 2002. "We don't ask why or when the people were cut off, we just switch them back on. Everyone should have electricity."

One of 25,000 employees who have lost jobs at Eskom since 1994, Bongani Lubisi arrived at the intersection of Maseka and Moema Streets one morning flanked by two recruits. "Red and white are used as live wires, and they are very dangerous," Lubisi said, showing the wires to the trainees as a crowd gathered.

"There's definitely been a revival of the struggle mentality," Lubisi told me later. He is twenty-eight, the father of a four-year-old boy. "We thought that when we got rid of the old government, our black government would take care of us. But instead the capitalists are getting richer while the working people lose their jobs and can't even meet their basic needs."

James Buthelezi is fifty-eight and has lived in his house on Maseka Street for as long as he can remember, and his electricity was disconnected for the first time in 2001. Twenty-eight people live in this five-room house and a toolshed-sized room in the backyard. No one has worked in months, and the family survives on Buthelezi's mother's pension, less than $125 a month. He showed me his unpaid bills, which totaled more than $3,000 in South Africa's currency, the rand, and hadn't been paid in almost a year. "When they came to cut off our electricity, we begged them not to," he said. "We told them that we had babies and elderly people inside. They didn't even pause."

"This culture of nonpayment that people say exists in Soweto," said Setshedi, "it's only because people don't have money to pay." Said Shadrack Motau, an SECC board member, "We did not give up our lives and the lives of our children only to let this brazen capitalist system exploit us even more."

The SECC's members have tried to talk to Johannesburg's mayor about the hardships endured by families like Buthelezi's, but he has repeatedly given them the slip. In the final weeks of 2001, more than twenty angry residents marched to the mayor's home, but again he ducked them.

Unable to cut off his electricity, they disconnected his water.

Part Two

CHICKENS COMING HOME TO ROOST

5

NEOLIBERAL NEGROES

Chicago and Democracy

> Contradictions between classes, even when only
> embryonic, are of far greater importance than
> contradictions between tribes.
>
> —*Amilcar Cabral*

Since its inception in 1969, the Congressional Black Caucus has grown from thirteen to forty-two members, all African American legislators elected to the U.S. House of Representatives and Senate. With its deep roots in the civil rights and labor movements, the progressive-minded caucus holds its Annual Legislative Conference every autumn in Washington, D.C., and thousands of conferees—wonks and clerics, mayors, celebrities and corporate executives—converge on the city in early autumn for an opportunity to talk policy and gossip with one another and the representatives they've sent to the nation's capital.

Unsurprisingly, "CBC week," as it has come to be known, is also a showcase for the African American elite—what one political scientist calls the "Black Enterprise [magazine] crowd"—to flex their hard-earned muscles, to network, even to flirt a little. It is a swank affair, and the soirees that typically follow the conference's daily seminars and workshops tend to be on the showy side, equal parts singles bar and Sunday church service.

Sponsored by AT&T, the 2006 reception for Illinois congressman Bobby Rush was more lavish than most. The soul food and champagne were a hit. A jazz band played with a light hand. Crisp white linens draped the dinner tables, and a pride of lobbyists, power brokers, and rainmakers prowled the chandeliered ballroom of the Grand Hyatt Hotel like big cats.

The king of the cats was unquestionably the sixty-two-year-old Rush, who moved through the crowd shaking hands and chatting up his constituents with an ease both regal and folksy. No one alive has traveled a greater distance to reach the orbit of American political power than Rush, the former minister of defense for the Illinois chapter of the Black Panther Party, a gun-toting revolutionary in a dashiki and dark sunglasses who fed poor schoolchildren, feuded with Chicago street gangs, and fled J. Edgar Hoover's FBI agents. Cofounder Huey Newton famously exhorted the organization to "serve the people," and through its national chapters the party organized free services such as clothing distribution, adult education classes, legal aid, pest control, plumbing and maintenance, transportation, drug and alcohol rehabilitation programs, ambulance programs, a breakfast program, food co-ops, and medical centers.

Many black Chicagoans of a certain age are stunned not so much by Rush's odyssey from fugitive-from-justice to seven-term lawmaker, or by the fact that someone once hunted by the establishment is firmly ensconced in it, but that he ever lived this long in the first place. He did, and nowadays he favors dark suits and silk ties rather than dashikis, and his receding hairline, peppered goatee, and thick glasses combine for an appearance that is senatorial yet avuncular, something, comically enough, of the lion from *The Wizard of Oz*.

A Democrat, Rush represents the "capital of black America," Illinois's First District, which includes a wide swath of Chicago's South Side and is home to more African Americans than any other congressional district in the nation. So safe is his seat that he easily turned back a challenge in the state's 2000 Democratic primary from a then fast-rising and ambitious state lawmaker named Barack Obama.

In March 2006, Rush sponsored a bill with Republican congressman Joe Barton of Texas and three other House Republicans to essentially repeal the longstanding principle of Internet neutrality and replace it with a pay-to-play arrangement. Since its introduction nearly twenty years ago, the Internet has allowed users to access any website or service without commercial interference from service providers. The Barton-Rush bill proposed to end the Internet as we've come to know it by requiring websites from Google to Wal-Mart to *Birdwatchers' Digest* to pay big phone companies like AT&T for the use of their landlines. If they did not, AT&T could relegate their websites to the Internet's slow lane, and anyone looking for them online could be redirected to an ad for, say, Quicken Loans or Domino's Pizza or any of the paying customers. The measure would also permit phone monopolies and cable franchises to enter markets without complying with local laws requiring service providers to make the same products and services available to all neighborhoods, poor and rich alike, and to set aside a designated number of television stations for noncommercial uses like public access television.

Rush and lobbyists for big telecom contend that deregulation will lower prices. Consumer advocates say that deregulation will lead AT&T to lower its prices about as much as it encouraged Enron to lower the cost of electricity. What is more likely, they say, is that the regulatory changes will result in a form of redlining in which big phone and cable companies ignore their networks in poor inner-city neighborhoods and instead funnel billions of dollars into affluent neighborhoods, which promise fatter profits. The Barton-Rush bill, in effect, would widen the country's already yawning digital divide, not close it.

After intense opposition from consumer groups and content providers like Google, the legislation failed, though Rush and others promised to introduce a similar bill in the future. What is unavoidable is this: Rush's campaign coffers and the community center he runs get a lot of cash from big telecom, and big telecom would get a lot more cash from a law curbing Internet neutrality.

At Rush's reception, he was introduced by Rodney Smith, AT&T's assistant vice president for federal relations, who strolled to the podium as glasses tinkled and the band fell silent. "I only have one brief comment to make about tonight's guest," he said. "I think all of us recognize that many Americans do not necessarily have nice things to say about our nation's political leaders, or, for that matter, those of us who work in the nation's capital. We're either bureaucrats or lobbyists. And some of this criticism is undoubtedly justified. But just let me make this point to all of you here tonight: there are some very dedicated men and women in both parties who

do their best to make our country a better place. And none
of them work harder for their country, their state, or their
district than our guest of honor. In fact, in Washington we
have a unique way of spelling commitment and integrity—
it's a four-letter word, and it's spelled R-U-S-H."

The view of Rush from Englewood, on Chicago's South
Side, is quite different. An expanse of rib joints, shoe stores,
empty lots, and CASH FOR YOUR HOME signs, Englewood is as
poor as the American city gets. Of the 83,000 people who live
in the neighborhood, 97 percent are black. One of every three
able-bodied adults is jobless. More people here die violently,
get sick, go to jail, and drop out of high school than in practically any other neighborhood in Chicago.

As recently as the 1930s, nine of every ten people who lived
in the neighborhood were white, mostly the families of Swedes,
Germans, and Irishmen who worked the stockyards just north
of Englewood. Construction on the Dan Ryan Expressway
in the 1950s uprooted thousands of white homeowners, and
the riots in 1968 uprooted thousands more. Blacks who found
work at U.S. Steel, just south of the neighborhood, began to
settle their families in the spacious bungalows and walkups
with big yards and wide stoops. The stockyards closed in the
early 1970s, U.S. Steel a decade later.

Today there are no grocery stores or movie theaters in
Englewood. The El no longer stops here. Englewood is pock-
marked with vacant properties. One end-zone-sized lot on the
corner of Sixtieth and Peoria is of particular concern to Jean
Carter-Hill, a retired schoolteacher and community activist.
Particles of lead used to paint Englewood's aged homes and
at old industrial sites have poisoned the soil and the air. The
broad consensus of the scientific community is that even

slightly elevated levels of lead pollute the air and can cause permanent neurological damage and reduced IQ in children, and many public health experts believe that lead contamination plays a role in the increased rates of asthma in aging inner cities.

Carter-Hill serves as the director of a grass-roots organization named Imagine Englewood If. Three years ago she and several other volunteers were scouring Englewood for sites to seed community gardens when they discovered that the lead levels in the soil at Sixtieth and Peoria are more than three times as high as what is considered safe by public health officials. The lot is directly across from Woodlawn Elementary School.

Imagine Englewood If has not contributed so much as a dime to Rush's campaign, or to any other political candidate, for that matter. Couldn't even if it wanted to. The operating budget is exactly $0. But what members of the organization want is not nearly as ambitious as changing the face of twenty-first-century communications. They want to breathe air that won't sicken them. They want the site across from the elementary school cleaned up to prevent the lead from seeping into the air that children inhale every day. "You see, this is partly how you get these high dropout rates and these developmental problems in our kids," said Carter-Hill. "We don't know how much crime is because these young men breathed in this stuff when they were kids."

Carter-Hill has led the community's effort to address the site's contamination. Finally, in the spring of 2006, a call to Obama's Senate office resulted in the construction of a fence around the lot. That will keep children from playing on the soil but won't necessarily keep them from breathing in the polluted air. "It's not exactly what we need, but it's a start," Carter-Hill said.

Touring the neighborhood with Carter-Hill one autumn afternoon, I asked, Did the group contact Rush's office?

She smiled.

"Hmm," she said. "Now, everybody knows that you can call and call and call Bobby Rush till you turn blue in the face." She held her hands out in front in a gesture of exasperation. "And nothing gets done."

THIS IS THE new global class war, a conflict that increasingly recognizes neither race, nor geography nor traditional alliances. Worldwide, widening inequality has increasingly estranged ordinary working people from the proxies they choose to represent them in democratic discussion.

What fuels this shift is the evolution of a modern postindustrial elite, an international cadre of politicians, corporate executives, diplomats, journalists, and bankers who have more in common with one another than they do with their countrymen or constituents. Across the globe, from the *favelas* to the townships to the *villas miserias* to any neighborhood located just off Martin Luther King Jr. Drive in inner-city America, the traditional champions of the poor, workers, consumers, and people of color are siding with big business. The story of globalization is in part a Shakespearean drama of betrayal: of working-class Zambians by a former trade union leader; of Argentines by the party founded by the populist labor minister; of Brazilian workers by a former lathe operator who lost a finger in an industrial accident; of black South Africans by the countrymen who liberated them; and of neighborhoods like Englewood by one of their own.

In each of these narratives, public space for ordinary people is shrinking. Wages and salaries in the United States now make up the lowest share of the nation's GDP since the government began recording the data in 1947, while corporate profits as a share of national income have climbed to their highest ratio since the 1960s.

The disparate trajectories are both the consequence of and the catalyst for profound changes in longstanding political alliances. Consider, as one example, that the Democratic Party—once the party of the American working class—raised $340.3 million in campaign contributions from big business in 2000, compared to $52.4 million from organized labor. It is not surprising, then, that the chief architect of the North American Free Trade Agreement was a Democratic president, Bill Clinton, who, along with Mexico's Harvard-educated former president, Carlos Salinas, lobbied for the 1994 law, although Clinton's Democratic base—especially labor unions—was staunchly opposed.

On newspaper editorial pages and television newscasts, globalization is often described as an inevitable process, a Darwinian winnowing that yields a modern state. But as the economist and writer Dean Baker has noted, the authors of the international trade rules could just as easily have rewritten labor laws and licensing requirements that shield such professions as medicine, journalism, and accounting from foreign competition, which would produce far greater savings to consumers than lowering restrictions on the sale and purchase of manufactured goods does. As one example cited by Baker, the only reason a publisher cannot hire English-speaking journalists from, say, India or South Africa and pay them half of what newspaper reporters earn at the *New York*

Times (and consequently charge less for advertising space) is that prevailing wage laws make it illegal. Workers at Wal-Mart have no such protections.

Similarly, consider that the World Trade Organization and NAFTA-style pacts require participating countries to strengthen laws protecting international patent rights, thereby increasing the price of anti-AIDS medicines and other drugs and the profits reaped by multinational pharmaceutical firms. "Free trade" is not so free when it suits big business.

Growing corporate influence only deepens the isolation of poor communities like Englewood from the representatives they send to city hall, state capitals, and Washington. Between 1989, when Rush first ran for Congress, and 2006, big phone and cable companies donated $114,082 to his campaign coffers; AT&T has chipped in more than half of that total, or $56,714. In addition, a charitable arm of AT&T in 1999 awarded a $1 million grant to an Englewood community center founded by Rush, who serves on the House Energy and Commerce Committee and its Internet subcommittee. Liberal bloggers and consumer groups have protested the grant as a clear conflict of interest. Rush has said there is no conflict. He and his wife, Carolyn, are on the center's board but not its payroll, he said. "I'm from the other side of town," he told reporters, referring to his South Side Chicago roots. "This is a bill that will make a difference in the lives of the people on the other side of town."

Of the forty African Americans in the House who voted on the Barton-Rush bill in July 2006, twenty-six joined Rush in supporting the legislation. (The legislation died in the Senate when Ron Wyden, a Democrat from Oregon, threatened to filibuster if it came up for a vote on the floor. A near-identical measure was introduced in 2008; again Rush was one of its sponsors in the House.) Rush was one of eleven black lawmakers who voted in 2005 for a successful GOP-sponsored bill to expand subsidies for big oil companies just as the industry was raking in record profits and consumers were paying record prices at the pump. That same year he was one of eleven African American lawmakers in the House to vote for an amendment limiting the liability of oil companies who pollute groundwater supplies with the toxic chemical MTBE. That bill passed as well.

To his credit, Rush did not join the ten CBC members who voted in 2005 for the Republican-led overhaul of the nation's bankruptcy law, a measure that will fatten the bottom lines of lenders while providing little relief for the majority of cash-strapped consumers seeking help. Neither did Rush join eight African American congressional legislators who voted for a GOP proposal to repeal the estate tax for the wealthiest taxpayers, even though fewer than 10 percent of all black households are affluent enough to take advantage of the tax break, which will further deplete the government's already thin resources for public schools, health care, and social services.

That the Democratic Party has long been ambivalent about its African American base is nothing new. But black voters are discovering that at all levels of government, the vote of their elected official cannot be taken for granted. Obama, the U.S. Senate's lone African American and as of this writing the 2008 Democratic nominee for president, has in his first three years on the job made little effort to balance the dueling priorities of his Wall Street donors and his heavily black constituency. He has voted against a measure to cap interest rates on credit cards at 30 percent, arguing that the bill was badly written, though Obama, a former constitutional law professor at the University of Chicago, made no attempt to revise or rewrite the bill. He voted for a bill to limit the liability of big business in civil suits filed by consumers injured and even killed by defective products by putting much of the litigation in federal court rather than the more populist state courts. He said he voted for the bill because suits tried in typically conservative federal courts are more likely to produce a verdict, while defendants in state court are more likely to negotiate an out-of-court settlement rather than risk a large judgment against them. He voted in favor of a NAFTA-like trade pact with the impoverished country of Oman, despite objections from labor unions in both the United States and the Middle East, who complained that the agreement would further lower workers' wages. He sided with mining concerns in voting against a measure to collect royalties of 4 percent on existing hard rock mining operations and 8 percent on new excavations and to force the industry to clean up abandoned mines. Obama said the legislation posed too large a burden for the already profitable industry and would deter investment and job creation. A lobbyist for a Nevada mining corporation contributed $2,300 to Obama's presidential campaign.

In fact, at almost every opportunity Obama as a presidential contender has chosen the interests of the monied, usually white elites around the globe rather than those of the often darker-skinned poor and working classes. He promised a group of radical Cuban exiles that he would uphold the longstanding U.S. embargo against that country's poor; he has repeatedly rattled his saber against Palestinian, Iranian, and Lebanese Arabs in a sycophantic defense of Israel; he has endorsed the illegal cross-border raids of Colombia's right-wing government in their war against leftist guerrillas and labeled as a U.S. enemy Venezuela's democratically elected president, Hugo Chávez, whose socialist government has dramatically improved the living standards of poor and working-class people. Again and again, in speeches even to predominantly black audiences, Obama has sounded the neoliberal mantra, railing against irresponsible black parents, but rarely, if ever, singling out for criticism the increasing cronyism between business executives and politicians or their effort to shut off the spigot of middle-class wages or the withering educational, health, environmental, and penal policies that have wreaked havoc on black families over the past thirty years.

For all intents and purposes, holding elected office in the United States is tantamount to being the member of an international parliament of brokers, shareholders, and politicians—globalization's governing class. Consider, for example, Congress's approval of a bailout plan that will benefit only creditors and bankers but not the taxpayers. Treasury Secretary Henry Paulson insisted that the final bill contain no real limits on executive pay and a provision allowing him to buy the commercial paper not just from Wall Street firms but from foreign banks as well. And while the banks did require an infusion of cash to avert a disastrous credit crunch, government bailouts around the world have typically recapitalized failing businesses by buying stock in the company or loaning money at stiff rates, resulting in a payout for the taxpayers down the road. By comparison, Obama objected to providing any substantial foreclosure assistance to homeowners on the grounds that it would invite "moral hazard," but he made no such objections to offloading Wall Street's reckless gambits onto taxpayers.

There is in Obama's appeal to African Americans a strong current of "middle-class black nationalism," according to the scholar and author Michael Eric Dyson. The goal of diversity has replaced the goal of equality in our political culture, but they are not one and the same. The majority-black city of Washington, D.C., for example, has one of the highest mortality rates in the Western Hemisphere. Yet former mayor Anthony Williams, an African American, closed the city's only trauma center in 2005 while putting his political muscle behind an effort to build a $611 million major league baseball stadium entirely on the city's dime. Seventy percent of city voters opposed the giveaway, according to polls. That is the same percentage of Chicagoans who endorsed a proposal requiring big-box retailers such as Wal-Mart to pay their workers a living wage and provide health care. Seven of the city's sixteen black aldermen, including Shirley Coleman, representing a slice of Englewood on Chicago's City Council, supported Mayor Richard M. Daley's veto of the bill in late 2006.

And in Springfield, Illinois's state capital, a coterie of black Chicago lawmakers led by state senate president Emil Jones, a political mentor to Obama, blocked efforts to rescind a rate increase of more than 20 percent for ComEd, the state's largest utility. A major donor to black lawmakers and several black mega-churches in the city, ComEd raked in record profits in 2005 but contended that it would go bankrupt without the rate hike.

Like South Africa's black townships, Latino and black neighborhoods such as Englewood are plagued by electricity shutoffs for nonpayment. Community activists in the neighborhood say they are inundated with calls from families who need help paying their electricity bills. Just as in Soweto, homes in Englewood go dark for weeks and even months at a time. In March 2006 three children were killed when a candle they were using for light set their West Side apartment ablaze. In arrears, the family had been without electricity for more than three months.

Rush, like Obama, Jones, Williams, and most of the CBC, is part of an evolving black political class in the United States that a friend of mine likes to call sardonically "neoliberal Negroes." Evidence of their growing solidarity with corporate interests abounds, even when they assume the traditional stance of black elected leaders. When a cadre of white southern Republican congressmen in 2005 balked at reauthorizing the 1965 Voting Rights Act, black lawmakers rallied support by lobbying their corporate donors to pressure the conservative lawmakers. "On the one hand, that was great, because who knows if we would have gotten the reauthorization passed without it," said one Capitol Hill aide who saw the lobbying campaign firsthand, "but you really did have this feeling of the ground shifting underneath your feet."

By most any yardstick, blacks represent the most reliably liberal voting bloc in the United States. Nine of ten African Americans who went to the polls in 2000 and 2004 voted for Al Gore and John Kerry. Black women are more likely to join a union than any other demographic group in the country. And a 2006 survey conducted by the Bay Area Center for Voting Research concluded that the most liberal American cities were, almost without exception, those with the largest black majorities. Detroit topped the list, followed by Gary, Indiana. The most overwhelmingly white cities were the most conservative. Provo, Utah, topped that list in a survey of the nation's 237 largest cities. That fulfills the predictions made nearly forty years ago by the conservative political analyst Kevin Phillips that a near-total political polarization along racial lines would usher in an era of Republican electoral dominance.

What Phillips did not account for are the profound fissures that have emerged within the black community over that time as well. As in South Africa in its post-apartheid era, the repeal of laws that parsed one race from another opened doors for educated, skilled, and connected blacks in the post–civil rights period at the precise moment that the global economy's diffuse corporate ethos was closing doors for the uneducated, the unskilled, and the disconnected.

In both the United States and South Africa, inequality among blacks is wider than at any time in history. And in many ways the glowing introduction of Rush by a corporate benefactor parallels the effusive praise heaped upon South African president Thabo Mbeki, an economist educated at the University of Sussex in England, by figures such as the former World Bank president James Wolfensohn, who often publicly lauded Mbeki's efforts to strengthen property rights, cap inflation, and deregulate the economy. I often thought that if I were the leader of a developing country, I would have considered a public backslap from Wolfensohn or any other global banking institution the kiss of death. It inevitably means that unemployment is high, wages are low, and your political support is dimming. That was indeed the case for

Mbeki, who was ousted as ANC leader and the party's presidential candidate in an internecine party coup in 2007.

The best-of-times, worst-of-times tonality is as true for black Americans as it is for South African blacks, both of whom have seen income disparities widen following the end of legally mandated segregation. Said the University of Maryland sociology professor Bart Landry, "I'm afraid that for black Americans, this is truly the Gilded Age."

"SOMEBODY GAVE YOU a bad report."

This is Rush delivering the sermon from the sprawling oak pulpit of his Englewood church on a September Sunday afternoon. He was ordained a nondenominational minister in 2002, three years after his twenty-nine-year-old son was gunned down in a street robbery on Chicago's South Side. In 2005 Rush moved to this eighty-four-year-old Gothic-style church with towering stained glass windows, cracked plaster, and water-stained ceilings, which sits in the shadow of the Dan Ryan freeway.

"You hear the report that there are no jobs, and you say, Why do I need to look for a job? I know they aren't going to hire me."

The sermon is from the Book of Numbers, chapter 13, in which Moses sends an advance team to scout Canaan for the Israelites. They return with "an evil report of the land": Canaan is indeed the land of milk and honey, but the cities are walled, the people strong. Their advice is to steer clear of the Promised Land.

"Somebody gave you a bad report, and you believed the bad report. They told you that the white man is so great and so powerful that you can never compete with him. They told you that your education is so inferior that you can never lead a large corporation. You hear the report that there are no jobs, so you know they are not going to hire you. A bad report."

Rush roams the pulpit while he speaks, speaking in the familiar lyrical cadence of the black church, using a single phrase, "a bad report," repeatedly, like the hook of a catchy pop song as the momentum builds to the big, booming finish.

"Fear holds you back," Rush exhorts the congregation, maybe forty-five parishioners, making the hulking church resemble an empty football stadium. "You got to do something different. You got to rise up, get up and go. Don't waste God's miracle. Some of us have been in the wilderness for too long."

Much like Obama's speeches to predominantly African American audiences, Rush's proselytism is at its core a paean to self-reliance, once the center of gravity of the Black Panthers, now a principal pillar of the conservative movement promoting austerity in the relationship between public resources and the challenges facing poor and working-class people. In a 2003 *Chicago Tribune* profile of Rush, he said, "Government will never liberate us. . . . We have to assume a lot of that responsibility for ourselves and I don't see Congress or elected office as being a cure-all for our problems. At the end of the day it can help deliver the resources, but it doesn't have the ability to transform lives and transform communities. Ultimately, you've got to make up your mind to change yourself."

Rush, the profile's author wrote, sounds at times "more like George W. Bush or Ronald Reagan than a liberal black Democrat from an inner-city district." That would have seemed unimaginable forty years ago. In their ten-point platform appealing for land, bread, housing, education, clothing, justice, and peace, the Black Panthers were also in the vanguard of the American political left. The party's socialist strategies, revolutionary zeal, and guns made it, as J. Edgar Hoover famously wrote in 1968, the "greatest threat to the internal security of the country." "It was always about injustice," Rush told the *Chicago Tribune.*

Rush was the right-hand man of Fred Hampton, the chairman of the Panther's Illinois chapter. A skilled organizer who coined the term "rainbow coalition," later used by the Reverend Jesse Jackson in his groundbreaking 1984 presidential campaign, the charismatic, twenty-one-year-old Hampton was slain as he slept—an FBI informant had drugged the Kool-Aid he and his lieutenants had with dinner—in an early morning raid of the Panthers' West Side headquarters. Chicago police described the gun battle as a shootout, but an independent forensic investigation later concluded that of the more than ninety shots fired, no more than a single shot was fired at the police, and that probably by the fatally wounded Mark Clark in a death rattle.

Rush had left the apartment only hours before, and the following day police raided the apartment where he lived with his wife and two young children, only to find that he had fled. His lawyers arranged for him to surrender to a black police commander at a Saturday meeting of Jackson's social service organization, Operation Breadbasket. Police kept him for less than an hour and he was released.

When Chicago's revered first black mayor, Harold Washington, fought bitterly against the city's white aldermen and state representatives in the "Council Wars" in the 1980s, Rush, then an alderman, was Washington's unwavering lieutenant. Labor unions, civil rights organizations, and liberal watchdog groups consistently give him high marks for his voting record. The independent group the CBC Monitor awarded him a score of 85 for his 2006 voting record on issues most relevant to poor and minority communities. (By comparison, the CBC Monitor awarded John Conyers [D-Michigan] and Maxine Waters [D-California] perfect scores of 100; younger lawmakers like Harold Ford [D-Tennessee] and Al Wynn [D-Maryland] scored less than 50 percent.)

In the midst of his 2000 reelection campaign against Obama, Rush launched a community development project, Rebirth Englewood. Acquiring vacant lots from the city for $1 and leveraging corporate donations and government grants and loans, the congressman planned to attract middle-class families to Englewood by building 550 homes over the next five years, with prices starting at $165,000 for the four-bedroom units. Rebirth Englewood has broken ground on a $1.2 million technology center for job training. Following a surge in violence in 2005 in which a ten-year-old Englewood girl was fatally shot, Rush coaxed state and city officials, ComEd, JPMorgan Chase, the Chicago White Sox and Bulls, and others to contribute more than $1 million for a summer jobs program for 952 youths—250 of them from Englewood—paying hourly wages of $7 to $10.

A pastor here once described Rush as "the Scottie Pippen to Hampton's Michael Jordan." He didn't leave footprints quite as large as Hampton's or even a few others in the movement, said Phyllis Offord, a lifelong Chicago resident and administrator for a Chicago nonprofit organization, who remembers running into Rush periodically in his Panther days. But, she said, "He was always cordial and respectful, and you could tell he was very smart. They were all very intellectual men, and they were challenging everything. They were leaders that you were automatically just drawn to. If you were black and living in Chicago there was nothing like seeing the Panthers march [downtown]. They brought this whole change of thinking and they were such prideful men." She pauses for a moment, then adds, "And they were ours."

Rush's most ardent critics would never describe him with the acerbic language blacks typically reserve for the worst forms of racial treachery—"Uncle Tom" or "sellout"—which are often uttered in private conversations about Clarence Thomas or Condoleezza Rice, for instance. Rather, many in Englewood are resigned to the likelihood that Rush, a U.S. congressman who earns $150,000 annually while the median household income in Englewood is slightly more than $18,000 annually, is no longer "ours."

DAYS AFTER RUSH'S posh 2006 reception in Washington, Carter-Hill and Yusuf Hassan take me on a tour of Englewood, cataloguing trouble spots and grievances and their community wish list. We stop outside Englewood High School just as classes are letting out for the day, and parents park curbside waiting for the phalanx of schoolchildren as they pour from the building. Honeybees swarm the car in the Indian summer warmth, forcing us to roll up the windows while we talk.

Nearly eighty years old, the school was converted into a charter school four years ago. It is much improved, Hassan and Carter-Hill agree, but it does the community little good. Less than 20 percent of the student body actually lives in Englewood. Most are middle-class kids from other neighborhoods.

"Our kids most times don't qualify to get in," Carter-Hill says.

"The school board will have a meeting and pretend to listen to us, but then they do what they planned to do anyway," Hassan says. "It's all for show."

"We've got all these vacant lots that the aldermen could sell [at steep discounts] to someone from the neighborhood, but they always seem to go to the outsiders, like the Koreans," says Carter-Hill.

"That's why we got all these Athlete's Foots and sporting goods stores selling all this hip-hop stuff," Hassan says. "We don't need any more stores selling tennis shoes and baggy pants."

"It's just like all these liquor stores," Carter-Hill says. "All these problems we have with liquor stores in our neighborhoods, and Jesse goes and helps his son get a liquor distributorship," she says, referring to Jackson's youngest son, Jonathan, who is part of a group of investors who purchased a local franchise here nine years ago.

"Boy, if we could just get a little help from some of our so-called leaders, we'd be dangerous," Hassan says.

We start the car and drive on.

Carter-Hill and Hassan lay bare their disillusionment as we talk. It is as if, ironically, the slow disintegration of the manufacturing sector has done to the inner city precisely what many fear Rush's telecommunications bill will eventually do to the Internet: create a two-tier system in which paying customers take priority over nonpaying customers.

"Englewood is low to the ground," says Hassan, "and Bobby does his thing on a different level."

Rush reflects the larger shift in the relationship between

voters and politicians in a shrinking democracy, said Robert Starks, a professor of political science at Northeastern Illinois University. "If you are running for office, you have to raise so much money, and if you are black, that means that you're always catering to the needs of the black middle class," said Starks, a key strategist for Washington's stunning mayoral campaign. "That's where a lot of your money is coming from. But their needs are different from the folks in the 'hood. They want set-asides [government programs in minority contracting]. The people in Englewood want jobs. They are not one and the same."

IN 1999 PRESIDENT CLINTON announced the launch of a federal program to spur economic development in urban areas at an Englewood elementary school, declaring that "there are people and places untouched by prosperity." Indeed, Englewood seems populated by citizens of another country at times, preoccupied with concerns that would resonate with squatters in Soweto or peasants in Bolivia. Young people here often greet each other with "Where you staying?" which they mean literally. With gentrification and the collapse of public housing, there are fewer affordable addresses in the city. Teenagers often crash for weeks at a time with a friend or relative, then move on to another. Without steady work, parents cannot easily afford the fees charged by public schools for basic supplies or day trips, a complaint I heard constantly while working as a foreign correspondent in southern Africa.

Obama's "post-black" presidential candidacy, which is causing a frenzy in the media and among the nation's elites, could just as well be the rumbling of some third-party candidate in New Zealand given the amount of buzz as it has created in Englewood. While speaking with Hal Baskin, a community organizer in Englewood, and other South Side residents, I was reminded of an African American politician in Detroit who spoke in 1992 of the chasm that separates the haves and have-nots in daily discourse. Just days before voters went to the polls to elect the first Democratic president in twelve years, he said to me in a private conversation, "The Dow Jones can go up five hundred points or it can go down five hundred points, it don't matter. Niggas will still be poor."

Two years after Clinton announced his redevelopment plans for Englewood, Baskin and other grass-roots leaders discovered that neither the mammoth $256 million project to relocate Kennedy King Community College from Englewood's west side to its east nor a $115 million effort to repair a stretch of the Dan Ryan freeway employed any blacks. "Right here in Englewood, we have enough untapped labor to tear China down to the ground and rebuild it again," said Baskin, who has twice run unsuccessfully for Chicago's City Council. "You got what will probably end up being $500 million in construction going on right here in this neighborhood, and no one thought that maybe a job or two would go a long ways toward the redevelopment of our neighborhood."

So Baskin began rounding up skilled, jobless workers from the neighborhood, marching to construction sites, and demanding jobs. If site managers refused, the protesters shut them down. Over a three-year period, police arrested Baskin six times for trespassing. But over that same period he and his band of demonstrators managed to land jobs paying an average of $31.55 an hour for 455 men and women. "I tell them, anyone I send to you, if they don't work out, you call me," Baskin said. "Never had anybody call me with a bad report."

Dionne Bender, thirty-seven and the mother of three, was in the middle of a divorce when she got the call from Baskin in September. The next day she joined Baskin and a dozen other protesters in a march on the Englewood construction site. She started work the next day at the community college construction site, where, she said with a deadpan delivery, "it's me and four Puerto Ricans blowing up a bridge. This makes a big difference in people's lives," she said. "Our politicians should be doing this, but they don't. We elect them and they take care of their friends and families and leave the rest of us to take care of ourselves."

Of the three aldermen, one congressman, two state legislators, and two U.S. senators who represent Englewood, only one, Senator Dick Durbin, is white. And yet, said Darryl Smith, a construction worker, "how come none of them helped us remove these obstacles? A lot of them are just selling out the community. These are the kinds of things we elect them to help with."

Smith is thirty-seven and the president of the Englewood Political Task Force; Baskin is a board member. Three years ago, Smith narrowly lost a race for a state representative's seat representing a portion of the South Side. He lost by fewer than 300 votes of the nearly 40,000 cast. He blames the Diebold voting machines for his loss.

Inside the task force's modest storefront headquarters, prodded by my questioning, Smith and Baskin began a spirited discussion on black elected officials and other leaders. "You know, these people have just lost touch with reality,"

Smith said, sitting at his desk. "They don't have any fight in them."

Baskin chimes in: "These ministers are too busy trying to cozy up to the mayor."

"And then you got people like Bill Cosby saying this nonsense about poor people misbehaving," Smith says of the speech the comedian delivered to the NAACP two years ago. "When you're that high, you really can't see low."

"They're not bad people," Baskin said. "But they're addressing their own, and they have a different agenda than most of the people who live in Englewood."

"And this is why the young people turn to the rappers for leadership," Smith said. "They're the only ones talking about their reality, not these politicians, these celebrities, and these, these"—he grimaces, as if in pain—"middle-class Negroes."

Carter-Hill told me she spends at least a few hours each day working on Imagine Englewood If and their issues: searching for more sites to plant community gardens, looking for training programs and grant money so that volunteers can go door to door and educate Englewood's residents about the dangers of lead poisoning and how to avoid it. "People are really crying out for some kind of leadership on these issues," she said. A board member who is a deacon at Rush's church was able to arrange a meeting with the congressman at his church in May, but nothing came of it.

Still, she is optimistic. She sees in Englewood a ferocious spirit of activism, in part because people don't believe government has any answers.

"I've always said there are only three kinds of power: God power, people power, and money power." She smiles.

"And we have two of them."

6

DEALS WITH THE DEVIL
AND OTHER REASONS TO RIOT

Malawi, Mexico, and Food

The day that hunger is eradicated from the earth
there will be the greatest spiritual explosion the
world has ever known. Humanity cannot imagine
the joy that will burst into the world on the day of
that great revolution.

—*Federico García Lorca*

Please forgive my ramblings," says the old man, sitting
listless and hunched over six small cobs of corn that are
drying in Malawi's tropical heat. "The hunger makes my
mind wander."

In his lucid moments, Lucas Lufuzi recites the numbers,
calibrating his catastrophe. Three days since he's eaten. One
son dead. Two grandchildren to feed. Two seasons of crops
spoiled by too few seeds, no fertilizer, and erratic weather—
rain one year, drought the next.

"I have never seen such starvation," he says to me, sitting
on the stool in front of his hut made with mud and straw. He
is so thin he looks as if he might break, and his stubble is so
pearly white on skin as fine and black as gunpowder that it
seems a magic trick. In this village just east of Malawi's capital city, Lilongwe, peasants have resorted to eating banana
stalks already plucked clean, pummeled into a lumpy mash

in wooden gourds. The mash is inedible, but it fills their stomachs for a few hours, until their bowels explode, sometimes in a fit of diarrhea, which neither the young nor the old are readily able to withstand in these conditions. "Eating the banana stalks," Lufuzi says, "that is the last kick from a dying mule. You are just trying to keep death at bay when you do that. I don't want to, but I fear I may have no choice soon."

The banana stalks are part of a growing international cuisine of desperation, the menu of last options that poor people turn to in the worst hunger they've ever known. In Burundi, villagers eat a porridge of black rice flour and rotting cassava leaves; in Somalia, a thin gruel made from the mashed branches of a thorn tree. Haitians eat biscuits kneaded from a yellowish dirt and water, nutritionless but filling. In the United States, grocery store managers in 2008 say that they can't keep enough Spam in stock. Here in Malawi, hospitals overflow, not just with the malnourished but with the hundreds of people who have been attacked by club- and machete-wielding mobs who accused them of stealing corn or other food. Just hours before we met up with Lufuzi, I had interviewed a patient at Lilongwe's main hospital who had lost two fingers in a daylight attack. "The people are crazed by this hunger," the man told us from a gurney in a hospital corridor. He would not say one way or another whether he'd actually stolen food, as had been alleged.

Outside Lufuzi's hut, I turn to my interpreter, a young Malawian woman who works for one of the local relief agencies, and ask her, "How can I help him? I'd give him money, but it won't do him any good if there is no food to buy." "Oh, no," says the young woman. "The stores have food. The mar-

kets have corn and the shelves are stocked. It's just that no one
can afford it," she says. I empty my pockets of the Malawian
currency that I had exchanged for dollars at the airport the
previous day. I don't know how much it is; certainly not more
than US$50, since I prefer to carry mostly dollars when I
travel through Africa. I'm ashamed it's so little, that there
are others who need help, that I am staying at a beautiful
hotel that offers a bountiful buffet, air conditioning, and my
favorite brand of whiskey. But with the crumpled bills in his
hands, Lufuzi grabs my right hand, cups it between his own,
and kisses it three times, like a bird catching a worm in its
beak. "Thank you," he says. "God bless you."

The international food crisis that culminated in wide-
spread rioting in early 2008 began here in southern Africa
in 2002, well before the cost of transport fuel skyrocketed
to historic highs. The United Nations Food and Agriculture
Organization estimates that 925 million people worldwide—
almost one in every six—are undernourished, and of that
number, 300 million are children who will go to bed hungry.
But the problem isn't scarcity. Bad weather, natural disasters,
and civil wars account for only 8 percent of the people in the
world who are underfed, according to the UN, and indeed,
the drought that afflicted Malawi in 2002 was relatively
minor. Worldwide, there is in fact more than enough food to
go around. Farmers in 2007 produced record grain harvests,
or about one and a half times global demand, and global food
production has been rising steadily for more than twenty
years—2 percent annually, on average—while population
growth has been falling at a rate of about 1.14 percent per
year. No, the fingerprints of the invisible hand are all over
this food crisis. By exhorting poor countries to treat agri-

cultural production as primarily a source of export revenue rather than a way to supply food for local consumption, and by encouraging the state to withdraw resources from crop development, global financiers have priced poor people right out of the market for food, just as they have priced them out of the markets for water, electricity, and housing. Food prices in sub-Saharan Africa began their sharp increase in 2001. Worldwide, the average price for corn has increased by 125 percent since 2005, rice has risen by 217 percent, wheat by 136 percent, and soybeans by 107 percent.

"There really is an Alice in Wonderland quality to the situation, isn't there? Water, water everywhere, yet not a drop to drink," says my interpreter as we duck inside an empty store where sacks of corn sit untouched. (The paraphrase is from the Samuel Taylor Coleridge poem "The Rime of the Ancient Mariner," not *Alice in Wonderland*, but her analysis of the absurdity of the crisis is astute.)

Inexpensive food is a thing of the past. The UN projects that food prices will continue to rise, by as much as 50 percent by the year 2016. With its evisceration of the middle class, globalization has sorted rich from poor in parceling out the world's food supply. By driving up the incomes of the comfortable and affluent, global finance has increased demand for agricultural products that fetch their sellers top dollar and are typically more expensive than staple foods like rice, corn, and potatoes, which are an integral part of the poor's daily diet. Commercial farmers in Malawi and southern Africa began replacing their wheat and beans with more lucrative tobacco more than a decade ago; Australian growers, who once fed more than 2 million poor Asians with their rice, converted their farms to vineyards and now produce wine for monied customers in the United States and Europe. Growers around the world sell their corn harvests to produce biofuels or to feed livestock, which earns them quite a bit more income than supplying food for people but reduces the amount of food available for consumption, thereby raising the price.

China, the home of one in every four people on earth, is chiefly responsible for the surge in consumption. Even though its economy is booming through the government's unorthodox Keynesian economic strategies, a majority of the Chinese remain rural and poor. But the growth in sheer numbers of the ranks of the affluent accounts for most of the increased global demand for agricultural outputs. Chinese consumption of meats and milk, for example, has tripled since 1990.

Like the World Bank's doctrinaire approach to Mozambique's cashew market, the global financial system's trade-first policies have pushed poor countries to use their agriculture for export revenue rather than to feed their own population. With no tariffs in their way, commercial farmers can make more money selling their crops abroad, which depletes the local food supply. As one example of the market's illogical savagery, Argentina had a record grain harvest in 2004. That same year, nineteen children died of malnutrition in the country, also a record.

Another factor in the crisis of unaffordable food is the global financial system's relentless campaign to reduce all manner of public spending, including spending on crop production, to keep inflation low in poor countries. This is having a particularly onerous impact on poor countries in sub-Saharan Africa and East Asia, where soils are depleted and climates are volatile. In the post-independence era, African governments heavily leveraged farming activity, providing inputs, extending credit, sharing technological advancements, and even building roads to get harvests to market. Now African farmers produce around one ton of grain per hectare, about a third of the yield per hectare throughout the rest of the world.

After winning independence from British rule in 1964, Malawian farmers—mostly smallholders producing for local consumption—had no trouble supplying this landlocked country with food for most of the thirty-three-year totalitarian regime of Hastings Banda, the country's self-appointed "president for life." With the government subsidizing fertilizer and seeds, crop production increased steadily until the late 1980s, when pressure from the World Bank and the IMF caused Malawi's government to wean its farming sector of state largesse. The result was, beginning in the early 1990s, one of the most "food insecure" countries in the world. Between 1990 and 2004, per capita corn production in Malawi fell by 40 percent. And with Malawians' wages shrinking as well, there has been little cash or tax revenue available to buy corn or other staple foods from abroad.

After Malawians suffered faminelike conditions for a third consecutive year in 2004, newly elected president Bingu wa Mutharika, a U.S.-trained development economist, waved off complaints from international donors and announced that for all Banda's Mao-style eccentricities and iron-fisted authoritarianism, he had had it right when it came to farm policy. Ahead of southern Africa's 2005 planting season, agriculture agents began to flood the Malawian countryside, distributing wads of vouchers to tribal chiefs and village leaders, who in turn doled out the coupons to small farmers. Growers then took their scrip to local feed stores and exchanged them for discounted high-yield seeds and 50-kilogram bags of fertilizer. Because the government guaranteed a minimum price for surplus corn at the end of the season, farmers were assured of at least a small profit.

The result: a record harvest in 2006, followed by an even bigger one in 2007, and yet a third bumper crop in 2008. When rioters took to the streets of Haiti, Somalia, Egypt, Uzbekistan, Mexico, and at least ten other countries in late 2007 and 2008, Malawians were eating better than they had in nearly a decade. Cash poured into government coffers. The only sector hurt by the shift in policy was the agribusiness dealers, who, with fewer crops available for export, saw their earnings decline by as much as a third.

Seeing Malawi's unqualified success, and hypocritically shut out of agricultural markets in the United States and Europe that are still protected by tariffs and subsidies, many developing countries have begun to turn away from lenders' structural adjustment programs to try their hand at stimulating domestic production. In just the past few years, Kenya has begun to provide subsidized fertilizers to small farmers. Ethiopia has banned cereal exports altogether and added a 10 percent surtax on imported luxury goods to finance wheat subsidies for the poor. Cameroon is coupling food subsidies with blanket pay hikes for all civil service workers to enable easier purchase of costly grains. In an attempt to depress market prices, Burkina Faso and Nigeria are releasing stockpiles of emergency grains to the market.

In West Africa, Sierra Leone and Liberia—which imports 90 percent of its staple food, rice—have announced government efforts to subsidize local smallholder rice production. And Ghana hopes to join research efforts in the development of a new, high-yielding rice that was created by the Africa Rice Center in Benin. Argentina's president, Cristina Kirchner, earned the wrath of her country's wealthy landowners in 2008 but avoided the lethal food shortages of previous years by taxing agricultural exports, cutting into farmer's profits but keeping affordable stockpiles of food in the country.

Malawi's green revolution is a flat rejection of global trade orthodoxy and represents a small nod to repairing inequities from the colonial period. Here in southern Africa, most of the arable land still remains in the hands of a tiny, mostly white elite, which sells its crops abroad. Malawi, Zimbabwe, Kenya, and other former British colonies developed one of the world's better commercial farming sectors beginning in the years after World War I, when returning soldiers—many of whom had never farmed in their lives—were offered free land, inputs, technical assistance, and low interest loans for equipment. It was common practice to forgive the loans of inexperienced farmers year after year until they managed a good harvest and could turn a profit.

Under the global trade consensus that has emerged since the late 1980s, many wealthy countries have drastically cut money for agricultural research programs that developing countries badly need to tackle soil, climate, and irrigation problems. As a group, wealthy countries cut donations for research in half between 1980 and 2006, from $6 billion to $2.8 billion when adjusting for exchange and inflation rates. The United States alone cut its support for agriculture in poor countries to $624 million from $2.3 billion in that period. That's money that could eliminate serious agricultural threats like the brown plant hoppers, gnat-sized insects that are destroying rice crops in East Asia, jeopardizing food security for millions. As one example, in the 1980s the International Rice Research Institute employed five entomologists, or insect experts, overseeing a staff of two hundred. Now it has one entomologist managing a staff of eight.

What little scientific research there is has been left largely to agricultural conglomerates like Monsanto and Archer Daniels Midland, which have been aggressively trying to expand the overseas market in genetically modified foods. When southern Africa first began experiencing shortages of affordable corn in 2002, the United States offered to donate genetically modified crops to aid in the relief effort. Malawi and other African nations refused the donations, drawing ridicule in the American press. But Africans had very real reasons to balk. First, they were following the lead of the European Union, which remains unconvinced that genetically modified products are safe and does not allow the food to enter their member countries. But even more, their reluctance stems from a World Trade Organization ruling that would call into dispute the ownership of a farmer's entire yield if even a single patented genetically modified seed were discovered on his soil. In short, WTO's intellectual property rules potentially pave the way for agribusinesses to expropriate an entire farm or harvest if even one of their patented seeds is discovered on that soil. It is not an overstatement to say that allowing genetically modified products entry is the camel's nose under the tent which could imaginably lead a sovereign country to cede commercial control of its entire food supply to a single foreign conglomerate. "They want to recolonize us," one southern African trade official told me in 2002, "and they haven't even gone to the trouble of being particularly artful about it."

Rising food costs have not been limited to the developing world, however. Food inflation in the United States reached its highest level in seventeen years in 2008, with prices overall increasing by nearly 5 percent over the previous year. The price of staple products has jumped even higher: milk and dried beans are up more than 17 percent; cheese is up 15 percent, rice and pasta 13 percent, and bread 12 percent. Hormel, the company that produces Spam, reported a 14 percent increase in profits for the year's first quarter.

The number of Americans receiving food stamps reached nearly 28 million in March 2008, about 1.5 million, or 6 percent more, than in the same month a year earlier. Food pantries in the United States have been stretched thin because more working people are turning to them when their paychecks don't make it. Demand for charitable food donations in 2008 was up as much as 20 percent over the previous year. Relief agencies around the country are serving "folks who get up and go to work every day," Bill Bolling, the founder of the Atlanta Community Food Bank, told *USA Today.* "That's remarkably different than the profile of who we've served through the years."

Anita Rhodes, a single mother of three living in the western Maryland town of Oakland, told National Public Radio that she has turned to shopping at a local grocery store that sells food past its expiration date. "The things there are all way, way past their due date, but I tried it," Rhodes said. "The first box [of cereal] I opened had bugs in it." She returned the box for a refund of its purchase price: $1. The family has been forced to cut from its budget paper towels, bottled water, chips, cookies, candy, and toiletries. "I don't even look at roasts right now," Rhodes said. If prices continue to rise, she told the reporter, she may be forced to take more drastic action. "I can shoot a deer," she says. "I can do that. I can shoot a turkey. So I will feed my kids one way or another."

THE INCREASE IN world hunger coincides with another trend that underscores the bipolar nature of global trade. The 925 million people suffering from hunger worldwide are outnumbered by the 1 billion people who are overweight. The main ingredient in this global eating disorder is corn, American corn specifically, each bushel of which is produced with a 50-cent taxpayer subsidy. Designed by the Nixon administration in the 1970s to curb a sharp spike in food prices, the subsidy has led to a proliferation of fattening processed corn-based products on dinner tables in the United States, in Mexico, and increasingly around the world as other countries develop a taste for American fast food, snacks, and microwaveable meals. The burden is borne mostly by the poor, who for US$1 can buy three to four times as many potato chips, Chicken McNuggets, cans of soda, and cookies—all made with corn—than they can carrots, fruit juice, or fresh fish. Americans' waistlines have expanded over the past thirty years, especially among the poor, who account for the majority of people classified as morbidly obese in the United States.

Raj Patel, an activist, writer, and former food analyst at Food First, explained the contradiction to a reporter in 2008: "In the past, we had a situation where the rich were fat and the poor were thin. Today our food comes from the sort of industrial market of highly processed food that extracts value from poor farmers and gives us processed, highly fatty food, a sort of fast food, as convenience food for people living in cities. Well, the upshot of that is that you've got both poor people who are going hungry and poor people who are predominantly overweight. I mean, it's a sad contradiction that today in the United States, the lower your income, the more overweight you're likely to be."

Obesity has in turn fueled a rise in the rates of cardio-vascular diseases, especially diabetes. In 2007 researchers with the American Chemical Association contributed their own findings to a growing body of data that suggest a link between high-fructose corn syrup, used to sweeten carbon-ated soft drinks and many other foods and beverages, and obesity and the onset of type 2 diabetes. In many countries, American-made corn-syrup-sweetened products like Coca-Cola and Pepsi began appearing ubiquitously on grocery store shelves, billboards, ads, and commercials in the 1980s, roughly a decade after the Nixon administration introduced its corn subsidy.

A few years back, a young Brazilian woman told me that while Coke became immensely popular among many of her countrymen, many others came to regard the soda as a sort of witch's brew, a slow-acting concoction that makes Ameri-cans fat, greedy, and ignorant. Once, she said, when she was a child of maybe ten or eleven, a television commercial or billboard spurred her to ask her mother if the family could try a bottle of the soda for the first time. "My mother was quiet a long time," the woman recalled, "and then she said, with this disgust dripping off her tongue, 'You want to drink the black water of American imperialism?'" To this day, the woman, now in her mid-thirties, told me, she has never had a Coke.

WITH A SWISS Army knife and a red nylon Nike duffel bag, Antonio Quinones cases the patio behind La Merced, the produce market in downtown Mexico City, which occupies an entire city block. This is where the vendors dump rotting lettuce, bruised tomatoes, blackened bananas, and other spoiled merchandise. On a March afternoon in 2008, Quinones is one of at least a dozen people staking out the market's refuse, hoping to find something salvageable—enough, maybe, for dinner.

"Mamacita," he says campily as he rummages through a carton of chilies, cornstalks, and sundry vegetables. He pulls from the scrum a giant, glistening red tomato with a crater-sized green-black tumor on its shoulder. "This is good," he says, holding the red orb up to the sky like a gold nugget. "You just cut off this bad flesh and it's good as new." He tosses the tomato in his bag and continues to pore over the offerings.

The price of cornmeal used to make tortillas, Mexicans' staple food, nearly tripled between late 2006 and early 2008, and the jump in price left Quinones regularly unable to buy meat, vegetables, or even beans after his weekly purchase of cornmeal for his wife and two sons, aged four and seven. He began rummaging through the trash at La Merced in 2007, shortly after the streets in Mexico City first erupted in protests against the rising cost of food.

Thirty-six and boyish-looking, with a tuft of jet-black hair that shoots out like a fuselage from under his Houston Astros baseball cap, Quinones left his smallholder farm in Oaxaca four years ago, unable to compete with the river of cheap American corn that began pouring into Mexico after NAFTA took effect in 1994. "I couldn't earn enough to feed my family," he says. So he moved to Mexico City, where he found work full-time at a warehouse, unloading industrial supplies. He earns the Mexican minimum wage of about $5 a day.

The deluge of American corn has washed away 1.3 million Mexican small farmers, who left to try their luck in the *maquiladoras*, or factories, on the Mexican border, or in the big cities in Mexico or the United States. With its heavy taxpayer subsidy, American corn is "the welfare queen of crops," says the food writer Michael Pollan. And its competitive advantage illustrates how U.S. trade policy—particularly NAFTA—is rooted not in ideology but in craven greed. Like trade pacts with other countries, NAFTA discourages Mexico from subsidizing its crops with taxpayer money, and eliminated, as of January 2008, all tariffs on two hundred American crops shipped into Mexico. In less than a decade, American agribusiness has all but cornered the Mexican corn market.

The tradeoff, as the Clinton administration's snake-oil salesmen reassured workers in both countries in the early 1990s, was that the Mexican peasants pushed off their land would head for the new American and Canadian factories opening up in the country and land jobs paying higher wages. And the influx of cheap American crops would reduce Mexicans' food costs.

But NAFTA did not modernize the Mexican economy; it infantilized it. It was evident almost immediately that displaced small farmers greatly outnumbered the number of new factory jobs. And what jobs there are don't pay all that well. In 2008 the Ford plant in Cuautitlán on the outskirts of Mexico City, announced that it would slash workers' salaries from $4.50 an hour to half that. General Motors is negotiating similar concessions with unions. And these jobs are the crème de la crème of Mexico's NAFTA windfall. The vast majority of workers toil, like Quinones, for something closer to Mexico's federally mandated minimum wage. In May 2008, as people like Quinones scavenged in garbage bins for food, Mexico's labor secretary said that there were no plans to increase the minimum wage for fear of igniting inflation.

That horse has already left the barn. With livestock and corn-based ethanol offering higher returns, American agribusinesses are using more and more of their crops for biofuels and for grazing—something that Mexican farmers never did before NAFTA, because they believe that *people*, not animals, should eat corn. Consumer demand for corn outstrips available supply. And so this is what NAFTA has wrought: between December 2006 and May 2008, the cost of basic foodstuffs in Mexico increased by 47 percent, while wages increased by 4 percent.

"NAFTA," says the World Bank chief, Robert Zoellick, "is one of the reasons food costs aren't higher." Quinones, an effusive, animated speaker with a dry wit, says that you don't need an economics degree to see that such remarks are ridiculous. Before NAFTA, he says, he never thought of moving to the United States; now he thinks about it at least once a week. "If my wife and I didn't have kids, we would have left already," he says. "That is the only thing holding us back. I have family in Texas and in California, and I know that it's no great life in the United States either. But at least there you can eat every day. Your kids can eat every day. It's not the struggle it is here. There are some days me and my wife go without eating just so the boys can get a little something in their stomachs.

"Man, you can't take away tortillas from a Mexican," he says, smiling. "That's a declaration of war." He closes his duffel bag after today's small haul: a half-rotten tomato, some wilted lettuce, and a few overripe peaches. "Tell me," he says sardonically, "when will Mexicans begin to see all these great benefits from NAFTA like we were promised? We are ready now."

7

THE PLAN

Washington, D.C., and Housing

Just because you're paranoid don't mean they ain't out
to get you.

—*Detroit mayor Coleman A. Young*

John S. Burroughs Elementary School sits in Washington,
D.C.'s far northeast corner, in an old streetcar suburb
known as Brookland, where you can still see the Victorian
cottages and tract homes ordered from the Sears, Roebuck
catalog almost ninety years ago. To get there from Capitol
Hill, you head north to Michigan Avenue, then east, past
Catholic University and its towering gold-domed basilica,
which shimmers in the sky like an eruption of lava. Veer right
at Monroe Street NE, and not far from the B&O Railroad
tracks, within sight of the Maryland border, John Burroughs
will appear, suddenly, on your left, as if in a hallucination. It
is only two floors, but the schoolhouse's brick exterior is deep
red, the color of the setting sun, and it straddles the edge
of a neatly mowed rectangular field that occupies nearly an
entire city block and even in the dead of winter gleams rich
and green. It is surrounded on all sides by charming old row

homes and wood-framed bungalows, like a moat protecting a sacred community fortress.

On the whole, educating children in the District is challenging, to say the least. About one in three children here are poor, more than in any other U.S. city, in a country with the highest rate of childhood poverty in the industrialized world. In conversations with people in several countries, I have over the years heard them describe poverty in strikingly consistent terms, as a sort of torture, a slow but inevitable death of the spirit that accrues from a thousand cuts by a dull knife, with the wounds inflicted earliest in life—some as early as the womb—the deepest and gravest. Thousands of schoolchildren enter kindergarten here every year with learning disabilities, illness, or emotional problems caused by premature birth, toxic lead paint, abusive parents or neglectful day-care providers, a steady diet of bad food or a bad fall that went untreated, or any of a number or combination of traumas. D.C.'s public schools spent about $8,800 per pupil in 2007, but the money doesn't go far, because so much is spent just trying to get kids to the starting line. Twenty percent of the school district's budget, for example, pays for transportation to special education classes and counseling services. Consequently, test scores are dreadfully low, dropout rates alarmingly high. And some schools are in bad shape because the District has lost more than a quarter of its population since its postwar peak of 800,000. To be sure, the city doesn't need its full inventory of buildings, at least not for classroom space.

John Burroughs, however, doesn't fit the mold. Burroughs's students in 2007 scored higher on standardized math tests than students at all but fourteen of the city's eighty-one public elementary schools. Their reading proficiency put Burroughs in the top sixteen. Enrollment is climbing. Parents are active. The principal is energetic. The roof is brand spanking new. "We love this school," said Maria Jones, who moved here from Oakland, California, in the 1980s to attend Howard University and never left. She lives with her husband and their five-year old daughter, Kia, in an immaculate wood-framed bungalow with a rambling porch directly across the street from Burroughs Elementary. "The school is one of the reasons we moved here," she says. "It's really the anchor of this community."

On a cold and sunless November morning in 2007, Jones was one of dozens of parents attending Career Day at the school, when word spread from city hall that the mayor and his schools chief had just announced plans to close twenty-three schools for poor performance and falling enrollment. Burroughs was on the list. Some parents cried. Most were merely speechless. Some reacted angrily.

"We don't meet any of their criteria," Jones said when I interviewed her on a bitterly cold Sunday morning in January 2008, as we took a tour of the school grounds. "We're not failing. We're a model school. That's what's so crazy about it. But everybody knows what this is. All you have to do is look around the city at all these upscale condos that are going up and all these charter schools that are opening up, and the developers have already been on record expressing their interest in this and other properties on the list. And if you look at them, all the schools on the list are right on the Metro Line. We know what time it is. The city wants to move us out so they can move in people who generate more profit. This is a land grab."

Washington, D.C., has over the past decade gone on what is essentially a liquidation sale of its assets, closing schools, firehouses, tenements, abandoned properties, college campus buildings, the city's only public hospital, a homeless shelter, a home for battered women, and another for abused children. Starting with the cheapest parcels in the close-to-downtown slums that were flashpoints for the 1968 riots and spreading in all directions, from the waterfront to far-flung middle-class neighborhoods like Brookland, developers have snatched up the property for little more than a song, pouring nearly $40 billion into top-end condos, big-box retail stores, cafés, and theaters between 1999 and 2007. Poor and working-class neighborhoods that had complained to their city councillor year after year about the dearth of redevelopment dollars suddenly faced a deluge of cash. Across the city, the preoccupied hum of jackhammers became the local anthem, and cranes hover in the sky like toy clouds. But it was clear from the start that the flood of money pouring into the city wouldn't just cleanse the grime, remove the dirt. It would wash some people away as well. Giddings Elementary School in northwest D.C. was converted into a private health club where memberships start at $100 per month. William Syphax Elementary in southwest D.C., built in 1910 and named for a Reconstruction-era educator renowned for his efforts to improve the District's segregated African American schools, reopened as Syphax Village, where condos and town homes sell for upwards of $400,000. The nearly 150-year-old schoolhouse in Logan Circle, Berret Elementary, is now the Berret School Lofts, offering high ceilings, cityscape views, and as much as 1,700 square feet for $385,000 and up. Bulldozers demolished more than 1,100 public housing units in southeast Washington to clear the way for a taxpayer-financed, $611 million major league baseball stadium. Corridors plunged into darkness by seething mobs forty years ago are now neon-lit pathways lined with bars, nightclubs, and restaurants serving fusion cuisine to K Street lawyers and Hill staffers. Menacing, boarded-up husks have given way to faux loft apartments, Starbucks, and Whole Foods, beckoning white suburban professionals. The new convention center opened downtown in 2003, a new sports arena in neighboring Chinatown a few months later.

The District's fire sale fueled what former Federal Reserve chairman Alan Greenspan once referred to as the market's "irrational exuberance," which pushed home values up to record highs and the poor and working class out. From 1999 to 2007 the average home price in the District more than doubled, from $189,000 to $469,000, while median household income fell 8 percent for blacks and 2 percent overall. Property tax bills have increased by an average of 30 percent each year since 1999. At Ann's Beauty Supply and Wigs in southeast D.C., not far from the Washington Nationals' new 42,000-seat baseball stadium, the yearly assessment skyrocketed to $16,000 in 2007 from $600 just three years earlier. A nearby foster-care agency contracted by the city to care for abused and disabled kids saw its tax bill increase from $9,000 in 2005 to $83,699 in 2007. At the Market Deli at First and L Streets NW, property taxes soared to $22,000; its assessment had been only $1,500 in 2004. Not surprisingly, Washington's poorest residents have abandoned the city in droves. Between 2000 and 2006, the District lost more than 21,000 of its African American residents—almost 10 percent—while the city's overall population grew by more than 30,000, to 572,000. The city's black majority dropped from 60 to 55 percent, and demographers expect that whites will outnumber blacks in D.C. by as soon as 2010. Already whites represent a majority of the city council for the first time since Congress approved limited home rule for the city thirty-five years ago.

"This is another city," Jones said as we sat on the railing outside Burroughs Elementary. "They are telling us, in a not very subtle way, that we no longer belong here. Chocolate City is gone."

Two local radio disk jockeys coined the phrase "Chocolate City" in the 1970s as a reference to Africans' search for community in a hostile place far from home. The term seems quaint, almost mocking now. What was once black Americans' imperfect piece of the pie, its gritty Promised Land, has evolved into the model of the neoliberal city, its transformation so stark that it represents a reimagining of the American metropolis. This is a city on the make, serving first and foremost the needs of foreign speculators rather than its indigenous population, by supplying the bricks, mortar, and other raw materials required by Wall Street for its reckless gambits.

Across the nation, in cities like D.C. and New Orleans, Oakland and Chicago, Miami, New York, Atlanta, St. Louis, San Francisco, and most every other urban center, local governments have helped trigger a gold rush in housing by redirecting their community's assets and tax dollars into the hands of investment bankers whose portfolios include top-end realtors, education management firms, retailers, hotel chains, and mortgage brokers. In the 1990s, U.S. cities began using surplus property, eminent domain, zoning ordinances, and empowerment zones to sell off just about anything big business had its eye on.

Siphoning off public land, tax revenues, and even local transit systems for use by private capital has coincided with a suddenly deregulated banking industry to create the subprime mortgage debacle and housing bubble that began to burst in late 2007. Wanting bigger and bigger profits, Wall Street's insatiable titans demanded more and more land and more and more mortgages, fueling the rise of the most overpriced housing market in U.S. history. The slow, inevitable collapse of that bubble produced the gravest worldwide financial crisis since the 1929 stock market crash. The remaking of Washington, D.C., and Congress's giveaway of $700 billion of taxpayers' money to take bad loans off Wall Street's hands illustrate how, in the new economy, wins are private affairs, losses public.

Between 2000 and 2006, home prices nationwide increased at an unprecedented rate, rising 74 percent, more than four times the historic trend. That means that housing was at its peak overpriced by about $8 trillion, or $110,000 for every homeowner in the country. As with the wildly overvalued tech stocks of the late 1990s, the gap between what assets are actually worth and what the market says they are worth represents the bubble. By the last quarter of 2007, housing prices had begun their descent, falling 6.7 percent from the previous year, and as much as 10 percent in Las Vegas, Phoenix, San Diego, and other cities whose real estate markets were sizzling just a few years ago. But that's just a warning shot. For home prices to be restored to historic norms they would have to plummet much further, by as much as a third of their 2006 peak, and that would lead to a decade-long stagnation, according to the Harvard economist Larry Summers, or, says the economist Nouriel Roubini, to "the worst housing bust ever."

The losses will not be limited only to the infamous subprime borrowers. The same kinds of loans that imposed inordinate risks on subprime borrowers have left many other homeowners vulnerable to foreclosure as well. Defaults are now hitting even well-off borrowers saddled with adjustable rate mortgages (ARMs), whose low introductory monthly payments are reset upward as interest rates rise. About a quarter of all home loans are ARMs, and subprime and Merrill Lynch economists have called ARMs "ticking time bombs" that can add another $100 billion to the $400 billion in losses for subprime and other borrowers. With a growing number of borrowers already owing more than their homes are worth and unable to refinance, some homeowners just walk away, leaving the keys in the mailbox. By the third quarter of 2007, the percentage of homeowners behind in their mortgage payments on all residential loans stood at a nineteen-year high, according to a Mortgage Bankers Association survey, and the percent of home loans in the process of foreclosure was the highest ever. By the summer of 2008, sheriffs across the country were reporting a marked increase in the number of evictions.

The collapse of the housing bubble dwarfs the implosion of the dot-com bubble in 2001, largely because there are more homeowners than stockholders and because millions of homeowners have already borrowed against the peak value of their home. Those debts will likely trigger an even sharper drop-off in consumer spending as the economy slumps further.

From John Burroughs Elementary, Maria Jones can see a
future that, if allowed to take its course, does not bode well
for her neighborhood, her city, her country, or her daughter.
She is forty-two, looks thirty-two, feels sixty-two, she says.
Tears begin to well up in her eyes as she talks about the
neighborhood's effort to fight the city's plan to sell the land
beneath their feet. "This is about people's lives, just regular
people trying to get through the day okay," she says, wiping
the teardrops from her cheek. "Instead of fixing the public
schools, they want to turn public education over to charter
schools. But charter schools by and large don't do as good
a job at teaching kids as the public schools, *and* they're not
accountable to parents or the school board or really anyone.
Their answer is to make everything a tradeable commodity,
to improve the city by putting it up for sale. All they're doing
is making everything look the same. D.C. used to be a city
that wasn't like any other city. New York used to be a city
that wasn't like any other city. We used to have the kids, the
beautiful little black boys and the Latino boys playing drums
on the paint buckets all around the city, creating something.
It was art. I haven't seen that in years now. I go to New York
now and I want to see the little neighborhood Italian shops
where all the men, you know, tawk—like—dis—he-ah,"
she says, breaking into an overwrought New York accent,
pounding her right fist into her left palm in exaggeration.
"Now, everywhere you go, it's all TGI Fridays and Starbucks
and white couples walking their dog, who is probably treated
better and fed better and housed better than a third of the
kids in the city." She laughs at her tears and her attempts at
mimicry, sniffs, dabs her eyes again. "I just think we're at a
critical fork in the road in deciding what kind of community

we're going to live in, what kind of world we're going to live in and our children are going to live in.

"Don't they see it? Capitalism is eating itself."

No sooner had firefighters doused the last of the fires in early April 1968, it seemed, than the rumors began to circulate: Washington, D.C.'s corporate executives and congressional power brokers had a shadowy plan to reclaim the city from its black majority. Many blacks here first remember hearing about the plan—"The Plan," as it came to be known—from Ralph Waldo "Petey" Green, a local radio disk jockey and television talk show host who was popular from the late 1960s into the early 1980s (and who was portrayed by the actor Don Cheadle in the 2007 movie *Talk to Me*). There was little consensus on how the plan would be carried out. The details were sketchy. Some people thought it would involve a form of "benign neglect," allowing the city to deteriorate until it was unlivable and ungovernable, and desperation and cheap land would clear the way for a takeover. In the 1980s, some people began to talk openly about how poisoning D.C. with crack cocaine was part of The Plan.

For all its élan and European architecture, D.C. is a southern town, unbearably hot in summer, deeply segregated, and inhabited mostly by a working class descended from slaves, denied full enfranchisement on Capitol Hill by a paternalistic cadre of wealthy, mostly white men, elected and unelected. Congress's longstanding oversight of local affairs and the "advisory role" of a self-appointed coalition of the region's top business executives, the Federal City Council, lead many blacks to suspect that their local elected officials aren't really pulling the strings. It's not unusual to hear blacks of a certain age describe the city's mayor as no more than a manager, or overseer, and the city itself as a plantation.

Many whites, if they had heard of The Plan at all, dismissed it as folklore, simple, uneducated paranoia, and chalked up the city's problems—its poor schools, poor roads, rising number of homicides, and lingering insolvency—to the mismanagement and corruption of the black political class, symbolized most profoundly by Marion Barry. Indeed, when Barry left the mayor's office following his fourth term, in January 1999, there were few signs of a revival of any kind. The District had experienced three successive annual operating budget deficits; half a dozen city agencies languished under court-appointed receiverships; and the city's fiscal affairs were managed by the Financial Control Board, created by Congress in 1995.

But within a matter of months, two political developments laid the foundation for the makeover of the nation's capital. First was the swearing-in of Barry's successor as mayor, Anthony A. Williams, a charmless, bow-tie-wearing, Harvard-educated attorney who had served as the Control Board's chief financial officer. Though both men are African American and Democrats, Williams is the anti-Barry. Despite his drug arrest, his late-night carousing, and his overall ineffectiveness as D.C.'s mayor, Barry remains widely popular with black Washingtonians for his Keynesian political impulses, creating, as one example, a summer jobs program for city youths that many here recall fondly as the first paycheck they ever received. Patrician and wooden, Williams is more wonk than populist, his economics more Friedman than Keynes. As board CFO, his aggressive cost-cutting and firing of hundreds of District employees made him an enemy of organized labor, and the thrust of his mayoral campaign was to attract 100,000 new residents to D.C. by slashing spending and improving the delivery of city services and education through the use of vouchers and charter schools. At one point he even told reporters that he would consider the adoption of a regressive flat tax in the District. "Washington, D.C., is open for business," Williams proclaimed repeatedly throughout his two terms in office.

The second seismic shift occurred nine months after Williams's inauguration, when President Clinton signed into law the Gramm-Leach-Bliley Act, which knocked down the New Deal's monument to consumer protection. When the Glass-Steagall Act was passed in 1933, one in five U.S. banks had failed, largely because they had invested depositors' funds in risky stocks. Glass-Steagall's firewall limited risks and profits. Wall Street began pressuring Capitol Hill to demolish that wall more than twenty years ago, and the Orwellian-sounding financial services industry was born, creating both mortgage-backed securities and the largest government bailout in the history of the world. In practice, unregulated speculation has yielded one unsustainable bubble after another, supplanting productive innovation with a high-stakes Ponzi scheme. This latest one was a shakedown, with wealthy corporate executives and shareholders pocketing more of homeowners' hard-earned cash. Once Wall Street was allowed to buy home loans and take them off the books of commercial banks, lenders were encouraged to extend artificially cheap mortgages to people who ordinarily wouldn't have qualified for credit (and many who would have but were told otherwise). For all its bundling of complex investment vehicles, for all the Ivy League pedigrees and ampersand credentials of the blue-blooded financiers who orchestrated the housing bubble, a child could have identified its fatal flaw: if the commercial bankers have no real stake in whether borrowers can repay the loan, they are bound to make one bad mortgage loan after another. Wall Street was a house of cards, collapsing in 2008. By June of that year, Wall Street banks had reported losses equal to one half of their total profits for the entire three-year period between 2004 and 2007.

This volatile credit market worked in tandem with the aggressive transfer of premium public land to swell, as if by steroids, the value of the nation's housing stock to a size that the U.S. economy could sustain for only so long.

Public schools were the low-lying fruit in Williams's effort to remake D.C. To be sure, the District's schools are, on the whole, dreadful. In its 1995 law mandating the creation of charter schools in Washington, Congress permitted corporations that own and manage charter schools to buy surplus city property at a 25 percent discount and choose which students to enroll. Concurrently, the measure does not require charter schools to comply with union contracts or systemwide performance standards for teachers or student achievement, nominally to encourage autonomy and community decision-making. Still, charter schools in D.C. have proven as woeful as charter schools elsewhere in the United States and the world at teaching kids from poor neighborhoods, generally producing even worse classroom results than their public school counterparts. Polls show that District voters adamantly oppose charters. But Williams, who during his tenure as mayor told reporters that he never made a major decision without first consulting the business interests represented by the Federal City Council, was not interested in doing the difficult and costly work of fixing the city's public schools. He preferred affluent, childless newcomers to the city, who made their decisions based on square footage, not classroom size. If they did have children, they'd almost certainly opt for private schools. The conservative and libertarian think tanks that have pushed the charter school movement have openly championed Milton Friedman's oft-articulated ambition to kill public education and the teachers unions and replace both with a private, for-profit system. Because public schools are funded on a per-pupil basis, every time a charter school opens, resources leave the public school system, programs are cut, teachers are laid off. In D.C., the loss of as few as five students in a single grade can result in the elimination of one faculty position, according to the teachers union.

Zein El-Amine, a housing activist here, said that he and other activists got a glimpse of the powerful forces driving privatization during a 2006 meeting with a D.C. councilman. Inside the councilman's office, decorated with ceremonial shovels from the many condos that had broken ground in his ward, a small group of activists complained about the latest round of closings. The activists acknowledged that D.C. didn't need all of its schools, with so many standing half empty. But with so many needs in the neighborhoods, couldn't those schools be "repurposed" as child-care centers, recreation space, or even office buildings, since the public schools continue to pay $7.5 million a year to rent administrative space from private developers while touting school closures as cost-cutting measures? In an unusually candid disclosure, the councilman conceded their points, El-Amine recalled, but told them that elected officials were under tremendous pressure from Congress and developers to "starve the beast."

"I'm not sure if we understood until that moment exactly how antagonistic was the relationship between the city's politicians and its institutions," El-Amine said. "There is no effort to reform public education, public housing, public health, such as it is. It is an effort to bankrupt these institutions, to shrink the public sphere and expand the sources for private revenue. In this way, it is very much like the structural adjustment programs imposed on developing countries by the World Bank and IMF. The city's public space is meant first and foremost to generate more wealth for wealthy people, just like the bridges and dams and roads in Africa and Latin America and Asia are meant to benefit the wealthy. We—and by we I mean the poor, the black, the people of color—have become eyesores to be disposed of quietly."

The players in D.C.'s charter school movement include some of the biggest names in the Wall Street–backed industry that began only a decade ago: Mosaica Education, Inc., Edison Schools, LearnNow, all based in New York; Ohio's White Hat Management; Virginia's Imagine/Chancellor Beacon Schools and Venture Philanthropy Partners, funded heavily by AOL; K12 Schools, based in Massachusetts, and California's New Schools Venture Fund, which announced in 2007 plans to open five charter schools.

How much has public education in the District changed? When Mayor Williams was inaugurated in January 1999, there were three charter schools in the city, with an enrollment of fewer than three hundred kids. When he left eight years later, there were sixty-six charter schools. His successor, Adrian Fenty, also African American and a Democrat, picked up where Williams left off, adding to the list of closures only weeks after taking the oath of office. Within a year of Williams's departure, D.C. was home to eighty-seven charter schools, with an enrollment of nearly 22,000, or one of every three children in the public school system. That is more than any other city in the country except New Orleans, post-Katrina.

Subsidizing the booming housing market through the sale of public property has been the most widely used tool in local governments' efforts to nudge poor people out of the city over the past decade. But politicians and their corporate doppelgangers are nothing if not ruthlessly creative. State lawmakers in Georgia used simple fiat to wrest control of metropolitan Atlanta's regional transportation system and turned its operations and management over to the local Chamber of Commerce, despite the fact that 90 percent of the transit infrastructure was financed by tax dollars from the city and neighboring DeKalb County, both majority black. Cities such as Philadelphia have used eminent domain to evict homeowners and clear the land for residential development projects with generic suburban names like Mill Creek. And in Chicago, Mayor Daley has created more than one hundred tax-increment financing districts over the past ten years. Sometimes called empowerment zones, TIFs freeze property taxes paid to the city's general fund at a certain level—say the amount collected in 1996. The increase in property tax revenues in following years—the increment—is funneled into the TIF to be used for discretionary development projects. By law the designation is reserved for blighted communities, but Chicago has poured much of the money into downtown and other gentrifying neighborhoods. In recent years the city has spent $46 million in TIF dollars to rehabilitate buildings on the north lakefront campus of Loyola University, a private institution that doesn't pay property taxes. About $6.6 million went to convert the historic Fisher Building into luxury rental apartments, another $2.5 million went to convert the Mentor Building into condos, and about $25 million went to convert or rebuild several hotels, including the Hotel Allegro, the Hotel Burnham, the Oxford House, and the Saint George. A big chunk of the money—roughly $60 million—went to rehab or rebuild the Chicago Theatre, the Goodman Theatre, the Oriental Theatre, and the Cadillac Palace Theatre. Between 2001 and 2006 alone, TIFs have diverted at least $350 million in property taxes—$88.1 million just in 2006—from Chicago's treasury, functioning as slush funds that mostly empower the mayor's office or city aldermen.

"It's a tax grab," said Valerie Leonard Moore, who heads a South Side Chicago neighborhood group fighting gentrification, which is driving elderly and working-class families from their homes in the North Lawndale community. This is consistent with black Chicago's own version of The Plan. When she was a child growing up in the 1970s, Moore said, her father would often voice his suspicions that city officials were allowing prices in poor black neighborhoods to plummet by allowing redevelopment to dry up. When prices hit rock bottom, developers would suddenly swoop in, buy up the properties, and move affluent whites in.

"He said that the changes would come in the form of 'benign neglect,' " Moore recalled. "And that is exactly what has happened. Except for when I went away for college, I've lived in this neighborhood all my life, and I've seen more money put into the neighborhood in the last three years than in the previous thirty combined. People are losing their homes they've lived in all their lives because they can't afford the property taxes anymore, or they're shut out of buying here because they can't afford the prices. You see this happening all over Chicago."

Across the nation, blacks are being displaced from the cities in unprecedented numbers, often moving to close-in suburbs or to regions in the South and Midwest where housing is cheaper. Between 2000 and 2006, New York City lost 50,000 of its 2 million African American residents; Oakland lost 30,000, or more than a fifth of its black population. Cleveland lost more than 20,000, or roughly 10 percent; Philadelphia 14,000, Atlanta 10,000, and St. Louis almost 7,000. Chicago lost just shy of 100,000 African Americans over the period, or nearly 10 percent of the black population.

When I moved to New York City in 2007, a group of young men often sat on the stoop outside the apartment I rented in a gentrifying section of Brooklyn. They were occasionally loud, and sometimes I would smell the unmistakable scent of marijuana wafting in the air, but they were approachable, civil, and orderly. Once, when I joined them outside for a cigarette on a hot summer night, I asked the young men why they always gathered *here*, on my building's stoop. One answered that his grandmother had owned this building for years, but when young, affluent white professionals began to move into the neighborhood, her property taxes skyrocketed. Unable to afford the assessment, the retiree sold the building to a young couple who carved it into rental units. She headed south, to North Carolina. The young man seldom sees her anymore, he told me. He had been close to his grandmother, he said, and remembered sitting on the stoop as a child, chasing fireflies or eating ice cream cones with other kids in the neighborhood. "I know it's not anymore, but this still feels like home to me," he said, with his friends nodding in agreement. "I used to sit out here with my sister and eat ice cream in the summer. This is the one place in New York where I still feel close to my grandmama."

That kind of loss has produced palpable tensions between well-off newcomers and a poorer, increasingly resentful, and often darker-skinned community. One extreme but still representative example occurred in a gentrifying North Oakland neighborhood in 2005, when a man who had recently moved there shot an unarmed black teenager in the arm as he turned to flee following an argument. The man, Patrick McCullough, who is also black, said that he shot the youth because he thought he was reaching for a gun. The boy, Melvin McHenry, denied this, had no police record, and said that McCullough regularly confronted and harassed young black men in the neighborhood. Police declined to press charges, but a community activist told local reporters that McCullough was an "agent of the state" and part of a broader conspiracy to push blacks out of the city.

At a Martin Luther King Jr. Day rally in St. Louis in January 2005, hundreds began booing, hissing, and chanting "Slay must go" as St. Louis mayor Francis Slay strolled to the podium and began his address. Slay's giveaways of public schools and housing and his police department's increasing harassment and abuse of young blacks had angered the black community. Likewise, blacks and Latinos in New York City have complained of escalating harassment by the police. In the first three months of 2008 alone, New York City police stopped and frisked 145,000 people, a record number. Available numbers don't reflect a racial breakdown, and police say that the stops represent a more aggressive policy in the wake of the 2005 bombing of a London subway. But civil rights groups in the city say that the police use the threat of terror as a ruse to harass and intimidate black and Latino youths, and have called for an independent investigation. In the District, neighborhood groups say they too noticed an increase in police harassment of minority youths starting with Williams's first term in office, and it has continued under his successor. In September 2007, an off-duty policeman fatally shot an unarmed fourteen-year-old boy in the head in southeast D.C. Neighbors of the boy told reporters that the shooting was an execution. In 2008 police began installing checkpoints on the perimeter of a mostly black, Trinidadian neighborhood in northwest Washington, demanding that motorists provide their names and the telephone numbers of the people they are visiting before allowing them to pass.

Tension caused by the displacement from the central cities has spilled over the city limits, into communities where poor families are finding some of the affordable housing that they need. The deepening concentration of poverty has caused homicide and violent crime rates to skyrocket in Chicago's southern suburbs, the East Bay communities that border San Francisco and Oakland, Newark, New Jersey, and Prince George's County, Maryland, outside Washington, D.C., which reported 173 murders in 2005, shattering the record of 154 set in 1991.

At John Burroughs Elementary, Maria Jones reflected on the recent changes in her adopted city—the resettlement of people of color, the brazen seizure of public resources, the checkpoints and increasing militarism of the police, the changing of D.C.'s essential character, and the explosion of violence on the city's borders—and sees not just a plan—The

Plan—but something even more repressive. "Prince George's has become like a refugee camp or a South African bantustan with all these poor people cramped tightly into these little spaces, little miserable spaces, and bodies just start dropping. I have never traveled to the Middle East, but D.C. reminds me of what the Palestinians are going through," she said, repeating an analogy I've heard close to a dozen times in conversations with working-class people in D.C., Chicago, New York, and the Bay Area. "This," she says, "feels like an occupation."

8

THINGS FALL APART

Chicago and Family

> The sea rises, the light fails, lovers cling to each other,
> and children cling to us. The moment we cease to
> hold each other, the moment we break faith with one
> another, the sea engulfs us and the light goes out.
> —*James Baldwin*

Rob: what r u wearing?

Sonia: sweats. big ol' baggy sweat pants and a big baggy
sweatshirt with a rip in it. Not cute

Rob: i'll bet u r WEARING them sweats.

Sonia: i look a mess. but i don't care. its cold and i'm comfortable and ain't nobody going to see me tonight but maybe
my mama.

Rob: i bet those sweats would look great—on my floor.

Sonia: you'd have to be my husband. or at least my fiancé for
all that to happen.

Rob: u accepting applications for the job?

Sonia: Boy, PLEASE . . .

That their romance defied both distance and reason did
not really matter so much to Sonia. She lived in Chicago,
Rob outside of Boston. She was lonely; he was online. His

flirtations appeared to her in the middle of a winter night, words brightening a dark computer screen and her cheerless heart, fastening to something inside her. Photographs were exchanged, narratives unfurled. Finally, after six weeks, they agreed: a tryst.

But Rob didn't show. Sonia wanted him to, but she knew he wouldn't. Still she'd hoped—prayed—quietly to herself, when she was alone in her car stopped at a traffic light, or brushing her teeth in the first light of morning, that he would get off that airplane in Chicago; that he would be as tall as he said, and kind and unmarried and gainfully employed, that his teeth would be straight and his confidence sturdy so that Sonia's ambition and education and downtown friends wouldn't cause him to fly into a jealous rage over the most innocuous casual remark or study group meeting. After nearly two years of dating a man named Anthony off and on and off again, she had developed an article of faith that the three most pernicious words in the English language are "Where were you?" "When you hear those words from a man," she told me over coffee one afternoon, "some shit" was sure to follow, sure as rain.

When she finally tracked down Rob by e-mail, days after his no-show, he came clean. He was not a telephone repairman but a parolee—something about the street life, a beef, and a pistol-whipping, though Sonia couldn't make out all the details in her shock and disappointment. He was living in a halfway house and getting good hours at a warehouse but no benefits. He couldn't afford to fly to Chicago—couldn't afford to fly anywhere—and it was just as well, he said, because Sonia was clearly out of his league.

"I knew all along," Sonia said later. "I mean, I didn't know specifics, but I knew that something wasn't right. If you're a black woman, you develop an antenna for these things. We learn to survive by expecting the worst. But I won't lie: I wanted him to come see me, I wanted him to be my Prince Charming, I wanted him to be 'the one.' I am thirty-three years old and I am ready—no, let me say I *want* to be married and have children, just like my mama was when she was my age and her mama was when she was my age. Why is that so hard nowadays?"

If there were a formula for joining the middle class, the ingredients and sequence would remain fundamentally unchanged from a century ago, or from one country to the next, not unlike that for Coca-Cola or the hamburger: graduate from college, marry after your twentieth birthday, bear children. It is the poverty slayer, the anthropological equivalent of a magic bullet. Here in the United States, wealth for African Americans is, on average, about 58 cents for every $1 in the hands of whites. But taking a spouse changes the odds, puts the wind at your back. A black married couple has about 88 cents in income and assets for every white couple's $1. What's more, children born to unwed mothers are far more likely than those born in wedlock to drop out of high school, go to jail, have emotional breakdowns, become addicted to drugs and alcohol, get pregnant as teenagers, and bear their own children out of wedlock. In so many words, anthropologists assert that if you're unlucky in love, there's a good chance you'll be unlucky in life, passing misfortune down like a curse to your kids and grandkids.

All of which is to say this: to truly get ahead, Sonia needs a man.

Childless and a year into a Ph.D. program in education

at DePaul University here in Chicago, Sonia would seem to have a lot going for her. She lives in the largest black community in the country. She owns her own home, a car, and even a small apartment building on the city's South Side, which she rents out to tenants with Section 8 vouchers. She earned about $40,000 in 2006 in rental income and from her part-time job as a youth counselor. And, truth be told, she is a catch: petite, personable, and pretty. With blond highlights in her hair, she resembles Mary J. Blige. She makes a mean vegetarian lasagna. "A brother could do worse than me," she says, smiling, over a caramel macchiato at Starbucks one winter afternoon. "Lot worse."

But timing is everything, and this is no time for love. In countries across the globe, fewer people are getting married than at any time in the past twenty-five years. Marriage rates are especially low in big cities like Chicago, São Paulo, Johannesburg, and Jakarta, where joblessness and wage inequality are highest. Between 1970 and 2005, the overall marriage rate in the United States declined by 22 percent, 38 percent for African Americans. For blacks in Chicago, marriage is approaching obsolescence. For every one thousand adult blacks living in the city, twelve people were married in 2006. That's six marriages, a rate that is comparable to that in Port-au-Prince, Washington, D.C., or the Gaza Strip.

No demographic group in the United States has been hit harder by the haymaker thrown by the restructured global economy than blacks, who famously migrated to Chicago from the Deep South to man its assembly lines, stockyards, passenger trains, and steel mills. Since the Reagan administration began aggressively boosting the value of the U.S. dollar in 1981, mostly through the manipulation of interest rates, Chicago has relied less and less on big shoulders to do its business. Successive administrations only deepened the trend, with trade deals that accelerated the exodus of smokestack industries to points south. This city, "Hog Butcher for the World, Tool Maker, Stacker of Wheat," as Carl Sandburg wrote in the eponymous poem over ninety years ago, lost 141,300 manufacturing jobs just in the five-year period between 2000 and 2005, more than any other city in the nation. What remains is an economy increasingly dependent on women. As recently as the 1970s, according to the Bureau of Labor Statistics, nearly one in three jobs in U.S. cities were in manufacturing. By March 2008, that ratio had declined to about one in ten nationally, or 13,643,000 jobs, of which 9,848,000 were actually in production. The hospitality industry employed 13,682,000 workers, meaning that here in the last best hope on earth, there are more maids, cashiers, and waitresses than assembly-line workers. Men in the prime of their working lives are now less likely to have jobs than they were during all but one recession of the past sixty years. When accounting for all men and not just those actively seeking employment, the Labor Department in its March 2008 report calculated a jobless rate of 13.1 percent for those in the prime age group. Only once during a post–World War II recession did the rate ever get that high. It hit 13.3 percent in June 1982, the twelfth month of the brutal 1981–1982 recession.

Without jobs, things fall apart. Every import costs jobs at home. Every job sacrificed to trade affects an American household. Similar to sub-Saharan Africa, the United States makes so little of value that if the country exported every single item manufactured within its borders in 2007—cars, coffee grounds, shoes, air conditioners, sofas, party favors, *everything*—it would still have a trade deficit of more than 5 percent of GDP.

That would not be so problematic if public education were helping to close the gap between the new economy and the old by preparing workers for jobs in high-tech industries. It's not. Since 1980 the federal government's share of spending on education has fallen from 12 percent of GDP to 8 percent, leaving state and local governments to pick up the slack, mainly through uneven property tax assessments which put poor communities at a competitive disadvantage. In 2006 Illinois spent on average $2,065 less per year on each student from a poor school district than it did on students who lived in wealthier districts, according to a local trade publication, *Education Week*. For every one hundred black boys who enrolled as freshmen in Chicago public high schools between 1990 and 1996, only three had earned college degrees ten years later, according to a study by Chicago Public Schools. With a college diploma more integral than ever to reaching the middle-class life, black women outnumber black men on U.S. college campuses by a ratio of three to one. Educators and psychologists say that boys are both more likely than girls to be identified as problematic by schools, law enforcement officers, and employers and more likely simply to give up when confronted with dismal prospects for the future, taking a fatalistic turn toward crime, drugs or alcohol, or plain idleness. Squeezed from the labor market and discouraged in the classroom, unskilled black youths have been shuttled off to jails—one of the few domestic growth industries of the past twenty years—Iraq and other faraway military encampments, or, worse, early graves. The dearth of manufacturing and the resulting trade imbalance have driven a wedge between the sexes. For every one hundred black women in Chicago between the ages of twenty-two and thirty-four, there are only sixty-eight black men in circulation. There are literally too few black men to go around. Nationwide, more than half of all women are single; for black women, the ratio is two in three. Forty percent of black women have never been married.

The global city is, like the ghetto, populated more and more by people going it alone. On Chicago's South Side, in Soweto and the slums of São Paulo, and in the Paris suburbs and south-central Los Angeles, the corporate restructuring of the world economy has thinned what sociologists call the marriageable pool. A 2002 study by two economists at Hebrew University concluded that women were less likely to marry in cities where wage inequality for men was the highest. Growing income disparities, Eric Gould and Daniele Paserman wrote, was a proxy for diminished "husband quality."

Globalization pits men and women against each other, fueling greater miscommunication, jealousies, and even violence. Educated women like Sonia are confronted with an increasing number of potential husbands who earn less money than they do and travel in different professional circles. Sonia and many other women see that as a compromise they can live with, but men often find it unacceptable. In virtually every country I have visited in the past decade, I have heard women complain of a companion who is uneasy about the future facing him, disfigured by his resentments and insecurities: he finds his wife or girlfriend's paycheck a threat to his traditional role as the breadwinner or decision-maker in the relationship; he fears that she is better than he, that she is having an affair with one of the men at work or school who earns more money than he does, drives a nicer car, or hangs with a better crowd.

Paradoxically, the marriageable pool of women has been enlarged for young, single, professional black men, who recognize that their prospects put them at a premium and allow them to cast a wider net when searching for a wife. Eligible black men have seemingly limitless choices, and not just among black women. Black men enter interracial marriages at a higher rate—9.7 percent—than any racial or gender group other than Asian women. That's twice the rate of black women, who intermarry with other races less than anyone else in the United States.

"So here are your choices if you are a black woman," Sonia says. "I can share a man because he's dating another woman and she may be black, or Mexican, or white, or Asian. You see a lot of that nowadays. Or I can try to make peace with a blue-collar man who resents my education and always wants to know where I've been and who I had lunch with today and who might hit me or even kill me one day if the answer is not what he wants to hear. I can maybe date a white guy, but chances are not good that he will want to marry me. White men might want to fuck us, but they ain't usually trying to take a sista home to meet Mama, especially not a sista like me, who is darker than Halle Berry. Or I just go solo, maybe adopt or have a baby without a husband and raise it by myself."

The rules of international finance have made it harder for ordinary people to come by the tools to access the middle class: land, education, good jobs, health care, credit, water, electricity, union cards, and even husbands. Along with per capita GDP, household savings rates, and mathematical formulas measuring inequality, add another critical economic indicator to the list: marriage rates.

"To me, it is like we're living through this biblical plague," says Sonia. "Like the pharaoh ordered his guards to go into every home and strangle all the male babies in their cribs beginning thirty-five or forty years ago. And the community died with them."

"Sonia!"

She is sipping a $9 sour apple martini at Bar Louie on the South Side when her friend, Danielle, spots a man sitting alone at the bar staring at her. It is mid-December and classes at DePaul have finished for the semester, so Sonia is enjoying a rare weekday night out.

"That boy at the bar keeps looking over here." Danielle nods discreetly. "You know him?"

Sonia squints in the dimly lit room. "Uh-unh," she says to Danielle without turning to look at her. "I hope he ain't expecting me to walk over there and do his job for him. He better holla at me," she says, smiling at her theatrical bluster.

As if on cue, the man rises from his bar stool and walks over to the corner table where Sonia and Danielle are sitting.

"Sonia, right?" he says, still standing.

"Uh . . . yeah," Sonia answers in surprise, drawing the word out as if she's unsure.

"I'm Lawrence," he says, extending his hand. "We went to Hirsch together. I was a year behind you."

"Ohhh," Sonia says, grabbing his hand enthusiastically. "Riiiight." She has no idea who he is. But he is not at all bad-looking, nearly six feet tall, dressed sharply in a crisp white button-down and dark slacks—no jeans hanging off his ass, which signals to Sonia that he has somewhere to be during the day where that would be frowned upon. And he's confident, no doubt about that. Sonia senses an opportunity.

"This is my friend Danielle," she says to him. "Danielle, Lawrence." She points at each of them. "We went to high school together at Hirsch," she says to Danielle, who shakes Lawrence's hand, smiling in approval.

"You mind if I sit down?" Lawrence asks, even as he is pulling a chair from the table.

He fills her in on the past fourteen years of his life: no kids, no wives, no ex-wives. He works as a paralegal at a downtown law firm and is taking classes at Harold Washington, the community college. He hopes to be a lawyer. Sonia asks him why he rarely spoke to her in high school.

"You always looked mean," he says, smiling.

"I was *focused*," Sonia corrects him, then reciprocates with her own post–high school narrative, though she never mentions Anthony, the on-again, off-again boyfriend she has been dating for two years now. Nine years her senior, Anthony broke up with her again about ten days ago. The last straw this time was her inaccessibility during the last two weeks of classes, when she was studying for finals and finishing a paper. They saw each other only twice over that span, and Anthony was upset that Sonia was too tired and too busy to cook or have sex. For her part, Sonia says she didn't put up much of a fight.

"I tell Anthony: 'If you know I got a thirty-eight-page paper due, why would you ask me to come over?' It's sabotage. I'm real clear about what I'm trying to do professionally, and getting this degree in education is crucial. Anthony doesn't understand that, or he says he doesn't understand that, and he doesn't like that I am not always available to him, at his beck and call. In his mind I'm not traditional enough. I'm not home fixing dinner. I'm not home waiting for him in makeup and a negligee. I'm not pumping out babies. The truth is, I'm okay with seeing him once a week while I'm in school. If we saw each other five times a week, it wouldn't change the dynamics of our relationship, because it wouldn't change his insecurity."

Besides, she says, it wasn't her unavailability that was his problem. That same week he discovered that he owed the IRS about $2,500 in back taxes. This, Sonia suspects, is as much the catalyst for their most recent breakup as anything. Anthony is an exterminator, and he is acutely self-conscious about how much he earns—about $40,000 annually. "That tax bill is what really had him frustrated," Sonia says. "He wants a stay-at-home woman, which is fine, but he's not in a position to let me stay at home. So because that's always in the back of his mind, everything reminds him that he's not the man he wants to be, and he projects what he sees as his failures onto me. It would be great if we could live the fairy tale he has in mind, but we can't. That's just not the way the world works these days. He can't seem to get his mind around that."

But this is last week's news, and Sonia is not concerned about Anthony at the moment. She and Lawrence are clicking.

"Yeah, we could do a movie," Sonia says to Lawrence.

"Have you seen *Dreamgirls* yet?" Lawrence asks

"I haven't."

They exchange numbers, and after ninety minutes, a plate of bruschetta, and two more sugary martinis for Sonia, Lawrence puts down $40 on the $80 bar tab and rises from his chair to leave. Sonia rises, and as she and Lawrence say goodbye, she says, "It's so good to see someone from the old neighborhood who's not dead or on drugs."

"Dig it," Lawrence says. He turns and walks out into the blue-black of a December night.

"Anthony."

A week later, Anthony has apologized and returned to Sonia's bed. In the middle of the night, as Anthony tells the story to me, Sonia bolted straight up from a dead sleep and cried out for him.

"Anthony," she says again, and nudges his arm.

"What?" he answers, groggy, unmoving.

"Do you love me?"

"What?"

"Do you love me?"

"Yes," he answers. He still hasn't moved.

"Are we going to make it?"

"What?" Anthony asks. He is growling now.

Sonia repeats herself, slowly, pausing for a half-second between each word, her voice clear but soft.

"I don't know," Anthony says. "I hope so."

Sonia checks the clock. It is 4:23 a.m. She lies back down and burrows in behind Anthony spoon-fashion, with her arms crossed under her chin.

"I'm always honest, especially since I went through treatment," Anthony says later of the conversation.

When I ask Sonia about it, her memory is vague. She

remembers only waking with a start from a dream—she can't recall what it was about—and checking the clock. "Anthony says I talk in my sleep all the time," she says. "I don't think I did that before we met."

That was before she was laid off from her job as a counselor in the city's health department, where she was drawing an annual salary of nearly $50,000. An older coworker advised her to buy an apartment building on the south or west side to rent out to families with Section 8 vouchers for some steady income. She did just that, settling on a hulking prewar four-flat in the Englewood neighborhood. She discovered a roach problem, and her caretaker, a former boyfriend who had done jail time on a manslaughter charge, found an exterminator: Anthony.

"We were standing in one of the apartments and she was talking a million miles a minute," Anthony recalled of their initial meeting. "She told me, 'Now, what you need to do is to go in there with some DDT.' 'Ma'am,' " Anthony said to her. " 'I can't use DDT. It's illegal.' "

Sonia wouldn't listen, but after fifteen minutes, Anthony said, he was able to convince her that he knew a bit more about the pest control business than she did. "She was a smartass," he says.

He was smitten. As he was finishing the job and the two were going over paperwork, he chatted her up, asking her about her work, her weekends, her husband. "I don't have a husband," she said.

They went on their first date a week later.

Anthony was carrying about seventy pounds more on his six-foot-one frame when he met Sonia than he is now. He attacks the treadmill six days a week—proof, he concedes, that addicts often recover by trading a bad habit for a good one. He spent the first decade after high school drinking, getting high, and getting by with close-to-minimum-wage odd jobs. "I worked just enough to get whatever I was drinking or smoking. I tried everything—and I do mean *everything*—except heroin," he says. He did six months in jail for a burglary, got another conviction for assault. Drunk on gin, he punched a girlfriend in the jaw during an argument. He was working as a chef at a four-star downtown hotel when he got fired—"I was always late; *I* would've fired me—and went on a month-long binge.

He was staying with his mother on the South Side when she confronted him about his drug problem, and Anthony stormed out of the house, looking so dirty and crazed, he says, that even prostitutes and other addicts crossed to the other side of the street at the sight of him approaching, the pavement opening up to him like the Red Sea parting before an addled Moses. Unsure of where he was going, he walked until he stumbled across a church-based treatment clinic. He had never noticed it before, but it stopped him dead in his tracks. "I just started crying, bawling right there on the street. I don't even know how long I stood out there, but it had to be a good twenty minutes, and when I was finished, I turned around, went back to my mother's house, grabbed a garbage bag full of clothes, and left. I told my mother, 'Okay, I'm going to treatment.' I was just tired."

So much of his addiction, he came to understand, was a result of the chaos and fear in his life. He and his brother were raised alone by their divorced mother, and his sobriety depends on stability, permanence, a sense that he is moving daily toward something better. By the time he came to terms with this, he was twenty-seven, had never held down a job for more than eighteen consecutive months, and had never dated a woman for more than two seasons. He wanted to make up for lost time. He wanted to find a decent job, marry, and have kids, at least one. It took a few months, but he caught on at a pest control company. When they laid him off, he started his own outfit. He dated women from the neighborhood, but no one seriously. Until Sonia.

"Sonia has an aura," he said to me over coffee. "The more you talk to her, the more you like her. She has this strength that lets you know that you're dealing with a *woman*. I've never known a woman who has so much on her plate. When I met her, I was having an argument in my head. It was like, 'You've never been with a woman like this before. Are you sure you're ready?' Within that first hour, I was thinking to myself, 'Let me try this.' "

They got along like a house on fire initially, although they are very different in some respects. "I like to roller-skate," said Sonia. "He doesn't. He loves karaoke bars. I don't. He doesn't like going downtown. I do. I love going to the show; he'd rather just wait for the bootleg version to come out." But Sonia was drawn immediately to Anthony's confidence, his devotion to his mother and brother and close-knit circle of friends, and his wit. "One of the first things I noticed about Anthony was that he is always together, always immaculately groomed, hair cut and shoes shined. Now I know it's just overcompensating."

Neither of them was making much money, but they still managed to eat out every few weeks. Despite her petite frame, Sonia is, by her own admission, an aggressive eater, and Anthony would crack her up when he'd ask the waiter if he could get her a bib. She didn't mind paying sometimes, because she knew Anthony wasn't remotely cheap. He loved to give her money to get her hair done, or her nails, or to buy a book for school. "If I call and say, 'I need to get my car fixed and it's going to cost five hundred dollars,' Anthony steps up," Sonia said. "I've always loved that about him. And he's probably the only brother I ever dated who could call me and say 'I need five hundred dollars' and if I had it, I'd break out my checkbook."

The problem is that Anthony's money problems eat away at his self-esteem more than his bank account. It's not that he doesn't work hard. He often works six days a week and will travel as far away as Indianapolis for a job. But he just can't manage to get ahead the way he'd like. Once, about a year into his relationship with Sonia, his car broke down for what seemed like the umpteenth time and he couldn't afford to buy a new one. Frustrated, as they lay beside each other in bed that night, he confessed, "I know I need to get my credit together if I'm going to be able to do anything for us."

Sonia assured him that she planned to stick around until he did, that he'd be okay, and so would the two of them. But the closer they became, the more self-conscious Anthony was about money and the unfamiliar white-collar world that threatened to take Sonia away from him. They'd be sitting together on the sofa, huddled under a blanket watching *Flavor of Love* or some other awful television show, and out of nowhere Anthony would ask, "Why me, Sonia? Why not a banker or a professor or a lawyer—you know, the people you associate with?" And she'd always answer the same: "Why *not* you, Anthony?"

Sonia always thought it ironic that in his demeanor and

appearance, Anthony is unbreakable, his mien a shield
deflecting judgment or doubt. But intimately he can be as
vulnerable as a child, his insecurities like bile, tasteless and
invisible until that moment when they bubble suddenly,
unexpectedly, to the surface, poisoning the air. Every once in
a while, Sonia is able to convince Anthony to let her treat him
to dinner at a chic new restaurant she's just heard of. They
had a great time at a Brazilian steakhouse, Fogo de Chão,
with the waiters shuttling out endless platters of cooked
meats for Anthony to pluck from the tray. But a week later
they were talking to friends when Anthony said, "Baby, what
was the name of that restaurant again? You're the smart one
in the relationship. You know I only have a twelfth-grade
education." Sonia answered, as she always responds to his
needling, in a calm, dry, tone intended to voice her displeasure but deny him the satisfaction of her rage: "Anthony, you
know I hate when you say that."

Anthony's jealousies are so small and misguided and *obvi-
ous*, Sonia told me. "I'm trying to create these vehicles right
now that will pay off later, not just financially but career-
wise. I'm at this point in my life where I'm asking myself,
what's my legacy going to be? Anthony doesn't understand
that."

"You know what?" Anthony said to me over coffee. 'I *don't*
understand. I don't understand why she can't get in that
kitchen sometimes. I don't understand why she's at her study
group at ten-thirty at night. I don't understand why when
I call her when she's supposed to get out of class at twelve-
thirty, she can't call me back until three-thirty, and I don't
understand why she doesn't understand that when that hap-
pens, I'm thinking, well, maybe she's out kicking it with her

professor. What do they make? They must make like ninety, a hundred grand a year, right? She wants me to be there, but I'm not there yet. I don't trust her like that yet. I love her, but I don't trust her."

DREAMGIRLS WAS A HIT. Sonia loved the movie. But her romance with Lawrence was stillborn.

She went to his apartment after the movie, and she detected a woman's touch in the matching placemats and neatly folded cloth napkins on the kitchen table. Later she tried to reach him on his cell phone at nine in the evening and he wouldn't answer. He would never tell her which law firm he worked for and once said he was going into the office on a public holiday. About three weeks in, he said that he was coming over to her house to visit her, but he stood her up, and when she asked him about it later, he said he'd had to go help his aunt who just got out of the hospital.

"His shit just didn't add up," Sonia said. "Every time you look up, there's something going on with him. It made me uncomfortable, and it was too early to be uncomfortable."

She told me this as we walked to her class on DePaul University's campus. The winter semester had just begun.

"It was good getting out to see a movie," she said. "Anthony and I don't go out much anymore."

Their breakups are so routine that in the past year, she had gone on dates with four other men whom she'd met during her hiatus from Anthony. She didn't feel guilty, she said, in part because she thought that Anthony dated other women during that time as well. "And you know, Anthony always breaks up with me on Thursdays. I've noticed the pattern with him. He breaks up with me then because that's when he feels the most emasculated if he doesn't have any money. And that's why I'm always meeting someone when we're going through our breakups. Because my first day as a free woman is always a Friday and so I go out to celebrate or mourn—I'm never sure which."

Sonia's class was small, eleven graduate students and the professor. There were eight women, five of them white. Three of the students were men: white, Latino, and black. They sat in a circle, and Reggie, the classroom's only black man, sat next to Sonia.

"Gimme that sweater, Reggie," Sonia said to him. He was wearing a colorful mock turtleneck.

"*Give* you? We can barter. What you got to trade that I'd be interested in?" Reggie asked.

Sonia batted her eyelashes as if she were the starlet in a silent movie. "I have only my undying friendship to offer you."

Their flirtations were innocent enough. Reggie was engaged, and one of only two or three black men Sonia had encountered as a student or professor since she entered graduate school. For a city with such a diverse population, this is a homogenous environment that affords few opportunities for the smattering of black women on campus to meet black or even Latino men.

Sonia is not necessarily opposed to dating white men. She dated one a few years back, and a few others have approached her on campus. But it's been her experience, she told me after her class ended, that white men fetishize black women and other women of color. "I know that in talking with my girlfriends who have dated white men, and in my own limited experience, white men typically seem to have this image, this fantasy of a hypersexualized, almost animal-like black woman. They want this experience but not a relationship— not a long-term one, anyway. I know this is not how every white man is, but from what I can see, white men *love* them some white women, and that's why most black women *love* them some black men. They don't all love us back, but most brothas don't really have any alternative. I mean, where would a brotha like Anthony come into contact with a white woman, let alone meet one who would put up with his shit the way I would or another black woman would? People don't want to own up to reality, but when you get right down to it, don't nobody want black people, and especially not black women, for any reason other than to fuck them in some ungodly way."

In class, the students discussed their dissertations. One of Sonia's classmates, a young black woman named Suzanne, was talking about the militarization of public education: "I mean, we put failing schools on probation. *Probation.* That's the language of prison, not education."

"And do you think feminists have adapted their struggle to this kind of postmodernist discourse?" the professor asked. He was white, in his early forties, with shoulder-length dark hair and a tweed jacket, jeans, and running shoes.

Sonia's dissertation was on something called "differentiated learning," or, as she put it in class, "How African American students in secondary urban settings experience education." She sat up straight in her chair and ratcheted up the volume of her voice and enunciated each word with precision. "So maybe Kwame comes to class with other ways of learning, other ways of knowing than does Kelly. Do standardized tests validate Kwame's brand of intelligence, his way of knowing, the same way they do Kelly's? Or, to look at it another way, Kelly does better on the test than Kwame because a lot of what she knows is on the test. What if a lot of what Kelly knows is not on the test, but a lot of what Kwame knows is on the test? Is there value in what Kwame knows, is what I'm asking."

THE SAME CHARACTERISTICS that draw Anthony to Sonia can repel him in a different context, a paradox he compares to someone who loves the water but is afraid of boats, or who likes ice cream but not milk. He loves it that Sonia is smart and independent and ambitious, and he hates it that she is smart and independent and ambitious.

Just a few days ago he was returning from a job when the tie rod on the truck he uses for work just snapped in two, south of the city. It was a Saturday afternoon, and so he called Sonia. No answer. He called again. Still no answer. Finally he called his mother, who rushed to give him a lift.

"I asked her about it that night, and she's like, 'I forgot my cell phone.' Who forgets their cell phone? That's like your watch. I know I don't look like Boo Boo the fool."

"Well Anthony, what do you want me to do? That's the truth. You want me to make something up that sounds better to you?"

"I want my woman to pick up her phone when I call her on a Saturday afternoon."

"Anthony," she all but yelled, "what could you possibly think I was doing? You think that I was with somebody else and then have you over my house that night? All that we've been through, I'm still *here*."

Later, as we had breakfast at a diner, Sonia said that she

had taken her phone with her but was at a conference of black women entrepreneurs and turned it off because she didn't feel like being bothered, but she didn't feel she could tell Anthony that without alarm bells going off in his head. "When we were arguing, in my mind I was thinking, 'Just go.' There are some days when I feel so strongly for Anthony. He is smart and funny and strong and good-looking and . . ." She stumbles here, searching for the right word. She leans forward, then collapses in her booth. "Anthony is the best man I know. He really is. But he wears me down with his jealousy and his fear. That's what it is. This world just makes us so fearful.

"And I just don't know that love can coexist with fear."

9

Sí; Cago; Voy

Chile, Venezuela, and Hope for the Future

> With its French horn and its Swedish academy, its
> American sauce and its English wrenches, with all
> its missiles and its encyclopedias, its star wars and
> its opulent viciousness, with all its laurels the North
> commands—but down here close to the roots is where
> memory no remembrance omits and there are who
> un-dies and who un-lives and thus, all together work
> wonders be it known: the South also exists.
>
> —*Mario Benedetti, Uruguayan poet*

Day breaks sunless and brittle on Chile's southern coast. In the Andean mountains above the bay, the town of Puerto Montt stirs to life: a slender boy with jet-black hair leads a mottled brown cow by a rope along a curving dirt road; a brigade of adolescent girls in plaid skirts and white blouses march giddily, carrying books in the crooks of their elbows; a stooped old man in a billed cap and worn corduroys trudges along the shoulder of a paved road. At Patagonia Salmon Farming, the first shift arrives just as the fine morning mist dissolves, and from the factory's hillside vista the harbor comes into sharp focus. The water tanks hum and spit gunmetal-gray fish onto a silver table in a room with a tin roof but no walls, where Jorge Almonacid and his eldest son, Jose, stand, waiting for them on either side, and slice their gills with one smooth, fatal stroke from their fillet knives before sending them on their way in a pool of ice and blood.

"I've worked here for nine years," says Almonacid, who is forty-six, his voice still hoarse from sleep and last night's tequila. "My son started three months ago. He's not as good with the knife as the old man, but he's not bad," he says, beaming contentedly. Jose smiles dutifully as he plucks a thrashing fish from the tray. "I was a farmhand for many years before, and I can tell you that I very much like it here better. This is a good job. The company takes care of you. Before the factories opened, you either made a living off the land or not at all. The best thing to happen to this part of the country was the salmon industry. We'd be lost without it."

Salmon illustrates how this country navigated the ebb and flow of a rerouted global economy better than any in Latin America and perhaps better than any developing country in the world. While neighboring countries soared and crashed and their citizens protested their stumbling economies and dwindling paychecks, Chileans punched the clock, selling more fish, fruit, wine, processed food, and metal products abroad than ever before. No other country in this part of the world has grown more since 1990, inspiring Wall Street, the White House, economists, and other gurus of unregulated capitalism to praise this eel-shaped nation of 17 million people as a shining example of what developing countries can accomplish if they tear down their walled-off economies and faithfully follow Washington's path to prosperity. When Chile inaugurated its first woman president, Michelle Bachelet, in 2006, U.S. Secretary of State Condoleezza Rice was in attendance, praising Chile as a "force for free economies throughout the region." A *Washington Post* editorial fawningly noted that Chile "increasingly looks and behaves more like a European country than one of its neighbors" and praised Bachelet because she "doesn't question the foundations of her nation's growing prosperity—which are the very free trade, foreign investments and free markets that elsewhere in the region are demonized as 'neoliberalism.' "

But the arc of Chile's salmon industry also illustrates how the "miracle of Chile," as Milton Friedman once called the country's capitalist reorientation, is really the most enduring myth of this postindustrial era. The country assembled Latin America's most dynamic economy by doing quite a bit more than simply stepping out of the way of the market's invisible hand. It was the Chilean government that in the mid-1980s, during the tail end of the brutal dictatorship of General Augusto Pinochet, began investing in the research that produced the technology for salmon cultivation for wide-scale commercial use. When the project became commercially viable, a nonprofit research agency funded by the government, the Chile Foundation, sold its stake to Japanese investors, in 1989. Today salmon is Chile's second largest export, after copper, bringing annual revenue of more than $1 billion and providing jobs for more than 100,000 people. And, tellingly, it got its start not from government's withdrawal from the marketplace, as neoliberal theory posits, but from government intervention.

Years before other countries began retooling their economies to suit Washington, Chile was the prototype, quickly reconfiguring its monetary and industrial policies and cutting social spending in the days following the violent U.S.-backed coup that toppled the democratically elected government of socialist president Salvador Allende in 1973. Thing of it is, the reforms failed miserably, producing manic cycles of booms and busts, rising unemployment, and widening inequality of the sort that would define the financial transitions of poor countries that began to follow Chile's lead a decade later. The irony is that just as most of Latin America was beginning to whittle government's role in business affairs, Chile was shifting course, reestablishing the influence of government in industry and trade. Not only has the Chilean government wielded influence in getting its key exports, from table grapes to goat cheese to sofas, to market, but it also has used legislation, regulation, and taxes to tame a feral free-market system that turned rabid on the country in the 1970s and 1980s.

Argentina and Brazil loosened restrictions on foreign exchange flowing in and out of their countries; having already been burned by the fickle cash flow, Chile slapped restrictions on it. While countries such as Bolivia, Venezuela, and Uruguay put the brakes on public spending in the 1990s, Chile more than doubled public expenditures on health and education over the same period.

Other countries have cut taxes since 1990; Chile nearly doubled its taxes on corporations over the same period. While Argentina was watering down its labor laws to lower costs and make it easier for employers to hire and fire workers, Chile was strengthening its labor legislation, doubling its minimum wage and requiring employers to extend jobless benefits to unemployed workers.

Brazil and Argentina fixed the value of their currencies at an artificially high price to combat inflation and spur imports. Chile's central bank, by contrast, devalued its currency and kept its exchange rate on a tight leash, tinkering with it on an almost daily basis to curb inflation but also to protect local industries from imports that would be made inexpensive by an overvalued peso.

Nearly half of all Brazilian workers did not have a job contract in 2005; for Chile, the figure was one in five. The number of Argentines living in poverty quadrupled between 1989 and 2002; over that same span, Chile reduced by half the ranks of the impoverished.

"What makes Chile different from the rest of Latin America," said Manuel Riesco, an economist with the Center for National Studies of Alternative Development in Santiago, "is not that we embraced the free market more than our neighbors. What we realized is that the free market is like a car. There is no doubt that it is the best way to get you from point A to point B. But you have to steer. If you take your hands off the wheel, you will end up facedown in a ditch."

Chile's economy is far from perfect. But its fast fall and slow slog back up the hill to solvency provide crucial evidence that there is a middle ground between a Darwinian brand of capitalism and a navel-gazing approach to socialism, and demonstrate that an export-led economy is best achieved by spending more and not less on infrastructure, human capital, and technology.

"The myth is that Chile's success is purely the result of fundamentalist free-market policies," said Dani Rodrik, a professor of international economics at Harvard University. "But the truth is quite a bit messier than that. Government activism and management in Chile did not stifle the power of the free market. It unleashed the power of the free market."

ON SEPTEMBER 11, 1973, as troops stormed the presidential palace, the 500-page economic plan of the military junta leading the coup against President Allende's socialist regime was being printed in the basement of a Santiago publishing house.

Like its neighbor Argentina, Chile is a demographic anomaly on the continent, populated almost wholly by whites, who can trace their ancestry to Germany, Spain, and other parts of Europe. The antipathy of the wealthy landowning elite—*la clase alta*—for the poor, labor unions, and Marxists is deep and shrill. Argentina's deafening protests against crime, corruption, and poverty, which became popular during the height of that country's fiscal crisis, actually originated in Chile in the early 1970s, when affluent women in the capital city, Santiago, wanted to voice their displeasure with Allende's land reform measures.

Convinced that he was a messianic figure rescuing Chile from a Communist menace like the one that had taken hold in Castro's Cuba, General Pinochet put his faith in a coterie of young Chilean advisers who had trained under Friedman at the University of Chicago's School of Economics, the academic vanguard of conservative free-market economics. Censoring the press, banning opposition political parties, and restricting union activity, Pinochet's repressive regime murdered an estimated 3,000 leftist dissidents, tortured another 30,000, and handed the "Chicago Boys," as they came to be known, a blank check to remake Allende's nationalized economy.

Nearly fifteen years before economists coined the phrase "Washington Consensus" and eight years before Reagan began dismantling the New Deal in the United States, Chile installed the world's first post–cold war template for a neoliberal economy. Pinochet slashed duties on imports, from an average tariff rate of 94 percent in 1973 to 10 percent by 1979.

He privatized all but two dozen of Chile's three hundred state-owned banks, as well as utilities and programs such as social security. By 1979 he had cut public spending almost in half and public investment by nearly 14 percent. He abolished the minimum wage, privatized the state's pension fund, lowered taxes, virtually banned union activities, and returned more than a third of the land seized under Allende's land reform program.

Monetary policy was liberalized on two important fronts. First, Pinochet allowed "hot money"—speculation on the currency market—to flow in and out of the country without obstacle. And in 1979, similar to what Argentina and Brazil would do more than a decade later, he fixed the exchange rate for Chile's peso, requiring the central bank to keep US$1 in reserve for every 39 pesos printed. This prevented the bank from merely printing money to pay bills and curbed an inflation rate that had soared to nearly 400 percent annually under Allende.

Pinochet's reforms worked like a fast-acting virus. A recession in 1975 caused Chile's economy to contract by 13 percent, its greatest decline since the Great Depression. The recovery that followed was fueled largely by foreign cash, which poured into the country as investors gobbled up utilities and stashed money in Chile's currency markets. The prices of imports fell sharply; between 1975 and 1982, the number of foreign cars sold in Chile tripled. Manufacturing shrank by 30 percent. Domestic savings plummeted. Wages fell, and the income gap between rich and poor widened by a factor of 50.

By 1982 Chile had accumulated $16 billion in foreign debt—the highest in Latin America—and foreign investment represented a quarter of the country's gross domestic product. The money flowing into the country flowed out just as easily, to pay debts for imported goods and through capital flight as investors soured on Chile's currency market. The economy had overheated and was now melting down.

"I don't think there is any question that Chile did not have the right policy mix in those days," said Hernán Somerville, president of the Chilean Banking Association and one of Pinochet's advisers at the time. "The government wasn't as diligent as it needed to be to effectively manage the markets and the economy. We needed a system with more balance."

With a third of the workforce unemployed and unrest growing, by 1984 Pinochet began to "reform the reforms," said Ricardo French-Davis, an economics professor at the University of Chile. Rather than fixing the value of the peso, he allowed it to "float" on the open market and reinstated restrictions on the movement of capital in and out of the country. He introduced banking legislation and increased spending on research and development efforts through the Chile Foundation and other collaborations between the public and private sectors. This led to the birth of the country's salmon farming industry.

Still, Chile's economic woes persisted. By 1989 real wages had declined by 40 percent from 1973, and the percentage of the population living in poverty had doubled, to 40 percent. The number of Chileans without adequate housing had also climbed to 40 percent, from 27 percent during Allende's last year in office. In 1989 Chile's poor consumed on average 1,629 calories a day; in 1973 their daily consumption had averaged 2,019 calories. Mindful that the economic policies of the Chicago Boys had produced two of the worst recessions in

Chilean history, in 1975 and again in 1982, Chileans began to refer to the cadre of advisers not as the Chicago Boys but as *Sí; Cago; Voy*, which means "Yes; I shit; I go."

And while the bloodiest spasms of state terror had occurred in the military junta's early years, the campaign of assasinations, rape, and torture continued. In 1985 the bodies of three men who were members of the Communist Party were found in a field near the Santiago airport, their throats slashed. The following year military officials doused an eighteen-year-old college student, Carmen Gloria Quintana, and Rodrigo Rojas, a nineteen-year-old photographer, in gasoline during street protests in Santiago, then set them alight. Rojas died. In 1989 a judge issued an arrest warrant for a twenty-one-year-old leftist, Marcelo Barrios Andres. When police caught up to him, they summarily executed him.

Growing pressure from both inside and outside the country forced Pinochet to hold a 1989 plebiscite that returned democracy to Chile. The new government dramatically accelerated the reforms, said French-Davis and others. Between 1990 and 2002, Chile doubled government spending on health and education and introduced tax incentives to businesses that provide job training, helping to increase the number of Chileans with higher education from 9 percent in 1992 to 16.4 percent by 2003. The number of professionals in the country expanded 124 percent over that period.

Successive governments led first by Chile's conservatives and then by its socialist party worked to restore workers' rights eroded by Pinochet's regime. Government strengthened trade unions' ability to negotiate collective bargaining agreements, introduced the continent's broadest unemployment insurance plan, and reduced from six months to one the period of time employees can work without a contract. Between 1990 and 1998, Chilean lawmakers increased the minimum wage by 87 percent, making it the highest in Latin America, said Yerko Ljubetic, Chile's undersecretary of labor under Bachelet's predecessor, Ricardo Lagos. "You can probably find cheaper labor in other Latin American countries," said Jose Luis Charpentier, the manager at the Patagonia Salmon Farm. "But you can't find better workers than we have here in Chile. Their productivity more than makes up for the difference in costs."

Chile pressed ahead with privatization, even selling its cash cow—the copper mines that are Chile's top export earner—without charging the royalties that are typically charged in transactions extending mineral rights. But Chile's regulations generally surpassed anything attempted by its neighbors, and the government's stringent enforcement of its contractual terms mitigated job losses and rising service costs passed on to consumers, said Ricardo Paredes, an economics professor at the University of Chile.

For instance, Chile's push to foster competition is a variation on the World Bank and IMF model, designed to benefit not just big business but consumers as well, by requiring that telecommunications and natural gas firms connect their lines with those of other providers. Chilean regulatory agencies set the price for those interconnections, resulting in the lowest-priced long-distance rates in the region (a phone call from Chile to New York City is actually less expensive than one in the other direction).

The low prices have attracted new businesses, in another illustration of how globalization can work for everyone if it's managed well. Delta Airlines, for example, opened a $4 million international call center in Santiago in 2002, employing seventy workers.

Since 1990 Chile's gross domestic product has grown by an annual average of 5.9 percent, the fastest on the continent and nearly twice that of Argentina and Brazil. When Mexico's sharp devaluation of its currency in 1995 plunged both Brazil and Argentina into mild recessions, Chile's economy was unscathed, largely because of government controls on foreign investment, which prevented speculators from withdrawing their cash from the country's stock and bond market when the economy took a sudden downturn. By limiting the volatility of the free market, Chile enabled its economy to grow 6 percent that year.

"What we learned from the seventies and eighties," said French-Davis, "is that you don't want too much foreign investment coming into the country. You want money coming into the country to go toward the development of technology, roads, job training, those things that will improve productivity. That's where government comes in. We limited the influx of hot money and encouraged domestic savings that we can use as a building block just as easily as foreign savings." Chile's domestic savings rate is the highest in Latin America.

While Chile's economy improved steadily over the 1990s, its neighbor to the east, Argentina, endured destabilizing cycles of boom and bust that culminated in a default on more than $140 billion in foreign loans in 2001, the largest sovereign default in history. Between 1989 and 2001, Argentina's unemployment rate nearly quadrupled, to 22 percent, in a chain of events that largely mirrored what had happened in Chile twenty years earlier.

"What happened to Argentina in the late nineties and into 2000, 2001," French-Davis said, "is almost identical to what happened to Chile in the late seventies and eighties. When people say that developing countries should do what Chile did, I always wish they would clarify what time period they're referring to. We've tried some very different things over the last thirty years."

U.S. diplomats, journalists, and business executives usually offer a pat answer when asked to explain the difference between Chile and other Latin American countries or another country with a copper-based economy, like Zambia. "Corruption," one journalist who worked in the region said to me in 2002. "Chile has a culture of transparency that many of these other countries do not," he said. This was before a 2004 probe by a U.S. Senate committee investigating money laundering in the wake, ironically, of the 9/11 terrorist attacks in New York and Washington uncovered that Pinochet and his cohorts had taken bribes and kickbacks from defense contractors and other business firms. Still, the notion of Chile's transparency endures, unholstered from the American political class's arsenal of "explanations that don't explain," as the slain Black Panther leader Fred Hampton once said. By definition, opening up to business means more deal-making, which means more opportunities for personal enrichment, whether legal or illegal. Would anyone argue that the United States, with a political system authorizing bribes to elected officials, became the world's richest nation because it is less corrupt than others? Or, to look at it another way, if Chile's culture of transparency is responsible for its steady economic growth, then how exactly did that ethos disappear for seventeen years?

With all of the country's progress, however, Chile's manufacturing output has dropped off dramatically since its peak
in the Allende years, and Chile's dependence on exports has
widened income inequality. According to a 2005 United
Nations Development Program report, the richest 10 percent
of Chileans have 50 percent of the wealth, a deeper concentration than in 112 other countries and only slightly better
than in Namibia. And trade union officials have criticized as
critical missteps Lagos's signing of a 2003 trade pact with the
United States and his government's efforts after 2004 to scale
back workplace protections for employees under the age of
twenty-one, and to remove the monetary controls on foreign
investment that curbed the market volatility of the early
Pinochet years.

In Puerto Montt, however, the future continues to look
bright. Patagonia Salmon celebrated record-breaking sales
of packaged fillets and steaks to the United States in 2005.
"I think the sky is the limit," said Charpentier, the factory
manager. "You know, our economy has been a little like the
three little bears. First we were too cold, then we were too
hot. Now I think Chile has gotten it just right."

In late February 1989, as Chileans were preparing to
go to the polls to end their country's disastrous experiment
with neoliberalism, rioters 1,800 miles to the north stormed
the streets of Venezuela's capital city, Caracas. What drew
their wrath was their president, Carlos Andrés Pérez, who
had been sworn in not even a month before, after a more
or less populist campaign during which he had referred
to the International Monetary Fund as a "bomb that only
kills people." Two weeks after his inaguration, in perhaps

the seminal bait-and-switch of the neoliberal era, a political maneuver that would later become recognizable to voters in South Africa, Brazil, Washington, D.C., and many other locales, Pérez unveiled an economic *paquetazo* that was spectacular for its conservative orthodoxy. In a letter of intention signed with the IMF, the basic premises of the Pérez plan were laid out as follows: government spending and salaries were to be restricted, foreign exchange rates deregulated, interest rates raised, price controls on food and fuel relaxed, a regressive sales tax introduced, import tariffs substantially lowered, and state enterprises privatized.

Venezuela's elites had been toying with market fundamentalism for several years, and poverty had been inching up, as had the price of gas, which is supplied by Venezuela's nationalized petroleum company, known by its Spanish acronymn PDVSA. But February 27, 1989, was the tipping point. It was a Monday, and over that weekend Pérez's liberalization of petroleum prices had kicked in, doubling prices both at the pump and at the fare box on public buses overnight. The fuse was lit during the Monday morning commute from Caracas's hilltop slums into the city, when students, maids, gardeners, and other workers in the informal sector discovered the hike in bus fares and simply refused to pay. Rioters overturned and burned buses, spat at drivers, and blocked major thoroughfares. Within hours it was apparent that gasoline prices had provided the spark for a much larger political conflagration. Rioters turned their anger on wealthy neighborhoods on Caracas's east side, setting fire to more than a thousand stores in the city and looting slabs of meat and bottles of champagne. "The people are hungry!" protesters shouted. "The people are angry! No more deception!" The violence spread to the suburbs, then to virtually evey major city in the country: San Cristóbal, Barquisimeto, Maracay, Barcelona, Puerto la Cruz, Mérida, Maracaibo, and Valencia.

Pérez put down the revolt by imposing martial law. A massacre ensued. In the barrios in and around Caracas, police dragged suspected organizers from their homes and opened fire on crowded street corners, apartment courtyards, and stairways. Within three days the riots had ended. Five thousand people had been arrested, and authorities estimated the number of dead at three hundred. The actual number, many here believe, is closer to three thousand.

Of the many bystanders taking in the events that unfolded in Venezuela's cities over those three days in 1989, one was a young lieutenant colonel in the army who was steeped in Marxist theory and the historical feats of Latin America's "Great Liberator," Simón Bolívar. That officer was Hugo Chávez.

The *caracazo*, as it is known, was the first uprising against the world trading system, and it set in motion a chain of events that led to an international resistance movement that is in its makeup, if not yet in its momentum, the offspring of the global abolitionist and anticolonization movement that began to take shape in the late nineteenth century. During the violent upheaval on Venezuela's streets nearly twenty years ago, the seeds of the postmodern struggle were planted, yielding Chávez's unsuccessful 1992 coup attempt and his eventual election to Venezuela's presidency; Bolivians' grass-roots campaign against privatized water; the Zapatistas movement in Mexico and resurgent landless people's and workers' movements in Brazil; protests on the streets in Seattle, Washington, D.C., New York, and Europe;

the effort led by South Africa's Treatment Action Campaign to make expensive, life-saving medicines available to poor people infected with HIV; and the elections since 2002 of at least eight heads of state in Latin America offering a sharp alternative to neoliberalism and a clean break from the Wall Street–designed policies of the lost years. To one degree or another, those countries have begun to jump back into the driver's seat to guide their economies down a path first blazed by Chile, and as a result they have shown signs of getting the old mojo back, with growth rates that are reminiscent of those of the continent's postwar period. Since 2004, Venezuela, Uruguay, and Argentina have recorded the fastest-growing economies in the Western Hemisphere, and growth in the region over the past five years has been stronger than in any comparable period since the Nixon administration.

Critics of Chávez and his antagonistic attitude toward the United States attribute Venezuela's growth to the surge in oil prices rather than his government's economic policies, but a glimpse at the continent's 2008 growth rates suggests a different narrative: countries with the fastest-growing economies—among them Venezuela, Argentina, Uruguay, Bolivia, and Panama—are led by globalization's heretics, like Chávez and Bolivia's Evo Morales; those countries pulling up the rear are led by true believers in the austere approach to global finance, like Mexico's President Felipe Calderón; and right in the middle of the pack is Brazil, which, under Lula, has assumed a relatively agnostic view of trade.

Inequality on the continent remains the highest in the world; the economies are still far too reliant on a few raw commodities; and the informal sector, prostitution, and criminal enterprises remain major sources of employment. But since the end in early 2003 of a devastating two-month-long general strike orchestrated by the country's business leaders (curiously similar to a U.S.-backed work stoppage in Chile during Allende's government), Chávez's policies have cut in half the percentage of Venezuelans living in poverty, from 55 to 27. If you include expenditures by the state oil company, Venezuela under Chávez has increased per capita spending on health, education, and social services by an astounding 314 percent since he took office. Previous rises in oil prices have not led to such sustained and sizable economic growth, nor to such benefits for the poor and working classes. Going against the grain, Chávez's Bolívarian Revolution is redistributing land; building homes; opening new schools, credit unions, clinics, day-care centers, after-school programs, and agrarian research centers; and collecting delinquent taxes owed by corporations. Inflation is high, at about 22.5 percent annually in early 2008, but much lower than the 36 percent annual rate when Chávez took office. Measured unemployment has dropped from 15.3 percent in 1999 to 9.3 percent in the first half of 2007, its lowest level in more than a decade. Formal-sector employment has increased from 45.4 to 50.6 percent of the labor force, and in a country with an income divide that has historically been eclipsed only by those of Brazil and South Africa, Chávez has whittled the gap between the wealthiest 20 percent of Venezuelans and the poorest 20 percent by nearly a third. "Without the *caracazo*," Chávez has said, "we wouldn't have been able to do it."

Chávez has expanded the number of primary-care physicians from 1,628 to 19,571. In 1998 there were 417 emergency rooms and 74 rehab centers; by 2008 there were 721 emergency rooms and 445 rehab centers. Since 2004, 399,662 people have had operations to restore their vision. In 1999, 335 HIV patients received free antiretroviral treatment from the government, compared to 18,538 in 2006. Nearly 2 million Venezuelan children were enrolled in a free school lunch program in 2006, nearly ten times more than when Chávez started the effort in 1999. Two thirds of the population has access to subsidized food. Enrollment rates have increased by 25 percent for preschool, 8 percent for primary education, 45 percent for secondary schools, and 44 percent for higher education. Over 1 million people participate in adult literacy programs.

What the numbers don't reflect is what it means to poor people—especially Venezuela's black and indigenous minorities—to live in a country that is finally, after centuries of exclusion, their own. "Our media and the rich people say such horrible things about the president, and I have to ask who they are talking about," Ana Maria Araujo said to me in 2004. She was forty-nine, black, and the mother of two teenage children, and she worked in a Caracas Internet café. "To me, he is a great man. He is a gift to poor people everywhere. I love the man because he is a good man—he speaks to us when no other president in my lifetime has even bothered to look at us. If Pérez had his way, I think he would've liked to have seen us all die. That's how much he cared about us." She was speaking only two days before protesters planned an anti-Chávez rally in the city. "Now the people have hope. People are not afraid anymore, because they feel as though we have rights. We can truly say that we are Venezuelans. We belong."

The juxtaposition of Chile and Venezuela is, to me, globalization's Rosetta Stone, the means for cracking the

complicated code of classic macroeconomic theory and under-
standing fully the relationship between the cold war and the
Washington Consensus. In plain view, Pinochet tortured
and murdered thousands, bankrupted his country, and didn't
hold an election for sixteen years, and the United States'
political class didn't say a word, except of course to praise an
economy that never existed and an ally against a threat that
was never as menacing as advertised. Chávez, in contrast, has
won three elections, all judged free and fair by international
monitors and each by an increasingly wide margin. There
were no Supreme Court reprieves, just as there are no cred-
ible accusations that he has killed, tortured, or jailed political
prisoners—not even the wealthy businessmen who conspired
to overthrow his government for a few days in 2002. Polls
have for years shown him to be the continent's most popular
elected head of state, and a 2007 survey showed that Venezuelans were more satisfied with their government than people
in any other country in Latin America save Uruguay. And
yet by marshaling the wealth that sits beneath Venezuelans'
feet to feed, teach, and house his countrymen and help
bail his neighbors out of debt, he is villified by elites in the
United States and Europe as some sort of vulgar clown whose
administration is intent on destroying his nation's economy
and encouraging terrorism.

The history of Latin America, in a nutshell, is the tension between *la clase alta*—the mostly white elites who own
the land—and the peasants and urban workers—often the
darker-skinned blacks, Indians, or some mixture of the two—
who built it. And in that battle Chávez has clearly chosen a
side. It is impossible not to notice the physical differences
between the blue-eyed, white-haired, and square-jawed

Pinochet and the swarthy Chávez, a man who can pepper his speech with language both coarse and poetic, who was born in a mud hut and descended from Venezuela's indigenous people, African slaves, and Spanish settlers. (I and some people I know were particularly mindful of Chávez's dark skin when, during a 2007 summit in Chile, Spain's King Juan Carlos I angrily told this elected leader of a sovereign state to shut up, using the familiar voice). It is equally impossible not to notice that a rally of Chávez's detractors is made up almost entirely of affluent Europeans from Venezuela's stock- and land-owning classes and reseambles, both aesthetically and rhetorically, a rally of the detractors of Evo Morales, Bolivia's first fully indigenous president. Conversely, Chávez's deepest support comes from the country's poorest citizens: blacks, who account for about 11 percent of the population, *mestizos*, and working-class whites. So too does Morales's political base, like Allende's and Castro's and Bolívar's and Haiti's Toussaint L'Ouverture's. Like most everyone else who has championed the cause or ordinary people, Chávez chose the wrong side in the eyes of the homogenous political class that rules the United States, Venezuela, and the global financial system. By using his country's oil revenues—profits that would otherwise go to the weathy—to give a leg up to peasants, blue-collar workers, and the jobless, not just in Venezuela but also in Bolivia, Brazil, Cuba, Haiti, Ecuador, El Salvador, and other countries, Chávez is leading what is effectively a modern-day slave revolt, a twenty-first-century Haymarket uprising, a Bolívarian independence movement to free the continent from the control of a corporate junta. This is ultimately what is unforgiveable, not that he is a Communist or supports drug trafficking or international terrorism or uses the wrong fork at state dinners. Those are canards, conveniently dragged out by the global ruling class to mask their true objections. The business executives and speculators and politicians and intelligentsia that form the international financial system hate Chávez for the same reason that poor people everywhere adore him, and for the same reason that Thomas Jefferson despised L'Ouverture two hundred years ago for first stirring in the mind of the slave that one intolerable, transcendent idea:

"We can take them."

NOTES

Overview

Data on **worldwide unemployment**: International Labor Organization, *Annual Report on Global Employment Trends*, 2008, at www.ilo.org.

On **workers' productivity and wages**: U.S. Department of Commerce, Bureau of Economic Analysis, *National Income and Products Accounts 2006*, at www.bea .gov.

On **CEO pay**: Paul Buchheit, "The Income Gap," *CounterPunch*, February 2, 2007, at www.counterpunch.org.

On **income inequality**: Thomas Pikkety and Emmanuel Saez, "The Evolution of Top Incomes: A Historical and International Perspective," National Bureau of Economic Research, January 2006, at www. nber.org/papers/w11995. See also Aviva Aron-Divo and Isaac Shapiro, "Share of National Income Going to Wages and Salaries at Record Low in 2006; Share of Income Going to Corporate Profits at Record High," Center for Budget and Policy Priorities, March 29, 2007, at www.cbpp.org.

On **education and household spending**: United Nations Development Programme, *Human Development Report, 2007/2008*, at http://hdr.undp.org/en/humandev.

Figures on **$1 a day**: World Bank, *Global Economic Prospects 2004* and *Development Report and World Economic Indicators*, published annually at www.worldbank.org.

Figures on **Latin American per capita income**: Mark Weisbrot, "Latin America: The End of an Era," Center for Economic and Policy Research, 2006, at www.cepr.net.

Figures on **world and sub-Saharan African income**: World Bank, *Development Report and World Economic Indicators 2008*, at www.worldbank.org.

On **Teamsters' pensions**: Mary Williams Walsh, "Teamsters Find Pension Funds at Risk," *New York Times,* November 15, 2004.

On **dental health**: Alex Berenson, "Boom Time for Dentists But Not for Teeth," *New York Times,* October 17, 2007.

On **life expectancy**: Pam Belluck, "Children's Life Expectancy Being Cut Short by Obesity," *New York Times,* March 17, 2005.

Data on **stock bubble**: Robert Kuttner, "America's Economic Perfect Storm," *Boston Globe,* December 12, 2007.

Figures on **U.S. manufacturing jobs**: U.S. Bureau of Labor Statistics, at www .bls.gov; see also AFL-CIO, "Jobs Crisis in America," at www.aflcio.org/issues/ jobseconomy/jobs/jobcrisis.

On **Brazilian manufacturing jobs**: Instituto Brasileiro de Geografia e Estatistica (IBGE; Brazilian Institute of Geography and Statistics), at www.ibge.gov.br/home.

On **South African manufacturing jobs**: Statistics South Africa, *Statistics South Africa Census of Manufacturing 2007,* at www. statssa.gov.za.

Data on **Argentine television manufacturing**: Larry Luxner, "Argentina 936 faces phaseout threat," *San Juan Star,* May 27, 1996. http://www.luxner.com/cgi-bin/ view_article.cgi?articleID=379.

On **Mozambican cashews**: Margaret S. McMillan, Dani Rodrik, and Karen Horn Welch, "When Economic Reform Goes Wrong: Cashews in Mozambique," National Bureau of Economic Research, August 23, 2002, at www.nber.org/papers/ w9117.

On **Zambian textiles**: Shantha Bloemen, "T-Shirt Travels," *Independent Lens* documentary film, April 22, 2001, at www.pbs.org/independentlens/tshirttravels/ film.html.

On the **San Francisco port**: Jaimal Yogis, "What Happened to Black San Francisco," *San Francisco Magazine,* August 2006.

On **Wal-Mart and China's industrial transformation**: Nelson Lichtenstein, ed., *Wal-Mart: The Face of 21st Century Capitalism* (New York: New Press, 2006).

On **South African unemployment**: Statistics South Africa, *Household Survey* and *Labor Force Survey,* 1993–2007, published annually at www. statssa.gov.za.

On the **Chilean economy**: Ricardo Ffrench-Davis, *Economic Reforms in Chile: From Dictatorship to Democracy* (Ann Arbor: University of Michigan Press, 2002).

1. A New Day: Zambia and Free Trade

Quotations and other details are taken from interviews and reporting I conducted in Lusaka, Livingstone, and Kitwe, Zambia, in December 2001 and January 2002.

Data on **Zambian export policies and reduced tariffs**: Dale Mudenda and Madenga Ndulo, "Trade Reform and Adjustment: Zambian Experiences 1980– 2003," United Nations Conference on Trade and Development, at www.unctad.org.

Figures on **Zambians living on $1 a day**: World Bank, *Development Indicators, Zambia*, published annually at www.worldbank.org.

Figures on **Zambian poverty, unemployment, and manufacturing sector**: Zambia Central Statistics Office, Living Conditions Monitoring Surveys, 1991–2006, published annually at www.zamstats.gov.zm/lcm. Also see Mudenda and Ndulo, "Trade Reform and Adjustment."

On **Zambian textiles and tariff reductions**: Grayson Koyi, "The Textiles and Clothing Industry in Zambia," Zambia Congress of Trade Unions, October 2005; Shantha Bloemen, "T-Shirt Travels," *Independent Lens* documentary film, April 22, 2001, at www.pbs.org/independentlens/tshirttravels/film.html.

Figures on **share of global trade and manufacturing activity in sub-Saharan Africa**: Alexander J. Yeats, Azita Amjadi, Ulrich Reincke and Francis Ng, "What Caused Sub-Saharan Africa's Marginalization in World Trade," World Bank, 1996, at www.worldbank.org/htm/dec/publications/abstracts97/06econ/econ16.html.

On **growth of world income**: World Bank, *World Development Indicators 2008*, at www.worldbank.org.

On the **number of African college graduates at Zambia's independence**: Colin Legum, *Africa Since Independence* (Bloomington: Indiana University Press, 1999), p. 15.

On **Zambia's debt**: World Bank, *Development Indicators, Zambia*, published annually at www.worldbank.org.

On **Mozambican cashews**: Margaret S. McMillan, Dani Rodrik, and Karen Horn Welch, "When Economic Reform Goes Wrong: Cashews in Mozambique," National Bureau of Economic Research, August 23, 2002, at www.nber.org/papers/w9117.

2. The Night Shift: Argentina and Monetary Policy

Quotations and other details are taken from interviews and reporting I conducted in Buenos Aires, Argentina, between February 2003 and February 2004 (interpretation and translation provided by Brian Byrnes, Fabricio Di Dio, and Jimena Aracama).

Figures on **Argentina's inflation rate, manufacturing activity, and unemployment**: National Institute of Statistics and Census, Argentina (INDEC), annual statistics, at www.indec.gov.ar.

Data on **informal-sector jobs in Latin America and Argentina**: Victor E. Tokman, "Integrating the Informal Sector in the Modernization Process," United Nations, 2006, at www.un.org/docs/ecosoc/meetings/2006/forum/Statements/Tokman.pdf.

On numbers of *cartoneros: La Nación*, general information, at www.lanacion.com.ar/nota.asp?nota_id=754169.

Figures on the **Chilean economy under Pinochet**: Ricardo Ffrench-Davis, *Economic Reforms in Chile: From Dictatorship to Democracy* (Ann Arbor: University of Michigan Press, 2002), pp. 113–118, 181–188.

Data on **inequality and economic growth in Latin America**: United Nations, *Social Panorama of Latin America*, published annually at www.eclac.org.

On the **Chinese yuan**: "The Chinese Yuan: Reevaluation by Stealth," *The Economist*, January 10, 2008, at www.economist.com/finance/displaystory .cfm?story_id=10499076.

Figures on **Argentina's economic collapse**: Mark Weisbrot, "Latin America: The End of an Era," Center for Economic and Policy Research, 2006, at www.cepr.net.

Data on **distribution of Argentina's GDP**: annual reports, INDEC.

Figures on **poverty, unemployment, crime, high school dropouts, single-parent households, and teen mothers in Argentina**: Personal communication from Artemio Lopez, polling director, Equis Research, at www.consultoraequis.com. See also United Nations, *Social Panorama of Latin America*.

Data on **marriage, divorce, and racial demographics**: annual reports, INDEC.

References to **lack of "personal responsibility" in African American community**: Orlando Patterson, "A Poverty of the Mind," *New York Times,* March 26, 2006; Michael Eric Dyson, *Is Bill Cosby Right? Or Has the Black Middle Class Lost Its Mind?* (New York: Basic Civitas Books, 2006); Juan Williams, *Enough: The Phony Leaders, Dead-End Movements, and Culture of Failure That Are Undermining Black America—And What We Can Do About It* (New York: Random House, 2006).

3. Life and Debt: Brazil and Interest Rates

Quotations and other details are taken from interviews and reporting I conducted in Rio de Janeiro, São Paulo State, Bahia State, and several other locations in Brazil between January 2003 and May 2004 (interpretation and translation provided by Phylis Huber).

Data on **Brazilian 2003 GDP and unemployment**: Instituto Brasileiro de Geografia e Estatistica (IBGE; Brazilian Institute of Geography and Statistics), annual reports, at www. ibge.gov.br/home.

Figures on **interest rates and debt payments**: Mark Weisbrot and Dean Baker, "Paying the Bills in Brazil: Does the IMF's Math Add Up?" Center for Economic Policy Research, September 25, 2002; Mark Weisbrot and Luis Sandoval, "Brazil's Presidential Election: Background on Economic Issues," Center for Economic Policy Research, September 2006, both at www.cepr.net.

Data on **Lula's approval ratings, banking industry profits, and wages**: quarterly and annual reports, IBGE.

Figures on **GDP growth in Latin America and Brazil**: Mark Weisbrot, "Latin America: The End of An Era," Center for Economic and Policy Research, 2006, at www.cepr.net.

On **racial disparities in Brazil**: annual reports, IBGE.

Data on **police shootings**: Global Justice, "Human Rights in Brazil 2003," Annual Report, at www.global.org.br/english/arquivos/JGAR2003English.pdf.

Figures on **Brazil's public school enrollment**: Brazilian Ministry of Education, annual reports, at www.mec.gov.br.

Data on **fertility rates in Brazil**: United Nations Development Programme, *Human Development Report 2007/2008*, at http://hdrstats.undp.org/countries/data_sheets/cty_ds_BRA.html.

On **land ownership**: Movimento dos Trabalhadores Rurais Sem Terra (Landless Workers Movement), various documents, at www.mstbrazil.org.

Data on **Kaiowá Indian suicides**: Antonio Brand, "Kaiowá and Guarani: The Fight for Land in South Mato Grosso," Universidade Católica Dom Bosco, Campo Grande, Brazil, 2004, at ftp://neppi.ucdb.br/pub/tellus/tellus6/TL6_antonio_brand.pdf.

4. Power and Light: South Africa and Privatization

Quotations and other details are taken from interviews and reporting I conducted in Johannesburg, KwaZulu-Natal province, Cape Town, Port Elizabeth, and other locations in South Africa between May 1999 and October 2002 (interpretation in KwaZulu-Natal by Enoch Mthembu).

Statistics on **utility rate increases and cutoffs in South Africa**: Municipal Services Project, University of the Witwatersrand, related background papers, at www.queensu.ca/msp.

Figures on **Cholera outbreak**: Dr. David Hemson and Bongi Dube, "Water Services and Public Health: The 2000–01 Cholera Outbreak in KwaZulu Natal, South Africa," Human Sciences Research Council, 2002, at www.hsrc.ac.zalstaff-publications-1333.phtml.

Figures on **housing, water, electricity, unemployment, and per capita income**: Statistics South Africa, annual reports, at www.statssa.gov.za.

Data on **privatization in Wales**: Caroline Van den Berg, "Water Privatization and Regulation in England and Wales," World Bank, 2001, at http://rru.worldbank.org/Documents/PublicPolicyJournal/115vdbrg.pdf.

On **water rates in Nicaragua**: "Report: Nicaragua," *Public Citizen*, at www.citizen.org/cmep/Water/cmep_Water/reports/nicaragua.

On **electricity in Pekin, Illinois**: Citizens Utility Board of Illinois, "ComEd/Exelon's Performance Under the Illinois Electric Service Customer Choice and

Rate Relief Law of 1997 and Beyond," at www.citizensutilityboard.org/pdfs/
NewsReleases/20060220_ComEdBodmerStudyFinal.pdf.

On **water in Saudi Arabia and Bolivia**: Maude Barlow, "Blue Gold: The Global
Water Crisis and the Commodification of the World's Water Supply," International
Forum on Globalization, 2001.

On **Argentine electricity**: "Brief Power Outage in BA," *Buenos Aires Herald,*
October 17, 2003.

On **Brazil and Peru electricity**: The Big Issues, Social Watch, at http://www
.socialwatch.org/en/informesTematicos/58.html.

On **California utility rates**: Jason Leopold, "The California Rip-Off Revis-
ited," *CounterPunch,* August 18, 2003, at www.counterpunch.org/leopold08182003
.html.

On **New York cutoffs**: Erik Eckholm, "Cutoffs and Pleas for Aid Rise with Heat
Costs," *New York Times,* April 25, 2008.

On **ComEd rate increase**: Citizens Utility Board of Illinois, Don't Get Shocked
Help Center reports, at www.citizensutilityboard.org/ciDontGetShocked.html.

On **Lesotho water project**: International Rivers, "Lesotho Water Project," at
http://internationalrivers.org/en/africa/lesotho-water-project.

On **cholera outbreak**: Hemson and Dube, "Water Services and Public Health."

African colonial development: Thomas Pakenham, *The Scramble for Africa:
White Man's Conquest of the Dark Continent from 1876 to 1912* (New York: Random
House, 1991), p. 273.

Story of the **Voortrekkers and Piet Retief**: Allister Sparks, *The Mind of South
Africa* (New York: Knopf, 1990), p. 91.

Figures on **Afrikaners' earnings**: C. W. de Kiewiet, *A History of South Africa:
Social and Economic* (Oxford: Oxford University Press, 1957).

Figures on **whites in poverty**: Statistics South Africa, annual report data tables,
at www.statssa.gov.za.

Story of **Coleman Andrews and South Africa Airways**: Sakhela Buhlungu
et al., eds., *State of the Nation: South Africa 2007* (Johannesburg: Human Sciences
Research Council, 2007), p. 214.

Data on **land reform**: Carolyn Dempster, "Eyewitness: Evicted and Homeless,"
BBC News Africa, July 12, 2001, at http://news.bbc.co.uk/1/hi/world/
africa/1436069.stm.

On **ANC AIDS policy**: Helen Schneider and Didier Fassin, "Denial and
Defiance: A Socio-Political Analysis of AIDS in South Africa," Centre for Health
Policy, University of Witwatersrand, Johannesburg, South Africa, 2002. See also
Jon Jeter, "Free of Apartheid, Divided by Disease: S. Africa's Response to AIDS,"
Washington Post, July 6, 2000.

5. Neoliberal Negroes: Chicago and Democracy

Quotations and other details are taken from interviews and reporting I conducted in Chicago and Washington, D.C., from June 2006 to June 2008.

On the **history of the Congressional Black Caucus**: Congressional Black Caucus Foundation, Inc., "Origins and History of the Congressional Black Caucus," at www.cbcfinc.org/About/CBC/index.html.

On the **history of the Barton-Rush bill**: Leutisha Stills, "The Good, Bad and Ugly of the Congressional Black Caucus," *Black Agenda Report*, fall 2006, at www .blackagendareport.com/001/001c_CBC-Monitor_fall_2006.html.

Text of **Rodney Smith's speech at CBC**: Personal communication from Claudia Jones, AT&T Public Affairs.

On the **history of Englewood**: Maria Lettiere Roberts and Richard Stamz, *Chicago's Englewood Neighborhood: At the Junction (Images of America)* (Chicago: Arcadia, 2002).

On **wages, salaries, and profits as a share of GDP**: Aviva Aron-Divo and Isaac Shapiro, "Share of National Income Going to Wages and Salaries at Record Low in 2006; Share of Income Going to Corporate Profits at Record High," Center for Budget and Policy Priorities, March 29, 2007, at www.cbpp.org.

On **President Salinas's role in NAFTA**: Jeff Faux, *The Global Class War: How America's Bipartisan Elite Lost Our Future—And What It Will Take to Win It Back* (New York: Wiley, 2006), pp. 24–27.

Data on **campaign financing**: Center for Responsive Politics, annual reports by candidates and donors, at www.OpenSecrets.org; and Campaign Finance Institute, annual reports by candidates and donors, at www.cfinst.org.

On **trade rules**: Dean Baker Beat the Press (blog), *The American Prospect*, various citations including http://www.prospect.org/csnc/blogs/beat_the_press_archive?month=10&year=2008&base_name=is_paulson_planning_a_last_min.

Figures on **Barton-Rush spending**: Martin H. Bosworth, "Congress Moves Quickly to Satisfy Telecom Demands," *Consumer Affairs*, June 10, 2006, at www .consumeraffairs.com.

On **Rush's relationship with Big Telecom**: Lynn Sweet, "Critics Blast SBC-Rush Relationship," *Chicago Sun-Times*, April 25, 2006.

On the **CBC report card**: *CBC Monitor*, annual reports, at www.cbcmonitoronline .org.

On **Obama's voting record**: Matt Gonzalez, "Count Me Out: The Obama Craze," *CounterPunch*, February 29, 2008, at www.counterpunch.org/gonzalez02292008.html.

On the **construction of the Washington, D.C., baseball stadium**: David Zirin, *What's My Name, Fool? Sports and Resistance in the United States* (Chicago: Haymarket, 2005).

On **Chicago's living wage ordinance**: "Mayor Vetoes Chicago Living Wage Ordinance Aimed at Big Retailers," *USA Today*, September 11, 2006.

On **ComEd's links to Chicago political figures**: David McKinney, Chris Fusco, and Carol Marin, "Joneses Plugged In to Power," *Chicago Sun-Times*, May 3, 2007.

On **electricity cutoffs**: "6 Children Killed in Chicago Apartment Fire," Associated Press, September 4, 2006.

Data on **relationship between African Americans and unions**: AFL-CIO, "African American Workers Want to Form Unions," at www.aflcio.org/mediacenter/resources/workers.cfm.

Quotations by Rush: Don Wycliff, "Soul Survivor," *Chicago Tribune*, November 16, 2003.

Story of **Rush and the Black Panthers**: Salim Muwakil, "The Battle for Fred Hampton Way," *In These Times*, March 31, 2006.

On the **history of Englewood**: Chanel Polk and Mick Dumke, "A Brief History of Englewood," *Chicago Reporter*, 2006, at www.chicagoreporter.com/index.php/c/Sidebars/d/A_Brief_History_of_Englewood.

6. Deals with the Devil and Other Reasons to Riot: Malawi, Mexico, and Food

Quotations and other details are taken from interviews and reporting I conducted in Malawi in May 2002, Mexico in March 2007 (interpretation by Ricardo Guzman), other locations in sub-Saharan Africa between May 1999 and November 2002, and other locations in Latin America between January 2003 and May 2004.

Data on **Spam**: "Spam Sales Rise as Consumers Trim Food Costs," Associated Press, May 28, 2008.

Data on **food costs and crop production**: Joachim von Braun, "High and Rising Food Prices," International Food Policy Research Institute, April 11, 2008.

On **Australian growers**: Keith Bradsher, "As Australia Dries, a Global Shortage of Rice," *International Herald Tribune*, April 17, 2008.

On **Argentina's export experience**: Larry Rohter, "Once Secure, Argentines Now Lack Food and Hope," *New York Times*, March 2, 2003.

Figures on **crop investment**: Jeffrey Sachs, "Save Africa from America," TomPaine.Com, at www.tompaine.com/articles/2005/06/22/save_africa_from_america.php.

On the history of **Hastings Banda and Malawi's agricultural policy**: "Malawi's Leader Inspects Crops and Finds It Good," *New York Times*, March 8, 1987.

On **Malawian agriculture since 2005**: "Can It Feed Itself?" *Economist*, May 1, 2008, at www.economist.com/world/africa/displaystory.cfm?story_id=11294760.

Examples of **international responses to the food crisis**: International Food

Policy Research Institute, "High Food Prices: The What, Who, and How of Proposed Policy Actions," at www.ifpri.org.

On **diminishing investment in rice production**: Blaine Harden, "Philippines Caught in Rice Squeeze," *Washington Post*, April 12, 2008.

On **Africa's resistance to genetically modified crops**: Jenny Clover, "Situation Report: Genetically Modified Foods in the African Context: Behind the Smokescreen of the Current Debate," Institute of Security Studies, October 2002. See also Robert L. Paarlberg, "The Global Food Fight," *Foreign Affairs*, May/June 2000.

Data on **rising food costs, consumer response**: Nicole Colson, "Tightening a Belt with No Notches Left," *Socialist Worker*, 2008.

Data on **obesity and the corn subsidy**: Michael Pollan, "In Defense of Food," *Democracy Now*, February 13, 2008, at www.democracynow.org/2008/2/13/in_defense_of_food_author_journalist.

Figures on **Mexican wages**: Laura Carlsen, "No Rest for Working Poor," *CounterPunch*, June 12, 2008.

Story of **Mexico's small farmers**: Michael Pollan, "A Flood of U.S. Corn Rips Mexico," *Los Angeles Times*, April 23, 2004.

7. The Plan: Washington, D.C., and Housing

Quotations and other details are taken from interviews and reporting I conducted in Washington, D.C., in January 2008.

Data on **child poverty rates**: Fact sheet, Campaign for U.S. Ratification of the Convention for the Rights of the Child, 2007, at www.childrightscampaign.org.

Data on **D.C. school funding**: Zein El-Amine and Lee Glazer, "The Evolution of Public Education: A Critical Look at Washington DC Charter Schools," white paper commissioned by Open Society Institute, March 28, 2007, at www.tilsonfunds.com/personal/KeepingthePromiseWhitePapers.pdf.

On the **community's response to school closings**: V. Dion Hayes and Michael Ruane, "Parents Slam School Plan at Hearings," *Washington Post*, January 18, 2008.

List of D.C. properties sold: Empower DC, List of Lost or Threatened Public Property, at www.empowerdc.org.

Figures on **D.C. real estate market**: Paul Schwartzman and Robert E. Pierre, "From Ruins to Rebirth," *Washington Post*, April 6, 2008.

Figures on **rising home prices**: The Washington Region Housing Market 2007, The 15th Annual George Mason University Economic Conference, www.cra-gmu.org/forecastreports/2007%20Housing%20Market%20Forecast.pdf.

Figures on **rising D.C. property taxes**: Robert E. Pierre, "Straining in the Stadium's Shadow: Soaring Taxes Put Youth Agency, Others in SE at Risk," *Washington Post*, March 26, 2008.

Numbers on the **changing racial makeup of D.C., U.S.A.**: U.S. Census Bureau, annual tables, 2007, at www.census.gov.

Data on the **U.S. housing bubble**: Dean Baker, "The Housing Bubble Fact Sheet," Center for Economic Policy Research, July 2005, at www.cepr.net.

Assessment of depth of economic slowdown: Lawrence Summers, "Wake Up to the Dangers of a Deepening Crisis," *Financial Times*, November 25, 2007.

Assessment of recession: Nouriel Roubini, "Risk of U.S. Recession and Implications for Financial Markets," January 9, 2008.

Figures on **evictions**: Damien Cave, "In South Florida, Evictions Spare Few," *New York Times*, June 4, 2008.

Figures on **falling housing sales**: James Hagerty and Kelly Evans, "Pace of Decline in Home Prices Sets a Record," *Wall Street Journal*, December 27, 2007.

History of the **Glass-Steagall Act**: Robert Kuttner, "The Bubble Economy," *American Prospect*, September 24, 2007, at www.prospect.org.

Figures on **D.C. charter schools, legislative history**: El-Amine and Glazer, "The Evolution of Public Education."

Story of the **St. Louis protest**: Don Fitz and Zaki Baruti, "St. Louis Mayor Booed Off the Stage," *CounterPunch*, January 31, 2008, at www.counterpunch.org.

On **searches by New York City Police Department**: Sewell Chan, "Police Stop-and-Frisk Encounters Soar," *New York Times*, May 6, 2008.

On the **Atlanta transit system**: Bruce Dixon, "Atlanta's Answer to America's Urban Transit Apartheid," *Black Agenda Report*, May 14, 2008, at www.blackagendareport.com.

On **D.C. checkpoints**: Sarah Abruzzese, "After Checkpoints, Gratitude and Deep Skepticism," *New York Times*, June 18, 2008.

On **Chicago TIF**: Ben Joravsky, "Can You Spot the Blight?" *Chicago Reader*, June 9, 2006, at www.chicagoreader.com.

On the **Oakland shooting**: Jim Herron Zamora, "A Neighborhood Reborn," *San Francisco Chronicle*, February 18, 2006.

Figures on **homicides**: Candace Rondeaux, "Homicide Rate Soars in Year's First Quarter," *Washington Post*, April 25, 2007.

8. Things Fall Apart: Chicago and Family

Quotations and other details are taken from interviews and reporting I conducted in Chicago between January 2006 and December 2007.

Figures on the **racial income gap**: Jared Bernstein, "Weaker Job Market Reopens Racial Income Gap," Economic Policy Institute, at www.epi.org/content.cfm/webfeatures_snapshots_200607.

Figures on **outcomes of children from single-parent households**: U.S.

Department of Health and Human Services, "Benefits of Healthy Marriages for Children and Youth," at www.acf.hhs.gov/healthymarriagebenfits/index.html.

On **worldwide marriage rates**: United Nations Department of Economic and Social Affairs, World Fertility and Marriage Database, at www.un.org.esa.

Figures on **loss of manufacturing jobs**: AFL-CIO, "Jobs Crisis in America," at www.aflcio.org/issues/jobseconomy/jobs/jobcrisis.

On the **trade deficit**: U.S. Census Bureau, foreign trade statistics, published periodically at www.census.gov/foreign-trade/www.

Figures on **federal education spending**: U.S. Congressional Budget Office, "Spending for Research and Development for Education," at www.cbo.gov.

Figures on **Illinois disparities in education spending**: "Funding Gaps," *Education Week,* January 5, 2006, at www.edweek.org.

On the study of **Chicago high school freshmen**: Jodi S. Cohen and Darnell Little, "Of 100 Chicago Public School Freshmen, 6 Will Get College Degree," *Chicago Tribune,* April 21, 2006.

On the **dearth of black men**: Salim Muwakkil, "Black Men Missing," *In These Times,* June 16, 2005.

On **inequality**: Eric D. Gould and M. Daniele Paserman, "Waiting for Mr. Right: Rising Inequality and Declining Marriage Rates," *Journal of Urban Economics,* 2003.

On **rates of intermarriage**: U.S. Census Bureau, "Race of Wife by Race of Husband," June 10, 1998, at www.census.gov.

9. Sí; Cago; Voy: Chile, Venezuela, and Hope for the Future

Quotations and other details are taken from interviews and reporting I conducted in Chile in December 2003 and January 2004 (interpretation by Pascale Bonnefoy).

On the **history and impact of Chile's salmon industry**: World Bank, "Chilean Salmon Exports," Technology and Growth Series no. 103, October 2005, at www1 .worldbank.org/prem/PREMNotes/premnote103.pdf.

Quote from Condoleezza Rice: Larry Rohter, "Chile Inagurates First Woman to Serve as Its President," *New York Times,* March 11, 2007.

On **growth rates in Latin American since 1990**: United Nations Economic Commission for Latin America and the Caribbean, "Social Panorama of Latin America, 2007/2008," at www.eclac.cl.

Figures on the **Chilean economy, 1973–2000**: Ricardo Ffrench-Davis, *Economic Reforms in Chile: From Dictatorship to Democracy* (Ann Arbor: University of Michigan Press, 2002). See also Ricardo Ffrench-Davis, *Reforming the Reforms in Latin America* (London: Macmillan/Palgrave, 2000).

Story of the **caracazo**: Carlos Alvarez, "Mass Uprising Against Neo-Liberalism Opened New Era in Venezuela," *Socialism and Liberation*, 2007; Hugo Chávez, speech to the twelfth G-15 summit, March 1, 2004.

On **Latin American growth rates since 2004**: "Social Panorama of Latin America."

On the **Venezuelan economy under Chávez**: Mark Weisbrot and Luis Sandoval, "The Venezuelan Economy in the Chávez Years," Center for Economic Policy Research, 2008, at www.cepr.net.

On **schools and health care**: Center for Economic Policy Research, "Social Spending in Venezuela 1990–2005," at www.cepr.net/index.php/venezuela.

INDEX

adjustable rate mortgages (ARMs), 147

Africa, xvi–xvii, xviii, 9–10, 128–31, 154

agriculture in, 16, 19–20, 126–27, 128–29

colonization of, xviii, xix, 6, 8, 10, 14–16, 87–91, 129, 131

deindustrialization in, xiii, xiv, 5–8, 9–11, 13–14, 17–19, 22, 165

educational system in, 16, 17, 22

foreign imports in, 6–8, 18–19

health care in, 16, 22

industrial development in, 15–16

natural resources of, 15, 87

per capita income in, xii, 9

poverty and hunger in, 4, 5, 9, 10, 11, 12, 13, 18, 20, 21–24, 63, 124–27

racial economic and educational disparities in, 14, 16

slaves from, xxi–xxii, 40, 58, 64, 149, 202, 203

socialist and centralized economies in, 16–17, 20, 22

unemployment in, 4, 5, 6, 7, 10–11, 18–19

see also blacks; *specific countries or regions*

African Americans, xxi–xxii, 38, 41, 56, 64, 99–123, 143, 145

displacement from U.S cities of, 142, 143–45, 148–49, 154, 155, 156–58, 159–60

gender disparities among, 166, 167–68, 176, 177, 179

interracial dating and marriages of, 168, 179–80

liberal voting bloc of, 108, 112–13

marriage rates among, xiv–xv, 161–80, 181–82

northern migration of, 44, 164

"The Plan" conspiracy theory among, 149–50, 156–57, 158, 159–60

police harassment of, 158–59

political and socioeconomic elite of, 99–114, 115, 116–18, 119–21, 122–23, 150, 154–55

race relations and economic disparities of, 41, 64, 66, 113–14, 121, 144, 149–50, 154, 158–59, 163

self-reliance principle and, 114–15

unemployment and, 103, 114, 115, 121–22, 164–65, 266–67

urban schools in, 103, 104, 141, 150, 163, 166, 180–81

see also women, black

African National Congress (ANC), 75, 76, 78, 82, 83, 85, 91–94, 114

Africa Rice Center, 131

Afrikaners, 87–90

agriculture industry, 126–32

in Africa, 15–16, 17, 19–20, 126–27, 128–31

in Argentina, 36, 128, 131

agriculture industry (*continued*)
free trade and, xiii, 17, 19–20, 126–29, 130–32, 134, 136–38
genetically modified foods in, 132
government spending and, 16, 17, 36, 90, 127, 128–32
in Malawi, 129–30, 131
in Mexico, 136–39
research programs in, 131–32
in South Africa, 90
U.S. corn subsidy in, 134–39
airline industry, 91–92, 192–93
alcohol, alcoholism, 30, 38, 71, 163, 166, 174
Allende, Salvador, 185, 188, 189, 190, 195, 199, 202
Almonacid, Jorge and Jose, 183–84
American Chemical Association, 135
American Water Works, Inc., 79
Amnesty International, 65
Andrews, T. Coleman, III, 91–92
Angola, 87
Annual Legislative Conference, 99–100, 102–3
Anthony (Sonia's boyfriend), 162, 170–71, 172–79, 180, 181–82
apartheid, xv, 64, 76, 78, 81, 82, 83, 84, 86, 89, 90–91, 92, 93, 94, 95
Araujo, Ana Maria, 200
Archer Daniels Midland, 132
Arevalo, Luciano, 71–72
Argentina, xix, xxi, 20, 25–34, 35–51, 90, 105, 188, 193
agriculture industry in, 36, 128, 131
black minority in, 28, 40–41
crime rate increase in, 37–38
currency devaluation in, 29, 33
current economic recovery of, 37, 63, 198
deindustrialization in, xiii, xiv, 27–28, 44, 45
divorce rates in, 38–40, 42
education in, 17, 38
exchange rates in, 27, 31–32, 33, 44, 186, 189
food crisis in, 128, 131
foreign imports in, 27, 32
foreign loans taken out by, 33, 193
GDP of, 36, 193
immigration into, 28, 29, 40, 44
los cartoneros ("box men") of, 26–27, 28, 45–49, 50

monetary policy in, 27, 29, 31–32, 33–34, 36–37, 44, 186, 189
post–WWII prosperity in, 27, 35–36
poverty rates in, 36, 37, 45, 187
privatization of utilities in, 45, 80
prostitution in, 25–26, 27, 28–31, 42–44, 49–51
slums of, 38, 40–42, 44, 105
trade deficit of, 33
unemployment in, xiv, 27–28, 30, 36, 37, 38, 39, 41–42, 45, 193
Asia, 18, 128, 131–32, 154
AT&T, 100, 101, 102, 107
Atlanta, Ga., 145, 155, 157
Atlanta Community Food Bank, 133
Australia, 87, 127–28
automobile industry, xiv, xxii, 27, 36, 137–38, 189

Bachelet, Michelle, 184, 185, 192
Bahia, 67–68
Baker, Dean, 106–7
Baltimore, Md., 41, 80
Banda, Hastings, 129
bankruptcy laws, 108
banks, banking industry, xix, 33, 108, 189
in Argentina, 32, 33
in Brazil, 53–54, 55, 56–57
in Chile, 33, 186, 189, 190
expensive loans in, xix, 53–54, 55, 56–57
hiking of interest rates in, 53–54, 55, 56–57
in U.S. financial and mortgage crisis, 34, 35, 57, 145–47, 151–52
U.S.'s deregulation of, 34, 35, 57, 146, 151
U.S.'s 2008 bailout bill for, xii, xv, xviii, 110–11
see also central banks
Barra da Tijuca Beach, 52, 55
Barrios Andres, Marcelo, 191
Barry, Marion, 150
Barton, Joe, 101
Barton-Rush bill, 101–2, 107–8, 119
Baskin, Hal, 121–23
Bay Area Center for Voting Research, 112–13
Belgian Congo, xx, 16
Bender, Dionne, 122
Benin, 131
Berret Elementary, 143
Berret School Lofts, 143

biofuels, 128, 138
Bispo, Catia Helena, 68
Black Panther Party, 100, 115–16, 117–18, 194
blacks:
  in Africa, xvii, 9, 14, 16, 87, 88–90
  apartheid and, xv, 64, 76, 83, 84, 90–91, 92, 93
  in Argentina, 28, 40–41
  in Brazil, 52, 58, 64–70, 73–74
  colonization of Africa and, 87, 88–90
  cultural contributions of, xxi–xxii, 40–41
  economic and educational disparities for, 14, 16, 41, 65, 66, 90–91, 144, 154
  slavery and, xxi–xxii, 40, 58, 64, 87, 149
  South Africa and impoverishment of, xv, 76, 83, 84, 90–91, 113–14
  Venezuela's Bolivian Revolution and, 200, 201–2
  see also African Americans; racial disparities; women, black
Boers, 89
Bolívar, Simón, 197, 202
Bolivia, 80, 120, 186, 197, 198, 202
Bolling, Bill, 133
Bond, Patrick, 81–82
bonds, 45, 53, 54, 56, 193
Brazil, xiv, xx, xxiv, 20, 40, 52–74, 105, 135, 186, 193, 196, 197, 198, 202
  blacks in, 52, 58, 64–70, 73–74
  credit crunch in, 54, 56, 57
  crime and law enforcement in, 60, 65–66, 73
  debt and, 54, 56, 64, 67, 70
  education issues in, xiv, 54, 57, 61–62, 65, 66
  fixing of currency value in, xix, 63, 186, 189
  GDP of, 53, 54, 69, 193
  government regulations in, 186
  health care in, 57, 62
  high interest rates and, xiv, 53–57
  land reform programs in, 70–71
  1960s–80s era of economic growth in, 62–63
  per capita income in, 62, 63, 69
  privatization of utilities in, 80
  race relations in, 64–72, 73–74
  religion and culture in, 52–53, 54–55, 57, 74
  slums in, 55, 57, 58, 60, 65–66, 67, 105

social mobility in, 55, 63–64
sterilization efforts in, 67–70
tribal reservations in, 67–68, 71–72
unemployment in, xiii, xiv, 53, 57, 62, 65, 71, 164, 187
wealth inequality in, 55, 63, 64, 70, 164, 199
British South Africa Company, 14
British West Indies, 64
Brooklyn, N.Y., 157–58
brown plant hoppers, 131–32
Buenos Aires, xiv, 25–32, 33, 36, 39
  Constitution neighborhood in, 20, 27, 28–29, 30, 44, 50
  crime in, 37
  los cartoneros ("box men") in, 26–27, 28, 45–49, 50
  prostitution in, 25–26, 27, 28–31, 42–44, 49–51
  slums in, 38, 40–42, 44, 105
  unemployment in, 27–28, 30, 39, 41–42
Bureau of Labor Statistics, U.S., 165
Burkina Faso, 130
Burundi, 125
Buthelezi, James, 95–96

cable companies, 101, 102, 107
Calderón, Felipe, 198
California, 80, 138, 154
Cameroon, 130
campaign contributions, 104, 106, 107, 109
Canada, 91, 137
Cape Town, xiv, 79
Caracas, 195, 196–97, 200
caracazo (Venezuelan uprising), 195–97, 199
Cardoso, Fernando Henrique, 64–65
CARE, 22
Carter-Hill, Jean, 103–5, 118–19, 123
cartoneros ("box men"), 26–27, 28, 45–49, 50
cashews growers, xiii, 19–20, 128
Castro, Fidel, 188, 202
CBC Monitor, 117
Central African Traders Ltd., 18
central banks, 32, 33, 53–54, 186, 189
Charpentier, Jose Luis, 192, 195
charter schools, 118–19, 142, 151
  public schools vs., 148, 152–55
Chávez, Hugo, 110, 197, 198
  Bolívarian Revolution of, xx, 199–203

Chávez, Hugo (*continued*)
  vilification of, 110, 198, 201–2
Chicago, Ill., 101, 107, 111, 117–23, 145,
    157, 159, 160, 161, 162, 166, 174
  Black Panther chapter in, 100, 116,
    117–18
  City Council of, 111, 116–17, 121
  community redevelopment projects in,
    117, 120, 121–22, 155–57
  destabilization of relationships in, xiv–
    xv, 163–80, 181–82
  Englewood neighborhood of, 103–5,
    107, 111, 112, 114–15, 117, 118–19,
    120–23, 173
  lead contamination in, 103–5, 123
  power shutoffs in, 112
  unemployment in, 103, 114, 115, 121–22
Chicago, University of, 33, 109, 188
"Chicago Boys," 188, 190–91
Chicago Public Schools, 166
Chicago Tribune, 115–16
Chile, xviii, 183–95, 199, 200
  Allende's socialist government in, 185,
    188, 189, 190, 191, 195, 199
  deindustrialization in, 195
  economic growth in, xx–xxi, 33, 184–85,
    186–87, 191–95, 198
  education in, xxi, 186, 191
  exchange rates in, 32–33, 189, 190
  GDP of, 190, 193
  government regulations in, xxi, 185,
    186–87, 190, 191–94
  government spending in, xxi, 185, 186,
    187, 189, 190, 191, 193
  labor reforms in, 191–92, 195
  land reform in, 188, 189
  monetary policy in, 32–33, 185, 186–87,
    189, 190, 193, 195
  Pinochet's reign in, 31, 32–33, 185,
    188–91, 194, 195, 201
  poverty in, 187, 190
  privatization in, 189, 192
  salmon industry in, 183–85, 190, 195
  unemployment in, 33, 186, 187, 190
Chile Foundation, 185, 190
Chiluba, Frederick, 5, 7, 8, 17, 21
China, xiv, 33, 70, 128
cholera, 21, 77–78, 84, 85–87
Chrysler, xiv, xxii
Cibils, Alan, 33–34
Clark, Mark, 116

Cleveland, Ohio, 157
Clinton, Bill, 8, 34–35, 106, 120, 121, 137,
    151
Coca-Cola, 135, 163
coffee, 15–16, 64
Coleman, Shirley, 111
colleges, 16, 65, 66, 121, 166, 178–79
Colombia, 40, 110
colonialism, xvii–xx, 13, 63
  in Africa, xviii, xix, 6, 8, 10, 14–16,
    87–91, 129, 131
  in South Africa, 87–91
ComEd, 80, 111, 117
Communist Party, Communists, xix, 188,
    191, 202
Congo, 16, 18, 87
Congress, U.S., 8, 35, 107, 110, 115, 145, 146,
    149, 150, 153
Congressional Black Caucus (CBC), 99–100,
    102–3, 107–8, 112
Conyers, John, 117
copper, 15, 16–17, 19, 185, 192, 194
Cordon, Cecelia, 29, 30–31
corn, 126, 127, 128, 129, 132, 134–39
corporations, xi, xv, xix, 8, 115, 117, 119,
    152, 155, 186, 199
  campaign contributions of, 106, 107, 109
  government subsidies for, 108
  political influence of, xv, 93–94, 102–3,
    105–14, 118, 119, 122, 145–46, 148,
    149–50, 151, 154, 155–56, 192, 202
  tax breaks for, xix, 8
  see also privatization
corruption, xii, 9, 150, 188, 194
Cosby, Bill, 41, 123
cost recovery measures, 78, 80–82, 86–87
crack cocaine, 149
credit, 54, 56, 57, 110, 129, 151, 152, 168,
    176
credit cards, 109
credit unions, xix, 199
crime, xii, xiv, 18, 104, 150, 166, 188, 198
  in Argentina, 37–38
  in Brazil, 60, 65–66, 73
  racial disparities in law enforcement and,
    65–66, 158–59
  U.S. rates of, 150, 158, 159
Criolla, 70
Cuba, 28, 40, 109, 188, 202
currency, xix
  China and value of, 33

devaluing of, 29, 32, 33, 186–87, 193

fixing exchange rates of, xix, 27, 31–34, 44, 56, 186, 189, 190

Latin America and value of, xix, 27, 29, 32, 33, 63, 186–87, 189, 193

South Africa and value of, xix, 78, 96

D'Adamo, Orlando, 42

Daley, Richard M., 111, 155

Danielle (Sonia's friend), 169–70

Dan Ryan Expressway, 103, 114, 121

da Silva, Isabella Lopes, 53

death squads, 65

debt, xi, xix, 17, 32, 201

Brazil and, 54, 56, 64, 67, 70

of Chile government in 1980s, 189–90

cost recovery measures and, 81–82

in U.S. financial crisis, 34, 35, 57, 147

see also trade deficits

deindustrialization, xiii–xiv, xxiii, 6–11

in Africa, xiii, xiv, 5–8, 9–11, 13–14, 17–19, 22

in Argentina, 27–28, 45

in auto industry, xiv, 27

exchange rates and, 27–28, 189

job loss and, xiii–xiv, xxiii, 5, 6, 7, 10–11, 22, 27–28, 45, 164–65, 166–67

in Latin America, xiii, 27–28, 44, 45, 189, 195

in U.S., xiii–xiv, xxiii, 8, 103, 164–67

in Zambia, xiii, xiv, 5–8, 10–11, 17–19, 22

Delta Airlines, 192–93

Democratic Party, U.S., 94, 101, 106, 108, 112–13, 150, 154

DePaul University, 164, 169, 178

Depieri, Andrea, 71

deregulation, xvi, xix, 34, 80, 113, 186, 189, 196

class wars and tensions increased by, xv, 102–3, 113–14, 119–20, 196–97

corporations and elite as main benefactor of, xix, 13, 19–20, 101–3, 106–10, 111–12, 113–14, 119–20, 127, 128

telecommunication industry and, 101–2

of U.S. banking industry, 34, 35, 146, 151

in Venezuela, 196

see also free trade; government regulations; privatization

Detroit, Mich., xxiii, 113, 121

Dingane (Zulu chief), 88–89

divorce rates, 38–39

dollar, value of, 27, 34–35

Domingo, Oscar "Paulito," 42

Dominican Republic, 28

dot-com bubble, 147

dropout rates, 17, 38, 103, 104, 141, 163

drugs, 30, 38, 43, 60, 65, 71, 163, 166, 174, 202

for HIV infection, 93–94, 107, 198

Durbin, Dick, 122

duty-free shipments, 5, 7, 188

Dyson, Michael Eric, 111

East Asia, 18, 128, 131–32

Ebrahim, Jim, 18

economic sanctions, 94

education, xi, xix, xxii, 36, 70, 78, 90, 115, 168, 171

in Africa, 16, 17, 22

in Argentina, 36, 38

in Brazil, 54, 57, 61–62, 66

charter schools and, 118–19, 142, 148, 151, 152–55

Chile's spending on, xxi, 186, 191

in colleges or universities, 16, 65, 66, 121, 166

dropout rates in, 17, 38, 103, 104, 141, 163

fees and tuitions for, 17, 22, 62, 73, 120

gender disparities in, 166, 177, 179

government cutbacks on, xi, 17, 54, 57, 61, 62, 151, 153, 166

privatization and, 78, 142–43, 148, 152–55, 158

racial disparities in, 16, 41, 65, 66, 166

standardized tests in, 141, 180–81

in U.S. inner cities, 103, 104, 141, 150, 163, 166, 180–81

in Venezuela, 199, 200

in Washington, D.C., 140–43, 150, 151, 152–55

El-Amine, Zein, 153–54

electricity, privatization of, 78, 79, 80–82, 102

activist groups and, 75–76, 94–96

power shutoffs due to, xv, 75–76, 78–79, 80, 94–96, 112

rising prices due to, xii, xv, xix, 76, 80, 111, 127

in South Africa, xv, 76, 78–79, 80–82, 94–96, 112

electricity, privatization of (*continued*)
    in U.S., 80, 111–12
Embabe, 76–77
Empangeni, 76–77, 83–87
Englewood High School, 118–19
Englewood Political Task Force, 122–23
Eskom, 75, 76, 80–82, 94, 95
estate taxes, 108
ethanol, corn-based, 138
Ethiopia, 130
Europe, xiii, 13, 14, 16, 62, 128, 130, 188,
        197, 201, 202
    colonization of Africa by, xviii, xix, 6, 8,
        10, 14–16, 87–91, 129, 131
European Union, xii, 132
exchange rates, fixed:
    in Argentina, 27, 31–32, 33, 44, 186, 189
    in Brazil, xix, 186, 189
    in Chile, 32–33, 189, 190
    deindustrialization and, 27–28, 189
    inflation and, 27, 31–34, 56, 186, 189
export taxes, 19, 33, 131

factories, xxii, 3, 8, 15, 18, 36, 44, 84, 137,
        183–84, 195
    closing of, xiii–xiv, 5, 10–11, 18–19, 45,
        103
    textile, xiv, 5, 6–8, 10–11, 16, 18–19
favelas (Brazilian shantytowns), 57, 65–66,
        67, 105
Federal Bureau of Investigation (FBI),
        100, 116
Federal City Council, 149, 152–53
Federal Reserve, U.S., 144
feijoada, 58, 59
Fenty, Adrian, 142, 154–55
Financial Control Board, 150
food crisis, xii, 124–39
    in Africa, 12, 17, 124–27, 128–29, 130,
        132
    globalization and, 126–32, 134–39
    obesity epidemic and, 134–35
    price inflation in, xi, xii, 126, 127, 128,
        130, 133–34, 138
    underfunded agricultural research in,
        131–32
    in U.S., 125, 133–39
food stamps, 133
Ford, Harold, 117
Ford Motor Company, xiv, 137
foreclosures, xviii, 147

foreign loans, xix, 5, 17, 31, 82–83
    of Argentina, 33, 193
    of Brazil, 56, 63, 64
free trade, xx, 3, 5–10, 17–24, 63, 106–7,
        109, 134, 165–67, 188–91
    African deindustrialization due to, xiii,
        xiv, 5–8, 9–11, 17–20, 22, 165
    agriculture and, xiii, 17, 19–20, 126–27,
        128–29, 130–32, 134, 136–38
    Chile as model for, 184–87, 192–93, 198
    global food crisis and, 126–29, 130, 131,
        133, 134–35, 136–39
    importing of cheap foreign goods in, 6–8,
        18–19, 27, 134, 135, 136–37, 138,
        186, 189
    international movements against,
        195–99
    Latin American deindustrialization due
        to, xiii, 27–28, 189, 195
    in Mexico, 134, 136–39
    unemployment and, 5, 6, 7, 10–11, 18,
        19, 22, 27–28, 78, 165, 166–67, 190
    U.S. deindustrialization due to, xiii–xiv,
        8, 165–67
    see also globalization
Freitas, Jocelino, 66
French-Davis, Ricardo, 190, 191, 193, 194
Friedman, Milton, xv–xviii, 32–33, 153,
        185, 188

gasoline prices, xi, 108, 126, 196
Gatchell, Howard, 19
Gates, Bill, xx
gender disparities, 166, 167–68, 176, 177
General Motors, xiv, 137–38
genetically modified foods, 132
Georgia, 155
Ghana, 7, 87, 130–31
ghettos, U.S., xiii, xxii, xxiii, xxiv, 40–41,
        56, 105
    in Chicago's South Side, 101, 103–5,
        107, 111, 112, 114–15, 117, 118–19,
        120–23, 156–57, 164, 167, 169, 173,
        174
    education and public schools in, 103, 141,
        152–54, 163, 166
    lead contamination in, 103–5, 123, 141
    power shutoffs in, 80, 112
    redevelopment in, 117, 120, 121–22,
        142–45, 153–54, 155, 156–58,
        159–60

unemployment in, 103, 114, 115, 121–22, 164–65, 166–67
see also slums
ghost trains (*el tren phantasma*), 26, 28
Giddings Elementary School, 143
Glass-Steagall Act (1933), 151
globalization, xvi, xvii–xviii, xxii, 38, 106, 186, 188
    agriculture and, 17, 19–20
    Chile as model for managing of, xx–xxi, 184–87, 192–93, 198
    class wars and, xii, xv, 92–93, 95, 96, 103, 105, 113–14, 118, 119–20, 122–23, 148, 158–60, 188, 196–97, 201, 202
    colonialism vs., xviii–xx, 10
    corporate influence and, xi, xiii, xv, xix–xx, 15, 94–95, 102–3, 105–14, 119, 145–46, 148, 149–50, 151, 154, 155–56, 192, 202; *see also* privatization
    crime rates and, *see* crime
    curbing inflation as goal of, xix, 27, 31, 32–34, 56, 128, 138
    deindustrialization and job losses due to, xiii–xiv, xxiii, 4, 5–8, 9–11, 13–14, 17–19, 27–28, 45, 164–65, 166–67
    efforts to reverse, xx, 195–203
    female migration as spurred by, 44
    global food crisis and, *see* food crisis
    government spending curbed by, xi, xix, 9, 17, 54, 57, 61, 79, 83, 85, 127, 128–29, 137, 153, 166, 185, 186, 187, 196
    inequality gap and, xi, xii–xv, xix–xx, xxi, 37, 55, 63, 64, 70, 91, 105–6, 107, 113–14, 121, 127, 154, 164, 169, 186, 189, 195, 198
    monetary policy in, *see* monetary policy
    supportive views on, xv–xviii
    see also free trade; privatization
gold, 64, 89
Goldman Sachs, 35
gold standard, 32, 34
Google, 101, 102
Gore, Al, 94, 112
Gould, Eric, 167
government regulations, 106–7
    in Chile, xxi, 185, 186–87, 190, 191–94
    in labor law, xxi, 13, 106–7, 191–92, 195
    in telecommunication industry, 192–93
    Zambia's enforcement of, 16

    see also deregulation
government spending, xi, xix, 36, 54, 90
    on agriculture, 16, 36, 90, 127, 128–32
    benefits of increased domestic investment in, xxi, 9, 16, 36, 83, 85, 128–29, 185, 187, 190, 193
    in Chile, xxi, 185, 186, 187, 189, 190, 191, 193
    on education, xi, xxi, 17, 54, 57, 61, 62, 90, 141, 151, 153, 166, 186, 191, 199
    globalization and, xi, xix, 9, 17, 54, 57, 61, 79, 83, 85, 127, 128–29, 131, 137, 151, 166, 185, 186
    on health care, xxi, 16, 36, 57, 90, 186, 199–200
    in South Africa, 90
    uneven distribution of, 166
    in U.S., 108, 141, 151, 166
    in Venezuela, 186, 196, 199–200
    in Zambia, 16, 17
    see also subsidies, government
Gramm-Leach-Bliley Act, 151
grants, government, 117, 123
Great Britain, xvii, 17, 79, 80
    Africa colonized by, xviii, xix, 6, 8, 10, 14–16, 89–90, 129, 131
Great Depression, xi, 33, 189
Great Leap Forward, 70
Green, Ralph Waldo "Petey," 149
Greenspan, Alan, 144
gross domestic product (GDP), xxi, 42, 169
    of Argentina, 36, 193
    of Brazil, 53, 54, 69, 193
    of Chile, 190, 193
    of U.S., 106, 166
    of Zambia, 15
Guarani Indians, 68

Haiti, 28, 125, 130, 202
Hampton, Fred, 116, 117, 194
Harvard University, 41, 106, 147, 187
Harvey, David, xviii
Haselau, Peter, 85
Hassan, Yusuf, 118–19
health care, xi, xix, 90, 108, 111, 125, 154, 168
    in Argentina, 36
    in Brazil, 57, 62
    in Chile, xxi, 186, 191
    cholera outbreaks and, 85–86
    nationalization of, 16, 36, 90

health care (*continued*)
  rising prices in, xi, 94, 107
  South Africa's HIV epidemic and, 93–94,
     198
  Venezuela's expansion of, 199–200
  in Zambia, 16, 22
Hebrew University, 167
Hemson, David, 86–87
high-fructose corn syrup, 135
HIV epidemic, 86, 93–94, 198, 200
Hlatshwayo, Zakes, 93
Homestead Act (1862), U.S., 70
Hoover, J. Edgar, 100, 116
Hormel, 133
hotel industry, 55, 145, 156
  in Zambia, 3, 12–14
House of Representatives, U.S., 99, 101,
     107–8
housing, xi, 117, 120, 146–49, 154, 164, 173,
     190, 199
  evictions or foreclosures in, xviii, 78, 79,
     147, 155
  privatization of public land and, 78, 127,
     142–46, 148, 152, 153–54, 155–58,
     159–60
  property taxes and, 22, 144, 155–57
  rising prices in, xi, 144, 146–47, 157, 159
  U.S. mortgage crisis and, xiii, xviii, 34,
     35, 57, 111, 146–47, 151–52
  see also mortgages
Human Sciences Research Council (HRSC),
     86–87
hunger, xii, 124–26, 134
  in Africa, 4, 11, 12, 13, 20, 22, 23, 124–26
  in Latin America, 46, 190, 196
  see also food crisis; poverty
hyperinflation, 31

Iemanjá, 52, 53, 54–55, 57, 74
Illinois, 80, 101, 166
Imagine Englewood If, 104, 123
immigration, 28, 29, 40, 43, 44
import substitution, 16
import taxes, 5, 6–7, 8, 19, 130, 188
India, 20, 106
inequality gap, xi, xii–xv, xix–xx, xxi, 62,
     63, 105–6, 107, 127, 154, 164, 169
  in Latin America, 36, 37, 55, 63, 64, 65,
     70, 154, 164, 186, 189, 195, 198, 199
  race and, 14, 41, 65, 90–91, 113–14, 121,
     144, 154, 163

  in South Africa, 63, 90–91, 113, 114, 164,
     199
  in U.S., xii, xix–xx, 41, 63, 105–6, 107,
     113–14, 121, 144, 154, 163, 164, 169
inflation, xix, xxi, 32–34, 62, 63, 79, 113,
     128, 138, 199
  exchange rates and, 27, 31–34, 56, 186,
     189
  of food prices, 126, 127, 128, 130, 133–34,
     138
  interest rates and, 53–54, 56
  see also prices
*Inquiry into the Nature and Causes of the
     Wealth of Nations, An* (Smith), 5
interest rates, xviii, xix, 35, 78, 109, 147,
     164–65, 196
  Brazil's recession and high level of, xiv,
     53–57
International Monetary Fund (IMF), xiv,
     xx, 5, 8, 17, 27, 53, 56, 73, 129, 154,
     192, 195–96
International Rice Research Institute, 132
Internet, 101–2, 107–8, 119
interracial marriages, 168

Jackson, Jesse, 116, 119
Jackson, Jonathan, 119
Jakarta, 164
Japan, 62, 185
Jefferson, Thomas, 203
Johannesburg, xiv, 76, 82, 83, 89, 93, 94,
     96, 164
John S. Burroughs Elementary School,
     140–42, 145, 148, 159
Jones, Emil, 111, 112
Jones, Maria, 142, 145, 148, 159–60
JPMorgan Chase, 117
Juan Carlos I, King of Spain, 202

Kaiowá Indians, 71–72
Kaunda, Kenneth, 16–17, 20, 22
Kennedy, John F., 8
Kennedy King Community College, 121
Kenya, 87, 130, 131
Kerry, John, 112
Keynesian economics, xxi, 90, 128, 150
Kirchner, Cristina, 131
Kirchner, Néstor, 80
Kitwe, 18
KwaZulu-Natal province (South Africa),
     76–77, 85, 88–89

Labor Department, U.S., 165
labor laws, 13, 62, 106–7, 138, 186, 189, 191–92
labor unions, 8, 13, 79, 105, 106, 109, 116, 138, 151, 189, 195
Lagos, Ricardo, 192, 195
laissez-faire capitalism, 34
Landless People's Movement (MST), 71
land reform programs, xix, 57, 70
    in Brazil, 54, 70–71
    in Chile, 188, 189
    privatization as obstacle in, 92–93
    South Africa, 92–93
    in Venezuela, 199
Landry, Bart, 114
Latin America, 27, 33, 35, 40, 41, 154, 186, 189, 192, 197, 201
    currency devaluation in, 29, 33, 186, 193
    deindustrialization in, xiii, 27–28, 44, 45, 189, 195
    deregulation of foreign exchange in, 186, 189, 196
    economic growth in, 198
    efforts to reverse globalization in, xx, 186–87, 195–203
    exchange rates in, 27, 31–34, 186, 189, 190
    foreign imports in, 27, 32, 186, 189
    inequality gap in, 36, 37, 55, 63, 64, 65, 70, 154, 164, 186, 189, 195, 198, 199
    migration of women in, 28, 29, 43, 44
    per capita income in, xii, 62, 63, 69
    privatization in, 45, 79–80, 189, 192, 196, 197
    slavery in, 40, 58, 63, 64, 202
    unemployment in, xiii, xiv, 27–28, 33, 36, 37, 38, 39, 41–42, 45, 53, 57, 65, 71, 186, 187, 190, 193
    see also specific countries
Latinos, 56, 148, 158, 159, 179
Lawrence (Sonia's brief suitor), 169–70, 171–72, 178
lead contamination, 103–5, 123, 141
Lebanon, 110
Lesotho, 82
Lesotho Highlands Water Project, 82–83
Liberia, 130
Lilongwe, 124–25
literacy rates, 16
Livingstone, David, 14
Livingstone, Zambia, 3, 5, 14, 18

Ljubetic, Yerko, 192
loans, 90, 110, 117, 131
    deregulation and, 35, 57, 146–47, 151–52
    foreign, *see* foreign loans
    high interest rates on, xix, 35, 53–54, 55, 56–57, 147
    of relief agencies, 21–22
    see also mortgages
lobbyists, 100, 102, 109, 112
Lopez, Artemio, 42
Los Angeles, Calif., 38, 41, 167
Loyola University, 155–56
Lubisi, Bongani, 95
Lufuzi, Lucas, 124–26
Lula da Silva, Luiz, 54, 57, 64, 73, 198
    land reform efforts of, 70–71
Lusaka, xiv, 18

McCullough, Patrick, 158
Machado, Jonathan, 45, 47
Machado, Lucas, 45–46, 47
Machado, Maria, 47
Machado, Mario, 26–27, 47
Machado, Miguel, 26–27, 28, 45–47, 48–49
Machado, Romina, 47–48
McHenry, Melvin, 158
Madlebe tribe, 84
"maize meal," 12, 21, 22–23, 24
malaria, 21, 22
Malawi, 20, 124–26, 127, 132
    farming policy in, 129–30, 131
malnutrition, 71, 125, 126, 128
Mandela, Nelson, 78, 85
maquiladoras, 137
Maramba market, 3–5, 9, 10–12, 18, 20–24
Maroga, Jacob, 80–81
marriage rates, xiv–xv, 39, 164, 167, 168–69
Maryland, xxiii, 133, 159
Massachusetts, 154
mate, 46, 48
Mato Grosso do Sul, 71–72
Mbeki, Thabo, 85, 93–94, 113–14
Menem, Carlos, 36–37, 38, 45
Mentor Building, 156
Merrill Lynch, 147
Mexico, 106, 130, 134, 136–39, 193, 197, 198
Mhiyne, Nomsa, 84
Middle East, 109, 160
minimum wage, xxi, 138, 186, 189, 192
mining industry, 14, 84, 93, 109

M'membe, Fred, 10, 14–15, 20
Mohapi, Agnes, 75–76, 94–95
Moiloa, Sam, 83
monetary policy, 31–35, 78, 193
    in Argentina, 27, 29, 31–32, 33–34,
        36–37, 44, 186, 189
    in Brazil, xiv, xix, 53–57, 63, 186, 189
    in Chile, 32–33, 185, 186–87, 189, 190,
        193, 195
    deindustrialization due to, 27–28, 164–
        65, 189
    devaluation of currency in, 29, 33, 186–
        87
    fixing of exchange rates in, 27, 31–34,
        44, 56, 63, 186, 189, 190
    inflation and, xix, 27, 31, 32–34, 53–54,
        186, 189
    unemployment and, 27–28, 33, 37, 53,
        56, 57, 164–65, 187, 190
    in U.S., 34–35, 164–65
Monsanto, 132
Moore, Valerie Leonard, 156–57
Morales, Evo, 198, 202
Morro do Borel (Brazilian slum), 65–66
Mortgage Bankers Association, 147
mortgages, xviii
    adjustable rate (ARMs), 147
    bad debt in, 34
    subprime, xix, 146, 147
    U.S. housing crisis and, xviii, 34, 35, 57,
        146–47, 151–52
Motau, Shadrack, 96
Mozambique, xiii, 19–20, 128
Mthembu, Metolina, 76–77, 86
Muller, Mike, 83
Murray, Albert, xxi–xxii
Mutharika, Bingu wa, 129

Namakube, Judith, 11–12
Namibia, 91, 195
National Association for the Advancement
    of Colored People (NAACP), 125
Nationalist Party (Afrikaner), 89–90
Ndola, 19
New Deal, 35, 151, 188
New Orleans, La., 145, 155
Newton, Huey, 100
New York, N.Y., 145, 148, 157–59, 160,
    194, 197
New York Times, 106–7
Nicaragua, 79–80

Nigeria, 52, 130
9/11 terrorist attacks, 194
Nixon, Richard, 34
Nixon administration, 134, 135, 198
Nkosi, Victor, 92
North American Free Trade Agreement
    (NAFTA), 8, 106, 107, 109, 137,
    138, 139
nshima, 12, 13, 23

Oakland, Calif., xiv, 41, 142, 145, 157, 158,
    159
Obama, Barack, 101, 104, 108–11, 112, 115,
    117, 120–21
obesity, 134–35
O'Donnel, Mark, 18
Offord, Phyllis, 117–18
oil, 17, 108, 126, 198, 199, 202
Ojeda, Jose, 45–46
Oman, 109
Operation Breadbasket, 116
Operation Khanyisa, 94
    see also Soweto Electricity Crisis
        Committee
Ozuna, Sylvia, 25–26, 28–31, 42–44, 49–51

Palestine, Palestinians, 110, 160
Panama, 198
Parades, Ricardo, 192
Paraguay, 28, 29, 40, 45, 50
pardo (mixed-race), 64, 66
Paserman, Daniele, 167
Patagonia Salmon Farming, 183–84, 192,
    195
Patel, Ramesh, 19
patent rights, international, 94, 107, 132
Patterson, Orlando, 41
Paulson, Henry, 35, 110
PDVSA, 196, 199
Pedro I, emperor of Brazil, 64
Pepsi, 135
Peralta, Lorena, 39–40
per capita income, 168–69
    in Latin America, xii, 62, 63, 69
    in South Africa, 78
    in sub-Saharan Africa, xii, 9
Pérez, Carlos Andrés, 195–96, 197, 200
Perón, Juan, 36, 37, 90
Peru, 28, 80
peso, value of, 27, 29, 32, 33, 44, 187, 189,
    190

pharmaceutical companies, 94, 107
Philadelphia, Pa., 155, 157
Phillips, Kevin, 113
Pinochet, Augusto, 31, 32–33, 185, 188–91, 194, 195, 201
police, 38, 44, 71, 116, 121, 191, 197
    race and treatment by, 65–66, 158–59
Pollan, Michael, 137
pollution, 108
Port-au-Prince, 164
Portugal, 63
poverty, vii, xii, xiv, xxiv, 62, 70, 117, 159, 166, 203
    in Africa, 4, 5, 9, 10, 11, 13, 18, 20, 21–24, 63, 124–26, 127
    and African American displacement, 142, 143–45, 148–49, 154, 155, 156–58, 159–60
    African American elite and, 101–2, 103, 105, 107, 108–14, 115, 118, 119–20, 122–23, 150
    apartheid and, 90–91
    in Argentina, 26–31, 36, 37, 38, 41–42, 45, 46–49, 50, 187, 188
    in Brazil, 55–57, 60–62, 63–64, 67–72
    Chile's rates of, 187, 190
    cost recovery programs and, 80–82
    food inflation and, 125–29, 132, 133–34, 136, 138
    HIV epidemic and, 93–94, 198
    land reform and, xix, 54, 70–71, 92–93, 188, 199
    misconceptions on causes of, 9, 41, 70, 110, 123
    obesity epidemic and, 134–35
    privatization and, xv, 75–76, 78–79, 80, 84–87, 112
    relief agencies and, 21–22, 75, 76, 79, 94–96, 125, 133
    social mobility and, 55, 63–64
    in South Africa, 75–79, 90–91, 92–96, 112, 198
    sterilization efforts and, 67–70, 94
    on tribal reservations, 67, 71–72
    uneven distribution of wealth and, xi, xii–xv, xix–xx, xxi, 37, 63, 64, 70
    in Venezuela, 196, 199, 200
    in Washington, D.C., 141
    see also ghettos, U.S.; slums; unemployment
prices, 27, 196

copper, 16–17
    cost recovery measures and, 80–82
    of food, xi, xii, 126, 127, 128, 130, 133–34, 138
    in health care and medicine, xi, 94, 107
    housing and real estate rises in, xi, 144, 146–47, 157, 159
    lowering of, 189, 192
    of oil or gasoline, xi, 17, 108, 126, 196, 198, 199
    see also inflation
Prieto, Fatima, 42
Prince George's County, Md., 159, 160
private schools, 66, 73, 153
privatization, 75–96
    African American displacement and, 142, 143–45, 148–49, 154, 155, 156–58, 159–60
    in airline industry, 91–92
    anti-AIDS drugs availability impeded by, 93–94
    cholera outbreaks due to, 77–78, 84, 85–87
    class tensions increased by, 92–93, 95, 96, 148, 158–60, 196, 197
    colonization and, 89
    corporations and wealthy elite as benefactors of, 80, 81, 82–83, 94, 111, 119, 145–46, 148, 149–50, 151, 154, 155–56
    cost recovery measures and, 78, 80–82, 86–87
    crime increases and militarism of police due to, 158–59
    education and, 78, 142–43, 148, 152–55, 158; see also charter schools
    of housing and public land, 142–46, 148, 151, 152, 153–54, 155–58, 159
    land redistribution efforts and, 93–94
    in Latin America, 45, 79–80, 189, 192, 196, 197
    rising prices caused by, xii, xv, xix, 76, 77, 79–80, 82–83, 111, 127, 144, 146–47, 157
    in South Africa, xv, 75–79, 80–87, 91–96, 112
    of telecommunication companies, 78, 79
    in U.S., 79, 80, 111–12, 142–46, 148–49, 151, 152–60
    of utilities, see utilities, privatization of
property rights, 88, 89, 92, 113

property taxes, 22, 144, 155–57, 166
prostitution, xiv, 18, 71, 198
  in Argentina, 25–26, 27, 28–31, 42–44, 49–51
public schools, xix, xxii, 22, 78, 108, 199
  in Brazil, xiv, 57, 61–62, 66
  in conversion into charter schools, 118–19, 142, 148, 151, 152–55
  fees and tuitions for, 17, 22, 120
  lead contamination in, 104–5, 141
  privatization and, 142–43, 148, 152–54, 158
  in U.S. inner cities, 104–5, 141, 150, 151, 152–54, 163, 166, 180–81
  in Washington, D.C., 140–43, 145, 148, 150, 151, 152–54
  see also education
Puerto Montt, 183–84, 195

Quinones, Antonio, 136–39
Quintana, Carmen Gloria, 191

racial disparities:
  in Africa, 14, 16
  in Brazil, 64–72, 73–74
  in education, 16, 41, 65, 66, 166
  in employment and economic earnings, 14, 41, 65, 73–74, 90–91, 114, 121, 144, 163
  in law enforcement and police treatment, 65–66, 158–59
  in South Africa, 90–91, 113–14
  in U.S., 41, 66, 113–14, 121, 144, 154, 158–59, 163, 166
  in voting tendencies, 112–13
Reagan, Ronald, 34, 115, 164–65, 188
Rebirth Englewood, 117
recessions, economic, 45, 165, 193
  in Brazil, 53–57
  in Chile, 189, 190–91
regressive taxes, 151, 196
Reinert, Erik, 8–9
relief agencies, 21–22, 125, 133
Republican Party, U.S., 108, 112, 113
Retief, Pieter, 88–89
Rhodes, Anita, 133–34
Rhodes, Cecil, 14, 15
Rhodesia, xvii, xix
rice, 127, 130–32, 133
Rice, Condoleezza, 118, 184
Riesco, Manuel, 187

Rio de Janeiro, xxiv, 52–53, 55, 57, 58, 60, 65
riots, 92–93, 103, 143, 144, 149
  food crisis and, 126, 130
  in Venezuela, 195–97, 199
Robaldo, Herbert, 39–40
Roberto, Alaide, 58, 60, 72–73
Roberto, Aline, 62, 73–74
Roberto, Joequeline, 58–59, 60, 62, 73
Roberto, Jose, 60–61
Roberto, Paulo, 55–62, 66, 72–73
Rodrik, Dani, 187
Rojas, Rodrigo, 191
Roubini, Nouriel, 147
Rubin, Robert, 34–35
Rush, Bobby, 100–103, 104, 105, 112, 113, 115–16, 117, 119–20, 123
  Barton-Rush Internet bill of, 101–2, 107–8, 119
  in Black Panther Party, 100, 116, 117–18
  Englewood church sermon of, 114–15
  voting record of, 116–17
Rush, Carolyn, 107, 116
Rwanda, 87

St. Louis, Mo., 145, 157, 158
Salinas, Carlos, 106
salmon industry, 183–85, 190, 195
sanctions, economic, 94
San Francisco, Calif., xiii, xv, 145, 159
Santiago, 187, 188, 191, 193
Santos, Rosangela de Jesus, 69–70
São João de Meriti (Brazilian slum), 60
São Paulo, xiv, 53, 65, 164, 167
Saudi Arabia, 80
Seattle, Wash., 197
Section 8 vouchers, 173
Senate, U.S., 99, 104, 107–8, 194
Setshedi, Virginia, 95, 96
Shaka Zulu, 88
shantytowns, 38, 57
  see also slums
Shanzi, Betty, 11
Shanzi, Ennelis, 20–21, 23
Shanzi, Rose, 3–5, 10–12, 14, 18, 20–24
Sierra Leone, 130
slaves, slavery, 87, 203
  in Latin America, 40, 58, 63, 64, 202
  in U.S., xxi–xxii, 64, 149
Slay, Francis, 158
slums, 93, 143, 167

in Argentina, 38, 40–42, 44, 105
in Brazil, 55, 57, 58, 60, 65–66, 67–68, 105
police harassment in, 38, 65–66
power and clean water shutoff in, xv, 75–79, 80, 84–87, 94–96, 112
sterilization of women in, 67–70
see also ghettos, U.S.
slush funds, 156
Smith, Adam, 5
Smith, Darryl, 122–23
Smith, Ian, xvi–xviii
Smith, Rodney, 102–3
socialist governments, 20, 90, 110, 187
Chile's era of, 185, 188, 189, 190, 191
Zambia's era of, 16–17, 20, 22
Somalia, 125, 130
Somerville, Hernán, 190
Sonia, 161–64, 167, 168, 169–73, 175–82
South Africa, xiv, xx, 12, 13, 14, 75–96, 105, 106, 113, 160, 164, 196
African National Congress of, 75, 76, 78, 82, 83, 85, 91–92, 93, 114
apartheid in, xv, 64, 76, 78, 81, 82, 83, 84, 86, 89, 90–91, 92, 93, 94, 95
black poverty in, xv, 76, 83, 84, 90, 91, 113–14
cholera outbreaks in, 77–78, 84, 85–87
colonization of, 87–91
cost recovery measures in, 78, 80–82, 86–87
currency value in, xix, 78, 96
deindustrialization in, xiii
HIV infection epidemic in, 86, 93–94, 198
inequality gap in, 63, 91, 113, 114, 164, 199
land redistribution programs in, 92–93
per capita income in, 78
privatization in, xv, 75–79, 80–87, 91–96, 112
Treatment Action Campaign in, 198
unemployment in, xiii, xv, 77, 78, 90, 93, 95–96, 164
South Africa Airways (SAA), 91–92
Soweto, South Africa, 75–76, 78–79, 81–82, 93, 94–96, 112, 120, 167
Soweto Electricity Crisis Committee (SECC), 75, 76, 94–96
Spain, 64, 188, 202
Spam, 125, 133

standardized tests, 141, 180–81
Starbucks, 16, 148
Starks, Robert, 120
sterilization, 67–70, 94
stock market, xviii, xix, 146, 147, 193
crash of 1929, 33, 146
street vendors, xiv, 3–5, 7, 10–12, 18, 20–24
subprime mortgages, xix, 146, 147
subsidies, government, xix, 7, 16, 17, 33, 35, 37, 54, 90, 108, 200
in agriculture industry, xii, 17, 36, 90, 128–32, 134–39
for corporations, 108
on U.S. corn, 134–39
suicides, xxi, 71–72
summer jobs program, 117
Summers, Larry, 146–47
Sun Air, 91–92
Sun International, 13
SWAPP Ltd. Clothing, 19
Sweden, 63
Syphax Village, 143

Tanzania, 7, 18
tariffs, 5, 6–7, 8, 17, 19, 33, 63, 128, 130, 131, 137, 188, 196
taxes, xxi, 130, 131, 151, 155, 171, 199
in Chile, 186
corporate breaks on, xix, 8
estate, 108
on imports/exports, 5, 6–7, 8, 19, 33, 130, 131, 188
property, 22, 144, 155–57, 166
regressive sales, 196
repeal of import/export, 5, 6–7, 8, 17, 19, 63, 128, 137, 188, 196
U.S. corn subsidy and, 134–39
tax-increment financing districts (TIFs), 155–56
teachers unions, 152, 153
telecommunication companies, 78, 79, 107
Barton-Rush Internet bill and, 101–2, 107–8, 119
Chile's regulation of, 192–93
textile industry, xiv, 5, 6–8, 10–11, 16, 18–19
Thomas, Clarence, 118
tobacco, 127
Tom, Joshua, 22
Toussaint L'Ouverture, François-Dominique, 202, 203

trade deficits, xxi
  of Argentina, 33
  of U.S., xv, 165–66
trade unions, *see* labor unions
transportation, public, xix, 54, 57, 155
Transvaal region, 89
Treasury, U.S., xiv, xx
tribal reservations, 67–68, 71–72
Trinidade, Mauricio, 68–69
tubal ligations, 67, 69–70
type 2 diabetes, 135

unemployment, xi, xiv, xxi, 34, 113, 191
  in Africa, 4, 5, 6, 7, 10, 18, 22
  in Argentina, xiv, 27–28, 30, 36, 37, 38,
      39, 41–42, 45, 193
  in Brazil, xiii, xiv, 53, 57, 62, 65, 71, 164,
      187
  in Chile, 33, 186, 187, 190
  free trade and, 5, 6, 7, 10–11, 18, 19, 22,
      27–28, 78, 165, 166–67, 190
  in Latin America, 27–28, 30, 33, 36, 37,
      38, 39, 41–42, 53, 62, 65, 71, 186,
      187, 190, 193, 199
  monetary policy and, 27–28, 33, 37, 53,
      56, 57, 164–65, 187, 190
  racial disparities in, 41–42, 65
  in South Africa, xv, 77, 78, 90, 93, 95–96,
      164
  in U.S., xiii–xiv, xxiii, 103, 114, 115,
      164–65, 166–67
  in Venezuela, 199
unions, 8, 13, 79, 83, 105, 106, 109, 112,
    116, 138, 151, 152, 153, 168, 189,
    195
United Nations, 63, 127
  Development Program report (2005),
      195
  Food and Agriculture Organization of,
      126
United States, xii, xviii, xx, 13, 14, 16, 17,
    39, 62, 70, 73, 87, 109, 128, 130, 132,
    138, 185, 194, 195, 199, 201
  African American political elite in, 99–
      100, 104–14, 115, 116–18, 119–21,
      122–23, 150, 154–55
  auto industry in, xiv, xxii
  Chávez vilified in, 110, 198, 201, 202
  cheap exported goods of, xix, 7, 8, 32,
      134, 135
  crime rates in, 150, 158, 159

deindustrialization in, xiii–xiv, xxiii, 8,
    103, 164–67
deregulation in, xix, 34, 35, 57, 80, 146,
    151
education in, 103, 104–5, 140–43, 145,
    148, 150, 152–55, 163, 166, 180–81
food inflation in, 125, 133–34
foreign loans offered by, 31, 33
GDP of, 106, 166
gentrification in, 120, 121, 142–45,
    148–49, 152–58, 159–60
ghettos in, *see* ghettos, U.S.
housing bubble and mortgage crisis in,
    xii, xviii, 146–47, 151–52
inequality gap in, xii–xiii, xix–xx, 41, 63,
    105–6, 107, 113–14, 121, 144, 154,
    163, 164, 169
marriage rates in, 164, 168–69
monetary policy in, 34–35, 164–65
obesity epidemic in, 134–35
privatization in, 79, 80, 112, 142–46,
    148–49, 151, 152–55
race relations in, 41, 64, 66, 113–14, 121,
    144, 149–50, 154, 163, 166
slavery in, xxi–xxii, 64
subsidized corn exports of, 134–39
trade deficit of, xv, 165–66
2008 bailout bill passed in, xii, xv, xviii,
    110–11, 146, 151
2008 financial crisis in, xiii, 34, 35, 57,
    146–47, 151–52
unemployment in, xiii–xiv, xxiii, 103,
    114, 115, 164–65, 166–67
value of dollar and, 27, 34–35, 164–65
see also African Americans; *specific states
    or cities*
Uruguay, 186, 198, 201
U.S. Steel, 103
utilities, privatization of, 22, 45, 75–87,
    94–96, 102, 197
  in Latin America, 45, 79–80, 189, 192, 197
  losses of electrical power due to, xv, 75–
      76, 78–79, 80, 84–87, 94–96, 112
  rising prices caused by, xii, xv, xix, 76, 77,
      79–80, 82–83, 111, 127
  in South Africa, xv, 75–79, 80–87, 94–96,
      112
  in U.S., 79, 80, 111–12

Vareso, Emilion, 44
vendors, street, xiv, 3–5, 7, 10–12, 18, 20–24

Venezuela, 40, 110, 195–205
  caracazo uprising in, 195–97, 199
  Chávez's Bolívarian Revolution in, xx, 199–203
  economic growth in, 198–201
  government spending in, 186, 196, 199–200
  land reform in, 199
  unemployment rates in, 199
Victoria Falls, 3, 12–13, 14
villas miserias (misery villages), 38, 41–42, 105
vineyards, 127–28
Voting Rights Act (1965), 112
vouchers, 54, 129, 151, 164, 173

wages, 13, 78, 111, 113, 130, 164
  decrease in, xi, 44, 62, 106, 109, 129, 137–38, 189, 190
  gender disparity in, 167–68, 171
  racial disparity in, 65, 90, 144, 163
Wall Street, xii, xviii, xx, 33, 36, 56, 108, 151, 154, 184, 198
  2008 bailout bill for, xii, xv, xviii, 110–11
  in 2008 financial crisis, 35, 146–47, 151–52
Wal-Mart, xiii, 101, 107, 111
Washington, D.C., xxiii, 111, 140–45, 148, 149–55, 159, 164, 194, 196, 197
  Brookland neighborhood of, 140–42, 143, 148
  CBC's Annual Legislative Conference in, 99–100, 102–3, 118
  education in, 140–43, 145, 148, 150, 151, 152–55
  "The Plan" conspiracy in, 149–50, 159–60
  privatization and gentrifying of neighborhoods in, 142–45, 148–49, 151, 152–55, 159–60
Washington, Harold, 116–17
Washington Consensus, xx, 188, 201
water, privatization of, 22, 79–80, 82–87, 197
  access to clean water shutoff due to, 76–78, 79, 84–87
  cholera outbreaks due to, 77–78, 84, 85–87
  cost recovery measures and, 86–87
  in Latin America, 79–80, 197

rising prices caused by, xii, xix, 77, 79–80, 82–83, 127
  in South Africa, 76–78, 79, 82–87
Waters, Maxine, 117
Weisbrot, Mark, 34
Werneck, Juanita, 70
Williams, Anthony A., 111, 150–51, 152–53, 154–55, 159
Williams, Juan, 41
Wolfensohn, James, 113
women, xii, xxi, xxiii, 18, 64, 71, 168, 188
  Brazil's sterilization of, 67–70
  family destabilization and, xiv–xv, 38–40, 42, 71, 161–80, 181–82
  in labor force, xiv, xxi, 165, 167
  Latin American migration of, 28, 29, 43, 44
  prostitution of, xiv, 18, 25–26, 27, 28–31, 42–44, 49–51, 71, 198
  as single or teenaged mothers, 30, 37, 39, 40, 42, 163
  on tribal reservations, 67–68, 71
women, black, 112, 182
  in Argentina, 28, 41
  Brazil's sterilization of, 67–70
  destabilization of relationships and, xiv–xv, 161–80, 181–82
  and gender disparities in education and income, 166, 167–68, 176, 177, 179
  interracial dating and marriage of, 168, 179–80
Workers' Party, 54
workforce, 111
  Chile's job growth in, 185
  deindustrialization and, xiii–xiv, xxiii, 5, 6, 7, 10–11, 18–19, 22, 27–28, 164–65, 166–67, 189
  gender disparities in, 167
  labor laws and, 13, 62, 106–7, 138, 186, 189, 191–92, 195
  racial disparities in, 65, 90, 144, 163
  summer job programs and, 150
  training programs for, 117, 123, 191, 193
  wage decreases in, xi, 44, 62, 106, 109, 129, 137–38, 189, 190
  women in, xiv, xxi, 165, 167
  see also unemployment
World Bank, xiv, xx, 5, 8, 17, 19, 27, 53, 56, 73, 78, 80, 82, 113, 128, 129, 138, 154, 192

World Trade Organization (WTO), 94,
     107, 132
Wyden, Ron, 107–8
Wynn, Al, 117

Zambezi Sun (hotel), 12–13
Zambia, xiv, 3–24, 63, 105, 194

free trade and, xiii, xiv, 5–8, 10–11,
     13–14, 17–19, 22
Zambia Association of Manufacturers, 7, 18
Zapatistas movement, 197
Zimbabwe, xvi–xvii, 3, 12, 14, 87, 131
Zoellick, Robert, 138
Zulu tribe, 83, 84, 88–89, 94